Seeds of Hope

Young Adults and the Catholic Church in the United States

Tim Muldoon

Paulist Press
New York/Mahwah, NJ

Cover design by Joy Taylor
Book design by Lynn Else

Library of Congress Cataloging-in-Publication Data

Muldoon, Tim.
    Seeds of hope : young adults and the Catholic Church in the United States / Timothy P. Muldoon.
        p.   cm.
    Includes bibliographical references.
    ISBN 978-0-8091-4514-0
    1. Church work with young adults—United States. 2. Young adults—Religious life. 3. Catholic Church—United States. I. Title.
    BX2347.8.Y64M85 2008
    282'.730842—dc22

                                                                    2007035418

Published by Paulist Press
997 Macarthur Boulevard
Mahwah, New Jersey 07430

www.paulistpress.com

Printed and bound in the
United States of America

Contents

Acknowledgments

I am grateful to many people who have helped bring this project to fruition. First, thanks to Liz Walter, formerly of Paulist Press, whose enthusiasm helped me identify the major themes of the book. Second, I am grateful to the thoughtful editing of Christopher Bellitto, whose keen historical sense has helped me to bring nuance to a number of issues addressed in the text. Third, I am thankful for my colleagues in the College Theology Society and Catholic Theological Society of America, who have provided stimulating food for thought about the state of the Catholic Church and Catholic faith in the United States. Finally, I am extremely grateful for the ways that my students at Mount Aloysius College challenged me with their questions, trusted me with their stories of faith, and demanded of me explanations for just about everything having to do with God, faith, and the Church.

Chapter 2 was influenced by my essay entitled "Constructing a Post-postmodern Theology," in *The Josephinum Journal of Theology*, Fall 2001. For a broader treatment of the themes in chapter 5, see my articles "Postmodern Spirituality and the Ignatian *Fundamentum*," in *The Way*, January 2005; "Shepherding the Postmodern Flock," in *Chicago Studies* 42/1, Spring 2003, pp. 81–92; "Why Young Adults Need Ignatian Spirituality," in *America*, February 26, 2001, pp. 8–14; and "Starving Outside the Banquet Hall: Faith Formation for Young Adults," in *The Living Light*, Fall 2000, pp. 35–43. Chapter 6 emerged, in part, from research that led to the essay "Postmodern Moral Theology and Holiness" in *Moral Theology: Fundamental Issues and New Directions*, edited by James Keating (Paulist Press, 2004).

Thanks to the editors and readers of these publications for their comments, which have helped me to formulate more clearly the challenges facing the Church as it ministers to young people today.

Finally, I am deeply indebted to colleagues and students at Boston College and to the many people who have contributed to The Church in the 21st Century Center. Immersion in a community that takes seriously questions about the Church today has given me great hope for its future, even amid uncertain times.

Chestnut Hill, Massachusetts
July 31, 2006
The Feast of Saint Ignatius Loyola

I met the future of America. I looked into the eyes of the future of America. The future of America is very bright, it's very hopeful, it's very promising. It's in the teachings of Christ. It's in your young people. America, best days are yet to come.

—Pope John Paul II[1]

Nothing is more practical than finding God, that is, than falling in love in a quite absolute, final way.

What you are in love with, what seizes your imagination, will affect everything. It will decide what will get you out of bed in the morning, what you will do with your evenings, how you will spend your weekends, what you read, who you know, what breaks your heart, and what amazes you with joy and gratitude.

Fall in love, stay in love and it will decide everything

Attributed to
Fr. Pedro Arrupe

Introduction
Is There Hope for the Catholic Church in the United States?

When Paul found himself speaking to a group of Athenian philosophers at the Areopagus, Luke the evangelist describes his eloquent attempts to use the language of philosophy in order to preach the good news about the risen Jesus Christ. I can imagine the scene: a passionate preacher of the gospel, one who has undergone a profound conversion experience and who has endured a great many persecutions for the sake of spreading the gospel, is hoping to persuade his interlocutors that the one true God has acted in human history in an absolutely profound way. From his second letter to the Corinthians, we have a clue about the kind of life Paul was leading:

> Five times I have received…the forty lashes minus one. Three times I was beaten with rods. Once I received a stoning. Three times I was shipwrecked; for a night and a day I was adrift at sea; on frequent journeys, in danger from rivers, danger from bandits, danger from my own people, danger from Gentiles, danger in the city, danger in the wilderness, danger at sea, danger from false brothers and sisters; in toil and hardship, through many a sleepless night, hungry and thirsty, often without food, cold and naked. (2 Cor 11:24–27)

In spite of all these hardships, Paul presses on with a kind of urgency that I marvel at. He is accustomed to being marginalized or the target of violence, so his situation in the midst of the Athenians is really nothing new.

In his address, which I once heard a bishop describe as Paul's most eloquent, but least accepted, Paul says the following to the philosophers:

> The God who made the world and everything in it does not live in shrines made of human hands…He made all nations to inhabit the whole earth, and he allotted the times of their existence and the boundaries of the places where they would live, so that they would search for God and perhaps grope for him and find him—though indeed he is not far from each one of us. For "In him we live and move and have our being"; as even some of your own poets have said, "For we too are his offspring." (Acts 17:24–28, emphasis added)

Paul's exhortation to the Athenians is a remarkable attempt to translate the fundamental good news about Jesus into a worldview that the philosophers might accept. He emphasizes that human beings are stung with the desire to know God, even in a world that is complex and that sometimes makes it seem as though God is far away.

For Paul, as for the other authors of the New Testament literature, hope was a gift of God because it was based in what they understood to be the consummation of human existence: eternal life with God, the evidence of which was the life of Jesus Christ. For them, this hope was so powerful and so profound that they were willing to risk everything in order to proclaim it. Paul's description of his life as an apostle manifests something of the depth of his commitment—he is saying, in essence, that he was willing to suffer any hardship in order to proclaim the good news about Christ.

The earliest Christian communities were communities of hope. The Church emerged from a crucible of suffering because it was founded on this deep hope in the power of Christ and of the gospel. Its treasure, we learn in a famous story about the life of Saint Lawrence, was not in its wealth or its buildings but in the faith of its people. What can we in the United States today, who live in a fractured Church, learn from these communities of hope?

At the beginning of the twenty-first century, we face challenges to our hope that are very different from the persecutions faced by the early apostolic and patristic-era churches. Then, proclamation of Christian faith was itself an act of hope, because before the age of Constantine, to be a Catholic was to be a possible target of violence. Today, at least in the United States, we benefit from the sacrifices of earlier generations who slowly overcame anti-Catholic sentiment to assume positions of leadership within our society. Our challenges are very different, because many of them come from within the very structures of the Church itself, while others come from the relationships that we in the Church have with the wider world. We proclaim a gospel of hope, but many experience a Church that sometimes obscures that hope. Within our Church are people who have been abused by priests; people who struggle with same-sex attraction and who do not see other Catholics as resources for growing in holiness; women who are perplexed by the absence of women in leadership positions; people who lament the polarization that exists on issues like the liturgy, the public voice of bishops, and the consistency of social teachings. The Church is an imperfect place even as it seeks to be an iconic witness to a God who speaks the gospel of love. Yet I am convinced that this sometimes dysfunctional Church nevertheless can be a place of grace and beauty, a place where we celebrate what is most noble in the human heart as it reaches, often in spite of itself, toward God—and, indeed, I am convinced that today we are deeply in need of this imperfect Church, even as we ask how it can be better.

I am only too familiar with the objections, which I encounter on a daily basis in my work: the Church is out of touch; it is a medieval construct with antiquated sensibilities and byzantine practices. The Church is a men's club whose leadership is so unaware of women's issues that it cannot possibly speak to their most profound yearnings. The Church is too European to speak to the emerging global order whose center of gravity is moving south and east. The Church is homophobic and unable to speak with any authority on human sexuality, especially after the sexual abuse crisis. The Church is divided among itself, with conservatives and liberals arguing over issues that many of its younger members don't even understand. The Church is removed from the rest of the world, seeking to advance its own peculiar worldview, either oblivious to or critical of the ways that the rest of humanity confronts the most profound existential questions about our future on the planet.

These are serious objections, and I do not pretend to minimize or ignore them. It is perhaps my peculiarly American[2] sensibility, though, that persuades me that citizenship in an organization is not the same as absolute acceptance of the current state of affairs. Instead, authentic citizenship has more to do with choosing to love those around us with whom we break bread. Being a Catholic today is not a historical given the way it once was, when generations shared faith the way they shared a family name. It is a deliberate choice to look at the world in a particular way, based not only on the teachings of Jesus, but also on the development of that uniquely "Catholic imagination." In my experience, it is precisely this imagination that enables people to negotiate the fundamental questions of human living in a graced manner. Catholicism is not simply about agreeing with what the Church teaches; it is about being invited to look at the world in the way that Jesus taught the disciples to, and to share with others a history of practice designed to lead us into greater communion with God and each other.[3]

I want to suggest in this book that active participation in the life of the Church is valuable to help younger Catholics—even those whose experience with the Church is ambivalent—to address the most pressing issues in our postmodern world, at both the individual and communal levels. Further, I offer reflections on some of the particular challenges facing the Church as it considers its younger members, suggesting ways consistent with its fidelity to the teachings of Jesus to be a catalyst for positive change in the world. Today, the global order is being shaped profoundly by nations and corporations that operate out of insufficiently expansive notions of self-interest. In such a context, religious communities—especially those of a global scale like the Catholic Church—have an important prophetic role. We need communities of people who share a faith that involves a truly "catholic" understanding of human flourishing. We need people who struggle daily to avoid unjust practices like purchasing goods made with sweatshop labor; consuming at a rate disproportionate with the rest of the world; neglecting the poor and disenfranchised members of society; engaging in sexual behavior that corrodes human dignity. We need people who choose to enter into solidarity with the suffering of the world, rather than pad their own nests. We need, in other words, a "corporation" or "body" that offers more than the individualistic, consumeristic, superficial, immature ethics of so much of contemporary culture.

While at times I lose optimism that the Church can fulfill these hopes, I am convinced of two things. The first is a practical recognition of the extent of the Catholic Church, both in the United States and around the world. This Church can exercise the kind of moral and political influence to counter those forces that destroy human lives because of crushing poverty and dehumanizing transnational corporate greed, to name but two examples. The second is a theological point. Cornel West once remarked that he was not optimistic about the future of race relations in the United States, but that he nevertheless had hope.[4] This remark offers insight into the perspective many U.S. Catholics bring toward their Church, and resonates well with the ancient understanding of the martyr (*martyrion*, Greek for "witness") as one whose self-sacrifice provided seed for the future of the Church. There are many signs that might lead the contemporary U.S. Catholic to despair, but to hope is to recognize that the life of the Church is ultimately the work of the Holy Spirit. We who value Catholic tradition often do so in spite of what the Church is actually up to, but mindful that the practice of Catholic faith is nevertheless an invitation to listen deeply to the call of God through the words and actions of Jesus.

SEEDS OF HOPE

[Jesus said,] "Listen! A sower went out to sow. And as he sowed, some seeds fell on the path, and the birds came and ate them up. Other seeds fell on rocky ground, where they did not have much soil, and they sprang up quickly, since they had no depth of soil. But when the sun rose, they were scorched; and since they had no root, they withered away. Other seeds fell among thorns, and the thorns grew up and choked them. Other seeds fell on good soil and brought forth grain, some a hundredfold, some sixty, some thirty. Let anyone with ears listen!" (Matt 13:3–9)

Jesus' parable of the sower is a blueprint for the future of the U.S. Catholic Church. There are many who seek to take the role of the sower—the one who distributes wisdom liberally across all ideological spectra, expecting it to take root and bear fruit in justice, goodness, and peace. Yet it is a sobering reflection; it suggests to us that social change is not as simple as speaking loudly about beliefs. For decades—indeed, centuries—Catholics have expected that their leaders would speak loudly, and thereby produce a yield of faithful followers. That model, while influential in the shaping of the modern world, is no longer sufficient. The future of Catholic faith cannot depend solely on good preaching or proclamation. The ground has become almost infertile, and must be worked before the seed can take root.

There is a note of hope, though, behind this sobering reflection. Jesus does not tell us in the parable how it came to be that some soil was rich. It is provocative to imagine that the rich soil became so because of the decay of refuse over time—a compost heap of abandoned ideas, worldviews that have grown passé, texts that have faded into the background of history. Decay of older matter fertilizes the soil, making it ready to produce new fruit. Perhaps this lesson also applies to social change for those of us who live in the shadows of the cultural revolutions of the twentieth-century Church. Perhaps even as conservatives and liberals, advocates of Neo-Scholasticism or of liberation theology, advocates of return to the Tridentine Mass or champions of liturgical change continue to wage their ideological battles amid the graying of the Vatican II generation, even now there are growing what Justin Martyr called in the second century "seeds of the word" among younger Catholics. Perhaps even as we witness the decay of public discourse among entrenched older Catholics, younger ones unaware of the nature of the current debates are discovering that the worldviews they have inherited from postmodern American society are suffocating. Many have recognized the weaknesses of these worldviews, and have begun to ask deeply spiritual questions—seeds that, if cultivated, will sprout into radically new expressions of Christian faith.

This book proposes ways of envisioning a Church that will cultivate these seeds of hope. It addresses two related concerns. The first is that of young people, many who have been raised Catholic, but who believe that the Catholic Church has become irrelevant and unresponsive to their needs. The second is that of older Catholics who are concerned by forces in U.S. society that seem to be eroding the faith of young people. What I propose in this book is that the hope of U.S. Catholicism is its unique power to invite young people to see the world in ways that challenge the extremes of postmodern American culture, ways that do greater justice to the fundamental yearnings of the human heart.

This book is at once a theological and a practical proposal. Theologically, it takes seriously our desires for meaning, for hope, and for justice, by paying attention to Catholic tradition as a deposit of wisdom about human flourishing in relationship with God. Practically, it recognizes the gross disparities in our nation and in our world, which hamper our abilities to live in communion with our brothers and sisters, especially in the developing world. It suggests that these disparities force us to confront how our spiritual yearnings must lead us to grow beyond selfish approaches to spirituality, and to confront fundamental questions about what it means to respond to the will of God in a fractured, unjust world. Personal spirituality is an important movement in the lives of all people, and it is good that we cultivate spiritual growth—as long as it does not descend into narcissistic idolatry of the self. Authentic spiritual growth must involve joining with others to address systemic questions about the social sins of poverty, racism, classism, sexism, and others. Ideally, a Catholic worldview ought to bind us together as a community of hopeful vision, one that seeks the will of God sometimes in union with, sometimes in contrast to, prevailing cultural norms. It ought to be a community in pilgrimage toward God. I want to suggest that to the extent that it seeks this kind of authenticity, it will not only attract young people in their hunger for spirituality; it will also be a transforming force in the world.

I seek to convey a hopeful picture of the Catholic Church in the United States even while recognizing its sins and limitations. For even in the wake of sexual abuse scandals, U.S. Catholicism holds a great deal of power to influence both members and the wider American society. Today, our challenge as Catholics is to recognize the way our Church has failed to follow Jesus' example, and to engage in the process of renewal. Forty years have passed since the close of Vatican II, which was the most significant renewal movement in modern Church history. Today, as the generation born after the Council reaches adulthood, we must again face the challenging questions that Christians of all ages must face: What does Jesus' teaching mean for us? How must I live? What must we do as a society to practice justice? In short, this book seeks to offer a model of how the Catholic Church in the United States can again respond to "the signs of the times." More fundamentally, it suggests that the Catholic Church is unique in its social and political power to foster a vision of human living that truly dignifies the person, often in contrast to the prevailing moral norms of popular culture in the United States (and indeed, the world). The traditional term used to designate the cultivation of such a vision, or worldview, is *formation*.

RELIGIOUS FORMATION?

The most significant barrier to the formation of young people today is the complexity of this postmodern world. There are so many competing voices and forces at work that the need for the shelter of community is ever present. Younger Catholics, who have grown up in an entirely post–Vatican II Church, have often not known the nourishing value of a culture of faith, as did their parents and grandparents. Even the population of younger immigrants is becoming more assimilated to contemporary U.S. culture than to the cultural Catholicism of their parents or grandparents. Several studies show that Catholics born after Vatican II have the least connection to the institutional Church, meaning that it simply does not represent for them the community that most shapes their worldview.[5]

In his book *All That's Holy*, Tom Levinson chronicles his pilgrimage across the United States in search of why people believe what they do.[6] Early in his travels, he speaks with a young Catholic Volunteer Corps[7] member, whose description of her relationship to the Catholic Church is illustrative of the attitudes many younger Catholics have. Of his conversation partner, he writes, "we shared both early religious disenchantment and popular cultural fluency." Levinson is inquisitive about her commitment to engage in social justice work even amid her ambivalence toward the Church. Her reply manifests a point that statistical evidence in the studies by Dean Hoge and others demonstrates is widespread.

> I just realized that I couldn't separate myself, and who I was, from my tradition of being raised Catholic. And I've come to think of it as not any better or worse than anybody else's tradition. It just happens that it's the tradition I was raised in. I think I really kind of came to terms with what that meant for me. It didn't mean that I had to embrace all the tenets or beliefs of the Church. It was okay that I didn't do that. I didn't have to leave the Church, either. But where at one point I felt like, oh, I've got to leave the Church, it's so terrible, and I'd ask friends, "How can you stay in the Church?" I think I came to the point where I felt like, this is my tradition. This is how I was raised.

The young woman describes the location of her faith in a way with which many older Catholics are unfamiliar. Having grown up within the sanctuary of a faith community, many view society from within the parameters of that community's perspective. Young Catholics, however, are at once insiders and outsiders with regard to the Church. They are insiders to the extent that they know some of the language and basic ideas, having gone through religious education. Yet they are also outsiders, seeing the Church as their parents' or grandparents' institution. Their formation has been more profoundly influenced by popular culture than by Catholicism, and so they are likely to see the terms of their faith through the lens of culture, rather than vice versa. Instead of standing firmly within the community of faith in order to critique U.S. culture, they stand firmly within U.S. culture in order to critique the Church. As a result, they are likely to appropriate only those elements of the tradition that do not threaten their cultural position.

If the communities to which we belong—especially at an early age—form our worldviews, then we must ask serious questions about the communities (formal or informal) that form the worldviews of young people. To be sure, there is still a population of young Catholics who have frequented youth ministry events and maybe even a World Youth Day or two. It is clear, though, that the contemporary U.S. Catholic Church is doing a poor job of welcoming Catholics born after the mid 1960s, who now comprise over forty percent of the Church. The majority of younger Catholics are part of the larger U.S. cultural landscape, and thus confront the issue of religious formation only obliquely. Many, at least among whites, are well educated. All live in a pluralist culture, meaning that there is a bewildering marketplace of ideas and worldviews. And they have come to the conclusion that individual conscience is the best guide to navigating this marketplace. They are American—strongly individualistic to the core, and will seek out what they need to know.

The Internet is the perfect medium in such a culture, an emblem of this marketplace of ideas. Yet it is still so new that we have not had the time to appreciate how it is changing our perception of ourselves. One thing, however, is clear: with the availability of more knowledge than we can ever use, people must learn what they wish to learn. *Information* is *formation:* the kind of people we become depends to a great extent on what we come to know.[8]

There is a religious dimension to this information-formation. The word *religion* comes from the Latin root *ligare*, which means "to bind," and carries a connotation of permanent relationship. All human beings are religious in one way or another. Our religion is that to which we bind ourselves in communion with others. Our religion is our worldview: it is the way we choose to live in the world, the way we choose to grow in community, the way we shape our individual choices, the way we structure our hope. Even before we learn something, we must deem it valuable—we must choose to pick up a specific magazine, turn to a specific channel, click on a specific Web site. What always lies behind our choices is the influence of a community, even if that influence is something we've never thought about. The things we choose to learn are valuable to us because they in some way help us to negotiate our lives in a complex world. We can learn a great deal about a person by simply paying attention to what keeps his or her interest. We learn something about how the person sees himself or herself in relation to others, something about what he or she deems important. There is something that binds people together who subscribe to *Sports Illustrated* or to *People*. There is a shared bond among people who watch *The Oprah Winfrey Show*. There is a common understanding among those who read the poetry of Maya Angelou or the novels of John Grisham.

How do young people learn the formative role of information? How are they formed by the information culture in which they live? If information in its many forms is so pervasive and omnipresent, how can we be certain that their formation is sound? How can we guide them toward formation that does justice to their true selves? These are only some of the questions that we must raise in the information age. Parents, schools, youth groups, and colleges and universities must ask them in a particular way, for they have privileged places in the formation of young people. In my own world of higher education, I see the beginnings of serious debate over this formative role of information. Religious leaders, too, are slowly coming to realize what is at stake. They see how young people are influenced more by popular U.S. culture than by the culture of the Church. They are beginning to understand the challenge of religious formation of young people who have been so systematically formed in a consumerist society.

The religion of the United States today is consumerism, and its influence is both subtle and pervasive.[9] From the earliest age, children are immersed in this religion.[10] They are taught its doctrines of buying and selling, learn its language through advertising and shopping, practice its rituals at birthdays and (its high holy day) Christmas. If information is formation, then perhaps the most fundamental formative aspect of consumerism is that so much information is related to buying and selling. Radio, television, almost all published media, and the Internet come with price tags. The most influential figures in the lives of young people are not in most cases religious leaders: they are entertainers and sports figures, people

11

whose interests are furthered by the vast economic resources that young people now have in U.S. society. Children, teenagers, and young adults hear messages over and over that form them as consumers, often to their detriment.

Ours is a culture of consumer choice: we can seek out exactly what we want, what will serve our every need. And we have come to believe that the same is true of spirituality and religion.

THE COMMODITIES OF SPIRITUALITY AND RELIGION

To be blunt, consumerism has convinced us that spirituality is another commodity.[11] In a way, consumerism has even created a market for spirituality. The number of books that deal with spiritual themes has skyrocketed in the last decade, and, more important, many deal with these themes completely apart from organized religion. This is a new state of affairs. The very notion of "spirituality" as distinct from "religion" is pretty new. For centuries, what we call "spirituality" was understood as necessarily related to a religious tradition: Christian spirituality was the practice of faith that one learned in church. In a consumerist culture, however, we believe that "church" comes with too much baggage—the unpleasant need to deal with other people, to learn doctrines, to perform rituals. There is a pervasive, though wrongheaded, dichotomy at work: religion is oppressive, outdated, structured to make people think and act the same, while spirituality is about personal meaning, the freedom to explore ultimate truth, the power to create a good life. Recent attention-getters such as *The DaVinci Code*[12] and the newly discovered "Gospel of Judas" suggest that the Church is the big, bad secret organization that squelches authentic spirituality by trying to create its own society of mindless, worshipping automata.

This false dichotomy thrives in U.S. culture today not only because of our individualistic ethos, but also because there are many who profit from it. The spirituality market is enormous. Consumers are spending millions of dollars on yoga, aromatherapy, massage, books, classes in meditation, and retreats to mountain getaways. Companies are happy to convince us that their product is what will lead us to more happy lives.

This attitude toward personal spirituality has affected all religions in the United States. According to recent polls by ABC News and CNN/*USA Today*, upwards of 95 percent of Americans profess belief in God, but actual attendance at churches on a regular basis is significantly lower. Spirituality is easier than religion, because it exempts us from the difficulties of communion and conversion.

The reason this dichotomy is so wrongheaded is that it fails to appreciate the depth of what it means to be human. There is a serious danger in an isolated approach to spirituality, because it is likely to be something we can easily manipulate to serve our own ends. It is not likely to challenge us too greatly, and it will not tell us when we are wrong. Spirituality isolated from religion runs the danger of narcissism and a kind of solipsism—which is to say that we can become our own gods. The logical extreme of this way of thinking is the belief that all of creation is ultimately here to make my life better.

There is also a social cost to this way of thinking. The consumerist view of spirituality has led to a disjunction between spirituality and the rest of our lives. We do not tend to see our spirituality as intimately connected to the kind of work we do at our jobs, the ways we relate to people in our lives, the choices we make with our money and time, the political decisions we make. As a result, on a global scale we Americans are overindulging in the world's resources.

Religious traditions have functioned in human history as depositories of wisdom: ways of thinking that help us to rise above the concerns of everyday life to glimpse something of what life is ultimately about. They bring with them moral demands, because collectively they pay attention to our innate tendency to act selfishly. The most universal of these commands is the golden rule, variations of which exist in all great religious traditions: love your neighbor as yourself. The most important reason we need the wisdom of religious traditions today is because this fundamental ethic challenges the core values of consumerism. Whereas the dynamic of consumerism is to gather things to ourselves, the dynamic of this religious ethic is the opposite: to open ourselves to others. And only religious traditions have the kind of influence to make people constantly confront this ethic. In the Catholic tradition, the foundation of this ethic is theological: people are created in the image of God, whose very being is the pure act of communion. As human beings, then, we realize our very reason for being when our lives are led not in pursuit of personal fulfillment, but in pursuit of communion with the other. Our moral heroes—figures like Martin Luther King Jr., Rigoberta Menchú, Desmond Tutu, Oscar Romero, Carlos Belo, Shirin Ebadi—are people motivated by faith to make the world more just.

SOCIAL JUSTICE

As the wealthiest nation in the world, the United States stands in an unequal relationship with other nations. We have decided collectively, if unconsciously, that our lifestyles are more important than our communion with the rest of the world. Our consumerist religious leaders—corporate CEOs and politicians—continue to ensure that our consumerism can thrive, even though some of its more extreme demands exact a huge toll on people in the developing world.

For over a century, the leadership of the Catholic Church has looked at the way that consumerism can hurt the human family. Beginning in 1891 with the document *Rerum Novarum* (On New Things, though published in English under the title "On the Condition of Labor"), Pope Leo XIII suggested that Catholicism must be in service to the greater good of all people around the globe, especially the poor, regardless of religion. This and subsequent papal encyclicals form the backbone of the tradition of Catholic Social Teaching (CST) that continues to this day. It is a sign of hope both for the Church in general and for the Church in the United States in particular.

The Catholic Church is moving south.[13] Industrialized nations in both Europe and North America are seeing signs of a waning faith, while the Church in the poorer nations of Asia, Africa, and South America are growing both in numbers and in vitality.[14] Can the Catholic Church in the United States, which has access to so many resources, really be in communion with Catholics in other parts of the world? Can those with two coats honestly break bread with others who have none? What is the role of a Church that is rich, but preaches a gospel of preferential option for the poor? How can U.S. Catholicism serve the greater good of the nation and the world?

These are the kinds of questions Catholics in the United States must ask. They are the kinds of questions that will help young people to see the Church as a place where people try to make the world better. They will help the Church to heal the divisions between conservatives and liberals, by focusing efforts on what is at the center of Catholic faith. They will move U.S. Catholics to understand their rich tradition behind the outward manifestations of faith, to learn the connection between desiring to do good, on the one hand, and expressing that spiritual desire in the contexts of private prayer and public liturgy, on the other. They will draw in younger people who have begun to see through the thin veneer that is consumerism, who have developed cynicism toward the world in which they live. Catholics in the United States must ask these questions because it will help them to live as a just community, a community that seeks to foster the good of the world by living in real communion with others.

PLURALISM

As early as 1972 scientists recognized the stakes involved in the patterns of consumption in the developed world. One observation worth noting comes from the book *The Limits to Growth*, published by a group of scholars at the Massachusetts Institute of Technology: "Probably only religion has the moral force necessary to bring about change."[15] Historically, the great religious traditions of the world have shaped people's lives to an extent unparalleled by any other system of thought and practice. Christianity is the largest of the world's religions, and the Catholic Church is the single largest body of believers, comprising about a sixth of the world's population. Catholicism is also the largest religious group in the United States, claiming about 22 percent of the population. And while it would be a stretch to say that the Church always speaks univocally, it is nevertheless true that U.S. Catholicism represents a significant political voice.[16] Making social justice concerns a significant focus of parish life has the potential of both revivifying existing structures within the Church as well as drawing together the passion that young people bring to their desire for making the world more livable. U.S. Catholicism is at a moment in its history when it can tap its own resources in order to speak to a new generation that is starving for spiritual food.

In a culture of religious consumerism, the Church is to many people only one choice among many—merely one of the items on the ideological smorgasbord. For many young adults, this point has been obvious for some time. The younger generations feel comfortable to select elements of religious and spiritual truth as they see fit (the so-called cafeteria Catholicism), having been formed in the tradition of consumerism. The positive side of this situation is that many young adults see basic similarities among religions, regarding them as constructive ways of learning the ultimate truth about life.[17] There is a negative side, though. Failure to see the legitimate doctrinal and practical differences among religions shows an unwillingness to critically engage what these traditions are really saying. It is easy to see similarities when one is standing too far away. Moreover, this cafeteria approach to spirituality leaves many still starving, having few criteria by which to judge the authenticity of their choices. How does one satisfy the inchoate desires to make life more meaningful, unless one has some models to follow?

A key reason many young people are reluctant to engage religious traditions on a deep level is because too often they see religious people who have little tolerance for, or understanding of, those who come from different religious traditions. It is understandable that someone should retreat into a safe personalized spirituality when he or she sees how poorly people from different religious traditions get along. Today, however, there are new signs of hope. Issues of social justice bring together people from different faith traditions, and their shared work crosses ideological boundaries. The shared work of justice can lead to deeper understandings of different traditions, as well as to the appreciation of how immersion in one tradition does not automatically mean the disdain of others. On the contrary, as many Buddhist and Christian monks have come to learn from each other, formation in one religious tradition often gives one greater appreciation of the gifts in other traditions.

In the Catholic Church, this point found expression in the 1965 document *Nostra Aetate* ("Our Generation," translated in English as the "Declaration on the Relation of the Church to Non-Christian Religions)". The bishops gathered at Vatican II recognized the wisdom that other religious traditions bring to the human family, and how this wisdom contributes to the flourishing of human society. There is great hope in further exploring the relationships between the Catholic Church and other traditions, even as we work together toward a more just order. And while the document represents only a starting point in the dialogues among Catholics and representatives of other religious traditions, it is nevertheless hopeful to recognize that the Church deems such dialogues valuable.[18]

WHAT THIS BOOK IS ABOUT

Chapter 1 looks at the state of the Church in the United States today. It includes sociological studies that detail the different concerns facing the U.S. Catholic Church: for example, the growing Spanish-speaking population; the immigrant Church; generational differences; the conservative/liberal divide; the gap between rich and poor; the legacy of the sexual abuse crisis. It also addresses the ways the twenty-first century offers new challenges to the Catholic Church both in the United States and around the globe. Most important, it focuses on how access to information has made young adults aware of the differences among people around the world, and how this awareness leads to questions about the nature of religious truth-claims. Especially in urban areas, where people from different backgrounds frequently interact, awareness of different religious traditions makes people raise questions about the extent to which any tradition can make ultimate claims to authority. Chapter 1 offers the thesis that the Catholic Church's claim to religious authority can no longer be regarded solely as a given because of its history. Its authority must be persuasive, and it must be offered—following the example of a gracious God—as a gift to all people for the sake of their ultimate well-being.

Chapter 2 takes up the point at the end of chapter 1, suggesting that the Church's social teaching is persuasive precisely because it draws from ordinary human experience and can lead people into deeper consideration of the gospel. To a culture influenced by consumerism, the Church's voice is strongest when it argues on behalf of the poor and disenfranchised. Catholic Social Teaching (CST) speaks to many young people in their desire for meaning, because it emphasizes our connectedness as human beings under God; it also addresses ecumenical, racial, and economic concerns. This chapter offers to the layperson a broad overview of CST, and explains why it speaks to the spiritual longings of people today. The aim is to connect spirituality to larger social questions, challenging the common misperception of spirituality as another consumer commodity.

Chapter 3 examines how a global vision, one that strives to be (in the fullest sense of the word) "catholic," will affect the Catholic Church in the United States. Following the work of theologians from other parts of the world, I focus on religion as a wisdom tradition that helps shed light on the mystery of human experience. The Catholic Church, as the single largest religious body in the world, must take leadership in fostering cooperation across religious traditions, as local churches are already doing in Asia, for example. Moreover, the U.S. Catholic Church, as the largest religious group in the United States (and the world), is in a particularly unique position. The United States is the most religiously and culturally diverse country in the world. I suggest that taking this view of other religious traditions is consistent with the Church's mission and is an integral development in fidelity to the teachings of Jesus. There is great hope in seeing the authentic practice of one's own faith as somehow related to the different religious practices of others. It is possible to celebrate one's own religious tradition while at the same time honoring those of others.

Chapter 4 addresses the regular practice of Catholic faith in liturgy, and raises questions about how it can more effectively respond to the different communities within the Church (described in chapter 1). It looks at the reasons Church attendance is down among young people, and offers a constructive proposal for drawing them back into the life of the Church. The basic argument is that there exists a disjunction between liturgy and ordinary life; and if liturgy more clearly speaks to the deepest needs of people it will draw them into communion. If liturgy celebrates our attempts to deepen our spiritual lives to make us more courageous in doing justice, people will want to be nourished by liturgy. It will become less a chore and obligation, more an opportunity and event.

Chapter 5 connects to the theme of chapter 4, offering a reflection on how to address what studies show are a strong interest in spirituality but a dropping interest in religion. The thesis of this chapter is that religious tradition is that which sustains spirituality, because of community, history, and liturgy. The challenge for the U.S. Catholic Church is to highlight the ways that Catholic tradition nurtures the spiritual life. The emphasis on social justice in chapter 2 leads to a picture of a Church that takes a prophetic stand against the excesses of U.S. culture, a Church that nourishes people's attempts to live meaningfully through practices of social justice and prayer.

Chapter 6 takes a look at the recent history of moral teaching in light of the sexual abuse crisis. It suggests that in light of the challenges the Church faces to regain public moral authority, the Church must lead by example first in those ways that address fundamental human rights. Pope John Paul II wrote eloquently about a culture of death, for example; the ways in which Catholics work on behalf of life issues offer witness. Similarly, to the extent that the Church has for decades worked to help those left out of our consumer culture shows a willingness to embrace so-called non-market values. Sexual ethics, which have been such a major part of Catholic teaching in the last four decades, will make more sense when seen against the backdrop of social justice teaching, for the emphasis both in social justice teaching and in sexual teachings is the dignity of the person.

In an age of cynicism, it is important to have hope. As a young Catholic theologian, I have great hope in my Church even though in some ways I am not particularly optimistic. What gives me hope is the fact that ours is a very long tradition, in which many good people have honestly tried to understand the ways God called them to live. Further, in looking at this tradition I see resources that

19

address the most fundamental needs of good people: some who have faith and practice it, some who have faith but do not practice it, and some who have faith but do not even know it. What is important for us who are Catholic in the twenty-first century is the recovery of that excitement that so animated the first disciples of Jesus—that sense of urgency that the gospel was truly good news, awesome news, for a world in desperate need of hope. Language, practices, traditions, and even doctrines can become reified and ossified when they fail to mediate this primordial hope that is the gift of the Holy Spirit. This book seeks to dwell on what Pope John XXIII called *aggiornamento*—Italian for "updating"—in reference to the work of the Church. I am part of the first generation born after the Council he called, a Council that sought to let fresh air into the musty halls of Catholic tradition. As a member of this generation, I know only a Church struggling to redefine itself. I and my peers have grown up in an organization with an identity crisis. And yet as we are now coming into positions of leadership within this Church, we recognize that even in spite of this crisis, it is a place where we have come to know something of the work of God. My hope, then, is for better understanding of the way people have come to know this God through the practice of Catholic faith, so that our shared energy in the practice of this faith can be a force for healing in a broken world.

Chapter One

The State of the Church

In his Nobel Prize–winning novel *Soul Mountain*, Gao Xingjian narrates the journey of the protagonist through contemporary China, as it moves through immense cultural change. The description of one of the characters is striking in its depiction of the way ancient practices fare in a postmodern society. It can be read as a cautionary tale for contemporary U.S. Catholicism.

The last surviving Master of Sacrifice has lived to a venerable old age because of his diligence in performing ancestor sacrifices. He recalls the days when they were performed on a grand scale, but laments that those days have passed:

> There is no-one else in sight on the desolate river bank, the doors of the houses are all shut and people are eating New Year's dinner. Nowadays, even if people do have an ancestor sacrifice it's just like a New Year's dinner. It's been shortened and simplified. People simply grow weaker every generation, nothing can stop this.[19]

Alone, the Master undertakes the careful preparations for the ritual: liquor, bean curd, rice cake, ox intestine, rice stalks. At one time there were many who took part in the ritual:

> In those days when he carried out ancestral sacrifices, he had twenty-four people at his disposal—two trainee masters, two supervisors, two men to handle the props, two overseers of the ritual, two persons in charge of the swords, two persons to pour the libation, two persons to make the food offerings, two dragon girls, two messengers, and several people to make pressed rice cakes.

What a splendid event it was! Three oxen were slaughtered and at times even up to nine.
…From the time of the ancestors these were the rules.

Today, the Master laments that things are different; the good days are over.

Now his teeth have fallen out and he can eat only a little thin gruel. He has indeed gone through good days but no-one comes to attend to him anymore. The young people have all the money. They've learnt to smoke filter-tip cigarettes, carry a screaming electric box and also to wear those evil black glasses. How can they still think about their ancestors? The more he sings the more wretched he feels.

Gao's description of the scene is compelling. As people from the nearby village hear what the old man is doing, they go out to help him, thinking he must be a poor beggar. They have forgotten him. He, however, with a feeble voice condemns their failure to offer sacrifice to the ancestors. Instead of listening to him, the people show pity because they think that he has lost touch with reality. In short, they have lost the ability even to recognize the ritual he has come to perform. Over time, the ritual became irrelevant to people because it no longer had any connection to their lives. In the language of anthropology, the ritual became a dead symbol. It may have originally carried deep meaning for the community, but over time that meaning was lost because it failed to sustain their imagination.

Gao writes of a situation in which a religious institution has been choked out by the changes in the modern world. Could Catholic Christianity in the United States be facing a similar future?

On the surface, the answer seems to be no. Catholicism is experiencing healthy growth in the United States, due largely to immigration.[20] Indeed, much of the future of U.S. Catholicism depends largely on the extent to which the Church involves the new immigrant communities. But other indicators suggest that there is cause for concern. Consider the following observations:

- Much of the immigrant population from traditionally Catholic countries is leaving the Catholic Church.[21]
- Among the youngest generation of Catholics (who now comprise close to half of the current U.S. Catholic population), both from immigrant and nonimmigrant communities, there is widespread apathy or antipathy toward the Church, and religious literacy among younger Catholics is low in comparison to Catholics of the baby boom and World War II generations.[22]
- Church attendance is statistically low among young adults; many do not regard organized religion as a key motivating factor in their lives.[23] The 2002 Gallup Index of Leading Religious Indicators showed the lowest level in American religious attitudes since the annual poll began in 1951, attributed to the sexual abuse scandal in the Catholic Church. These attitudes are not simply the result of the scandal, though; attitudes toward organized religion have been dropping steadily over the past four decades.
- The number of priests has fallen steadily over the last decade, and many parishes around the country are without a resident priest. According to projections, more and more Catholics will be unable to attend Mass on a regular basis.[24]

Observations such as these lead to many serious questions about the future of U.S. Catholicism. Why are so many young people ignoring organized religion? Why do so many children of Catholic parents seek spiritual meaning outside of religious traditions? Why are fewer people responding to the need for religious leadership?

Part of the answer has to do with the age in which we live. We fear religion as much as we need it. In the aftermath of the devastation at the World Trade Center in New York, a sign on one makeshift memorial put it best: "God, save us from those who believe in you." Nevertheless, Americans flocked to churches, synagogues, mosques, and temples in record numbers, at least for a time, after September 11. Televised interviews with religious leaders offered temporary moments of reflection on the collective need to find some scrap of meaning amid the horror of those days.

Ours is an age in which the very notion of religious tradition seems to be a double-edged sword. The violence of Muslim extremists today is only the most recent example in a long history of terror arising from religious convictions, including in many cases professed Catholic belief. The same religious traditions have produced zealots for war and zealots for peace: men and women whose wisdom reminds us that our attempts to find meaning must necessarily confront the depth and breadth of reflection that is unique to religion. For young Catholics in the United States, this paradox of religious tradition is obvious. Catholic tradition includes the legacy of the Crusades and the Inquisition, but it is also the spiritual home of figures like Francis of Assisi and Mother Teresa.

We can learn of the Church's dark secrets easily in an age of mass information, in which we can expose them to millions in an instant. For many, knowledge of Catholicism will have come only through the media coverage of the sexual abuse scandal, simply because it was the only information about the Church that was presented to them. In this information/communication age, we know only what is available to us, what we choose to hear. Unfortunately, for many young adults who have grown up Catholic, the answers are troubling: "We have heard pious platitudes disconnected from real life." "We have heard bickering right-wingers criticize liberals, and angry left-wingers criticizing conservatives on issues we don't understand." "We have heard debates about women priests, homosexuals, abortion, the use of obscure religious symbols and terms, birth control, and the death penalty." What many haven't heard, though, is anyone taking the time to tell them why they should be Catholic. Nor have they experienced the kind of welcome and inclusion they expect from a community of faith. As a result, many have simply stopped being Catholic in any meaningful way.

Nevertheless, young people have lived through a time that makes them raise profoundly spiritual questions, and they again confront the paradox of religion. They fear it, yet need it. And in this profound spiritual need is the seed of great hope for the future of the Church. The extent to which this seed bears fruit will depend on the way that Catholics practice a faith that engages the full reality of the postmodern, global world in which we now live.

THE POSTMODERN WORLD

The global reality involves two threads that, I hope, will come together in happy resolution. The threads can be roughly identified as North—the "old" Catholicism of Europe and North America, and South—the "new" Catholicism of Africa, Asia, and South America. The German theologian Karl Rahner suggested that Catholicism is experiencing its third wave; the first was the movement from the Jewish Church into the Gentile world in the first century, and the second was the movement of the Church into Europe during the Middle Ages.[25] This third wave of global Catholicism is taking place at the same time as another third wave, that of democracy. Samuel P. Huntington has described the growth of democracy in the world in three waves. The first wave followed the American and French revolutions; the second followed World War II; the third involves mainly Catholic countries in Central and South America, East Asia, and Central and Eastern Europe.[26] In short, we are seeing a parallel movement of globalization, both in the political sphere and in the Catholic Church.

The outcome of this story depends on a number of factors: social, economic, racial, theological, philosophical. And so it is difficult to predict how the story will end, whether it will be comedy or tragedy. History gives us plenty of examples when threads unravel in schism—the Catholic/Orthodox split in the eleventh century and the Protestant/Catholic split in the sixteenth century are two examples. I suggest that a great deal of the burden of this unfolding story lies on the shoulders of U.S. Catholics.

Why such a burden? Because the U.S. Catholic Church is the meeting place of North and South, old and new. Much of the growth of the Church is due to immigrants from Central and South America, as well as from Asia and Africa, and so the Church is in the midst of learning to navigate between the differing interests of (mostly) white middle-class and immigrant Catholics. Moreover, U.S. Catholics are caught squarely in the middle of global forces competing for their allegiance. On one side are forces of economic globalization, which involves national political systems, multinational corporations, international political bodies, and a host of nongovernmental organizations lobbying for various policies.

These forces have developed out of the economic systems that hold sway in the Western world, where an incredible (and tragically unfair) majority of the world's wealth remains. Perhaps the single most powerful impetus behind this force is the United States itself, with both its economic strength and its political and military power. The United States will play a major role in the trajectory of the world economy in the future, and this world economy will affect the price of food, access to clean water, availability of jobs, presence of health care, stability of local government, and many other day-to-day realities of billions of people.

On the other side are forces of religious ideas that jockey for the minds and hearts of ordinary people. There may be one recognizable organization called "The Catholic Church," which many would identify by pointing to the pope and the bishops—the magisterium or teaching office of the Church—but in practice it is probably more helpful to talk about the many Catholicisms that different people envision. U.S. Catholicism, like the United States itself, is a forum of ideas that are debated, weighed, accepted, or negated by millions, whether or not the magisterium endorses them. This forum has become fractious in the decades following Vatican II, the most significant meeting of Catholic bishops since the Council of Trent in the sixteenth century. Vatican II moved the worldwide Catholic Church into the modern age, but in so doing it ushered in a period in which different factions within the Church have sought to advance their respective agendas. At stake in this debate are basic questions that have been part of the landscape of Christianity since its earliest days: What does it mean to follow Jesus? How does Christian faith impact upon one's relationship to the community, the nation, and the world? What is a healthy relationship among faith, money, and power?

The middle-class majority of U.S. Catholics has great power, both within the U.S. political landscape and within the wider Catholic world. The United States is the largest and richest democracy in the world, while at the same time being the fourth largest Catholic country in the world (behind Brazil, Mexico, and the Philippines). And so U.S. Catholics are caught in the middle, facing the question of which force holds more sway in their decisions. Do middle-class U.S. Catholics identify themselves as Americans first, Catholics second, or vice versa? Is there a conflict between being American and being Catholic? If one is American, why be Catholic at all?

The ways that U.S. Catholics answer these and similar questions will have lasting impact not only on the Church, but also on the global economy. A cursory glance at the distribution of wealth in the world shows some alarming facts.

- Five-sixths of the world can be described as "developing," meaning that people live in considerably lower economic conditions than the average standard of living in the United States.[27]
- One-sixth of the world's population lives on less than $1 per day.[28] Another one-sixth lives on less than $2 per day.[29]
- Eleven percent of Americans experience hunger on a regular basis. According to the U.S. census, the number of hungry Americans has risen by 1.3 million since 2001.[30]

The middle-class majority of Catholics in the United States will grow increasingly distant from the rest of Catholics both within the United States and around the world if they ignore these facts. More tragically, perhaps, they will exacerbate the separation between Catholic faith and the global reality, thereby rendering it impotent to make social change. Perhaps most tragically, they will see it continue to wither, as young people perceive it as a kind of Gnostic superstructure that has nothing to say about the basic questions of meaning, of justice, and of peace. In short, if U.S. Catholics do not honestly confront questions about the intersection of faith and economics, their lives will be less like that of Jesus—the one who lived and worked among the poor and disenfranchised.

A MIDDLE-CLASS CHURCH

Even in spite of the ways that immigration is changing the face of the U.S. Catholic Church, it remains a largely middle-class organization. Historians have shown the ways that U.S. Catholics have climbed the social ladder over the last century and a half; in many ways, this group represents the ideal of the American Dream.[31] The vast influx of immigrants, beginning with the Irish after the famine of 1849 and continuing through waves of mostly European immigrants, changed the public face of Catholicism. The major struggle for these immigrant communities was to show the Protestant majority that they too could be good Americans—and out of this struggle, as Michael Budde suggests, developed a Catholic nationalism. This worldview held that to be Catholic was to be a good American: one who could work hard, contribute to the common good, and prosper.

Today, however, there is a critical challenge to this worldview: the movement of Catholicism into the third world. America's majority of comparatively wealthy Catholics—and by this I mean people who have reasonable food and water security, access to health care and employment, decent living conditions, and a living wage—represent a minority on a global scale. Budde writes provocatively that there is a tension that is developing in global Catholicism: "The U.S. Church is unlikely to break free of U.S. Catholic Nationalism and will be at odds with its Third World coreligionists on a range of theological and political commitments."[32] In short, unless U.S. Catholics begin to critically examine the relationship between economics and faith, there will develop a gulf between their practice of faith and the practice of the majority of the world's Catholics. U.S. Catholicism will become little more than a veneer of peaceful piety covering a fundamental alienation from the misery of the rest of the world.

Many younger middle-class U.S. Catholics have begun to see through this veneer. They wonder what point there is in preaching a gospel of love for one's neighbors—the real kind of love that has that edge of willingness to really give up something for the people you love—when they go to their suburban churches where so many people drive up in gas-guzzling SUVs and luxury cars. Many have confronted the bankruptcy of consumerism, recognizing that those who have become its saints—sports stars, CEOs, entertainers—are spiritually and morally infantile. They wonder where consumerism is leading them, and have begun asking whether it truly serves their deepest desires as human beings. As they look at their parents' generation, they wonder where the American Dream gets them.

Twenty-something Singaporean-British novelist Hwee Hwee Tan describes the kind of alienation that many young adults feel while looking at the effects of consumer culture. Many would call this description secular, but its roots are spiritual.

> I looked at my father. He stood outside the changing room, clutching my mother's handbag. For a horrible Mystic Meg moment, my future balloons into view: I will go to university, then wander into a job that pays me five figures, even though I don't Believe in what I am doing. I will spend eighty per cent of my life trying to help some MNC [multinational corporation] achieve complete and utter world domination of the chocolate biscuit market, and even though I know it is a complete pointless job, I cannot find more meaningful employment if I tried...I will become my father, the Husband-Waiting-For-Wife-To-Try-On-Dress, standing there with a glazed look, seeing nothing, bored, mindless, a living corpse, the man with the handbag.[33]

The disillusionment that many younger Catholics feel toward the Church is the sign of a spiritual hunger—the need to find some meaning in the disparities they witness in their lives, and the recognition that the Church does not address them. To them, the Church is a place where midlife suburbanites go to be comforted, to be told that their lives really need not change, that they are living the American Dream—the closest approximation of the kingdom of God on earth. The U.S. Catholic Church is their parents' church. It does not tell them why consumer culture is sucking the life out of them; it has not adequately invited them to participate in its life and transform its liturgy; it speaks archaically about sex and relationships; it offers pious thoughts dressed up in bland music and pop psychology–influenced homilies. It fails to teach them about the evils they see around them: racism, homophobia, drug abuse, poverty, and many others. And it fails to help them to know God.

Young people are seeing through the veneer of consumerism, but too often they do not see Catholic tradition as a sanctuary of hope. What is remarkable, though, is that studies hint that they nevertheless retain a connection to their Catholic roots—both young Hispanic and young white populations.[34] They may see the Church as hopelessly out-of date; they may see Catholics as hypocritical and biased; they may regard Church moral teaching as quaint, but irrelevant (if they regard it at all); they may look back on their religious education with cynicism; they may have stopped going to Church—and yet there is something in them that says "I am a Catholic." Why?

UNIQUELY CATHOLIC

The answer, I believe, is what theologians call the sacramental imagination.[35] It represents a certain way of looking at the world, a way of coming to know the presence of God in the most mundane, everyday realities of work and play, love and hate, suffering and death, pleasure and joy. There is a lasting impression made on those who are formed to see the world through this lens. Even if they choose not to practice their faith in a meaningful way, they may still retain a sensibility about the immediacy of God in human affairs. The sacramental imagination looks deeply at the real world, believing that there is a depth to things often hidden because of our inattentiveness. It represents a critique of the prevailing consumeristic norm.

Good

A classic presentation of this sacramental imagination comes from the writings of the fourteenth-century mystic Julian of Norwich. Julian's text is a reflection on what she called "showings"—images that God gave to her and that she reflected on in prayer.

And in this he showed me something small, no bigger than a hazelnut, lying in the palm of my hand, and I perceived that it was as round as any ball. I looked at it and thought: What can this be? And I was given this general answer: It is everything which is made. I was amazed that it could last, for I thought that it was so little that it could suddenly fall into nothing. And I was answered in my understanding: It lasts and always will, because God loves it; and thus everything has being through the love of God.[36]

For Julian, staring at a nut was a way of coming to awareness of the presence of God in the world. Julian lived alone, dedicating her life to prayer, and so all of her world was suffused with an awareness of the divine. The language and worldview that she used to make sense of reality were the fruits of late medieval English Christianity, though, and so many today would find her writings difficult to understand. What we can understand, however, is something of the passion she brings to bear on her daily experience. The text above, even though far from what many of us usually think about, manifests a deep spirituality unencumbered by false motives. She is not a mouthpiece for the Church; she is not advancing a cause; she is merely speaking from her heart, about an encounter with divine truth. And what is remarkable is its spontaneity.

Compare Julian's text with a much more contemporary one: a scene from the 1999 Academy Award–winning film *American Beauty*. Ricky, a drug-dealing videographer, is an odd high school-age young man. In one scene, he shows a classmate the video he shot of a bag being blown around in the wind. The video is nothing eye-catching; but Ricky's commentary is striking:

> It was one of those days when it's a minute away from snowing. And there's this electricity in the air, you can almost hear it, right? And this bag was just…dancing with me. Like a little kid begging me to play with it. For fifteen minutes. That's the day I realized that there was this entire life behind things, and this incredibly benev-olent force that wanted me to know there was no reason to be afraid. Ever.
>
> Video's a poor excuse, I know. But it helps me remem-ber…I need to remember…
>
> Sometimes there's so much beauty in the world I feel like I can't take it…and my heart is going to cave in.

Both Julian and Ricky are able to see more than just the mun-dane nut or bag—each item opens them to an even greater appreciation of reality, that which the British poet Gerard Manley Hopkins calls "the dearest freshness, deep down things." Both of these texts are examples of the sacramental imagination. One is representative of the great body of Christian spiritual literature, while the other represents a postmodern reaction against market value–dominated social order.

What is compelling about the second text is its freshness, especially since it unfolds in the midst of a narrative in which the main characters are jaded by their middle-class lifestyle. Ricky is a kind of imperfect mystic, not unlike so many of the characters from the biblical texts—a flawed person who chooses not to buy into the herd mentality, and chooses instead to go in search of God. He sees through the ways that the pervasive U.S. culture is in many ways an anti-culture, to the extent that it extols image at the same time that it hides the emptiness underneath it.

One of Jesus' critiques of the Pharisees strikes home in a similar way:

> Woe to you, scribes and Pharisees, hypocrites! For you are like whitewashed tombs, which on the outside look beautiful, but inside they are full of the bones of the dead and of all kinds of filth. So you also on the outside look righteous to others, but inside you are full of hypocrisy and lawlessness. (Matt 23:27–28)

Perhaps the single greatest critique that young people have of organized religion in general is hypocrisy. Such a critique tends to make practitioners bristle; they will adopt a defensive posture and offer reasons this critique is wrong. Let us consider this critique differently, though: it manifests a latent concern with religion. It is good when a young person criticizes the Church, because it shows that she or he is interested. Young people in the United States do not criticize the government of Ghana or the administration of the University of London, simply because these do not impact their lives. They criticize and complain about the Church, however, because they expect more. And we ought to show them how to get it.

interest

32

UNIQUELY AMERICAN

We in the United States have a political tradition based on the idea that it can be healthy when people argue about things, because when they take part in the political process they achieve a sense of ownership. Historically, Catholic leaders have been reticent to apply the model of U.S. democracy to the Church, because of the anti-hierarchical tendencies of the Protestant models of government that shaped early America. Yet there is a lesson to be learned: in a world where many government systems have fallen over the past two centuries, the U.S. model has had staying power. When revolutionaries in France, Venezuela, and even twentieth-century Vietnam sought a model for their declarations of freedom, they looked to our Declaration of Independence, in some cases lifting entire phrases from it. The reason, I believe, is that this document, and the government that sprang from it, rest upon what is ultimately a theological assertion: the human being is created free, and so leadership among free people must limit itself to the preservation of the freedom of all. There is something in our democracy that feeds our lives as individuals gather in community, and for this reason many have even gone to the extreme of seeing democracy as a kind of gospel unto itself—one that needs to be spread to other parts of the globe. It is, however, reasonable to ask why our democracy has worked, and what it might teach us as Catholics.

Perhaps the most basic answer is the one that is the most ripe for theological inquiry: democracy values the individual person by giving him or her a voice in the way the community lives. People do not like being told how to live; they prefer having the power of self-determination so they can choose how to live. They often prefer to make their own mistakes, rather than listen to an authority.

This basic observation suggests why people are drawn to stories about the struggles of the individual. Adam and Eve in the book of Genesis, Satan in Milton's *Paradise Lost*, the Pilgrims at Plymouth Rock, Muhammad Ali protesting the draft—all are stories about people rejecting some authority and choosing self-determination. From a theological perspective, we may make two observations. First, both the biblical tradition, beginning with Genesis, and the tradition of Catholic teaching dating back at least to Saint Augustine, suggest that God created human beings as free creatures, and that only in freedom can human beings respond to God in faith. God does not coerce us into faith, and as a consequence it is wrong to think that any human agency can be about forcing people's faith. (Note the difference between saying we "can" not force a person's faith, and we "should" not force a person's faith. The first is stronger, because it states that forcing faith is simply impossible—which is true.) The second observation is more complex: if a person's act of faith is free, it would seem that by choosing faith, a person effectively chooses (paradoxically) to place limits on his or her freedom. If I choose to have faith in God, I choose not to have faith in any other god (this is what Abram/Abraham chose when he cut a covenant with God). If I choose to act in faith toward the people around me, I relinquish the choice to do them harm.

People like to be free, but they also come to recognize their need for other people. The social contract thinkers who so shaped the U.S. Founding Fathers' vision of government believed that this recognition is what led people to establish agreements with those around them, forming the primitive societies that eventually flowered into great nations. Catholic teaching has never fully embraced any government theory, but it thrived under medieval hierarchical systems that (many thought) were based in the basic order that God created: giving divinely ordained law to human beings, who could interpret them and make human laws for the masses. The magisterium, moreover, is clearly hierarchical, based on the belief that God's revelation is a mystery that must be unfolded by the bishops gathered together in community—no individual is capable of discerning the fullness of truth.

U.S. Catholics live in the dual worlds of American social contract and Catholic hierarchy. They recognize the strengths of giving each person a voice, and will use democratic voting in many of their parish group meetings. But they also understand that God's laws are not democratic; that people will often act out of selfishness and bias, and that majorities can often be unjust, as in the case of America's embrace of slavery. They listen (sometimes) to their bishops and priests and sit quietly in church. Over the last thirty-plus years, though, U.S. Catholics have become accustomed to thinking of their faith in ways more amenable to democracy than to hierarchy. They want to assert their freedom of conscience and to have a voice in the affairs of the Church,[37] especially in the wake of the sexual abuse scandals. Groups that mobilized in the wake of these scandals, such as Voice of the Faithful and Your Catholic Voice, seek to give laypeople a role in the Church that they have not previously enjoyed. These groups are still comprised mainly of middle-aged Catholics, people who are accustomed to having some sense of cultural ownership of their Church. Their rapid growth in the months following the scandal demonstrates how different contemporary U.S. Catholicism is from its older iterations: pre–Vatican II Catholicism retained a clerical, hierarchical culture in which few would have thought seriously about galvanizing laypeople.

The age that U.S. Catholics live in today is divided. Pre–Vatican II Catholics grew up and lived in a Church that valued community, tradition, and ritual, and that extolled its leaders in the parish and diocese. They were taught to honor these leaders, who devoted their lives in service to God and who were thus chosen by God to lead them to the fullness of truth. Vatican II Catholics lived through a great transition; they learned the traditions and rituals of their parents, then lived through a period that changed them. Masses were in English, not Latin; music became contemporary; new churches in the round were built in the suburbs, and they moved away from their city parishes that looked like small cathedrals. These Vatican II Catholics saw that if liturgy and language could change, then tradition is not intransigent—they saw the possibilities for other changes as well, and started to work on them. The contemporary U.S. Catholic Church owes a great deal to this generation. They took their roles as "the people of God" seriously; became lay ministers and teachers; critiqued the clerical culture that had marginalized the majority of lay Catholics; moved into leadership positions at the parish and diocesan levels. But they also emphasized individual conscience over obedience to authority; took sides on contentious issues like liturgical reform, birth control, or the admittance of women to the priesthood; and sought to find balance between the Catholic culture of their youth and the American culture of their adulthood. This generation appropriated their roles as Catholics, both lay and religious, in radically new ways. Post–Vatican II Catholics, however, have grown up in the

35

midst of the deconstruction of the Church their grandparents and parents knew; they are like the children who are born after a war. The elders remember the beauty of the broken city, and hope for its return. The middle generation of cultural warriors fought for a cause, and in so doing they caused many of the city's buildings to fall; they know that in time the city will be rebuilt, for they have a vision of what it can be. The children, however, know only that they live in the midst of rubble. There are hints of what must have been grand parts of the city at one time; now, however, they wander amid the ruins wondering what they should do about it.

Pre–Vatican II Catholics lived in a hierarchical Church. Vatican II Catholics have sought a Church that is more democratic. Post–Vatican II Catholics are caught between competing models of community, competing models of Church governance, competing theologies. Is the Church more akin to a social contract, in which people gather together with a common cause, sacrificing their freedom for the greater common good? Or is it more like a hierarchy, in which the leaders guide their flock toward the fulfillment of God's will? More important, what is the role that the youngest generation of Catholics will play in this Church, which is at once their home and a place in which they have not been fully invited to share adult roles?

AUTHORITY AND AUTHENTICITY

The core issue for all Catholics, especially the youngest generation, is authority. The absence of many young Catholics from the pews is inversely proportional to their perception of the Church's authority: more absence, less authority. The task of the Church in the twenty-first century is the recovery of real authority.

It is no longer helpful to assume in a facile manner that the leadership of the Church is appointed by God to lead people, after the manner of Moses, into the promised land. The strictly hierarchical model of the Church that reached its zenith at Vatican I is only one way of conceiving of the structure of authority in the Church; the Church's history even in the United States includes very different examples.[38] On the other hand, we in twenty-first-century America cannot easily grant to democracy the status of panacea. When majorities rule, minorities are often crushed. A simple appeal to the need for democracy in the Church is insufficient.[39] There is a need for a third way.

That third way is the way of prophetic mission, in the sense that we find in the biblical stories of the eighth century BCE, the exile of Israel in Babylon during the fifth century BCE, and the teaching of Jesus in the first century CE. What makes this model of authority so important today is that it avoids falling into one of the two extremes that we find so prevalent among Christians today: those of fundamentalism and accommodationism. The former involves removing the Church from the rest of the world; the latter involves changing it so that it fits comfortably within the world. Prophetic authority is about seeking a just order: celebrating those tendencies in a culture that promote justice, and critiquing those tendencies that lead to injustices. The Catholic Church in the United States must be a prophetic force if it is to respond to the promptings of the Holy Spirit.

Social justice is the authentic and necessary manner of response for an organization seeking to do the will of God in a broken world. A more traditional rendering of the Church's mission in the world is that it is to respond to the commands of Jesus to preach the gospel and render *latreia*,[40] worship, to the one true God. In the postmodern age, however, the content of that preaching must be love of the other on both the personal and systemic levels, meaning that all Catholics must seek to understand the ways that their work, their entertainment, their purchasing practices, their relationships, their deepest longings are part of a system of global interrelations. Moreover, in its latreia, the Church must not rest content with repetition of words and practices as though they were removed from the rest of life. True latreia is the total offering of self and community to do the will of God. The Mass, in this context, is that community action that ought to most profoundly reflect the celebration of a community fully dedicated to the will of God at all times. The implication of such a vision of the Church—both in what it does on Sundays and in how it lives in the world the rest of the week—is that it must take a new look at what the Jesus of the Synoptic Gospels called in various places "the kingdom of God" or "the reign of God."[41] What does it mean to be part of a community that is trying to complete the work that Jesus began?

A prophetic Church must be built on the image of leaven. Leaven is unique and yet part of the whole, seeking its fulfillment by bringing the whole to its fulfillment. It is not separate from the whole, nor is it of the same stuff as the whole. A Church built on this image needs leaders who live in solidarity with the whole society: men and women, young and old, rich and poor, speaking the lingua franca of those whom they serve. Their authority would first be an authority of solidarity, meaning that their voices would be easily recognized by those around them simply because they understand their world. This authority would moreover be rooted in the gospel vision of the human condition before God, a vision that treats the individual person as far more valuable than the predominant market-driven ethic allows. Their mission would be to respond to the positive and negative forces that comprise the global reality of the twenty-first century. Paul Lakeland puts it well:

> Christian mission in the face of global capitalism is a blend of resistance and witness. It is not enough to name an evil. One must also offer an alternative vision of how to live…witness is not a full account of mission. To use traditional categories, witness is insufficiently evangelistic. Evangelism, in this sense, is persuasive life in the world.[42]

An authority built on prophetic witness would be an authority of persuasive life in the world. Such an authority would derive its persuasive power from the very fact that living according to the gospel is an authentic response to the very structures of human yearning. We are not solely economic beings, whose salvation is to be found in anything a person can buy or sell. We are beings designed for eternity, who must discern how to work with God in co-creation of temporal lives, in concrete circumstances, on pilgrimage toward heaven.

The story of Bishop Oscar Romero of El Salvador provides a good example of the movement from an older model of ecclesial authority to a model rooted in solidarity. When he was elevated to the episcopacy, he was an academic at heart, having immersed himself in the study of text in order to understand the breadth of Catholic tradition. Critics of his selection believed that he was too aloof from the population of El Salvador in the late 1970s, a population that was overwhelmingly poor and uneducated. El Salvador was a country of great economic polarity: a small minority of families controlled a vast majority of the wealth, leaving most of the population of farmers in destitution. Largely because of government policies that perpetuated this state of affairs, there was a great deal of civil unrest, to which the government often responded with brutality.

Early in his career as a bishop, Romero played the role of a Church leader who carried on the traditional relationship with the leadership of the government. As time went on, however, reports of military brutality led him to reconsider the way he perceived the Church's relationship to the government and the citizens. He came to understand that the country's Catholics were divided in their understanding of what the Church was supposed to do. The wealthy families, who held positions of power in the government, believed that the Church's role was to simply preach from the Bible and leave matters of state to the government. Poor families were looking for the Church to take a stand against the injustices all around them. They were already familiar with the many priests who sought to help them against the brutality of the military. Eventually, Romero came to the realization that the Church could not simply repeat pieties that did not address the fundamental political, economic, and often physical sufferings of the majority of its members. It had to speak in prophetic resistance to the injustices of the government and the military; and in doing so, it had to withstand the brutalities that were then turned against its own priests and nuns. Romero himself was assassinated in 1980, an event that he himself had anticipated: "I do not believe in death without resurrection," he said. "If they kill me, I will be resurrected in the Salvadoran people."

The example of Oscar Romero is difficult for us who live in a comparatively peaceful relationship with the culture in which we live. Yet it nevertheless represents a model of Church authority that is instructive. Romero's authority was not simply a function of his office as bishop: were that the case, all the Catholics of El Salvador would have granted it to him immediately upon his accession to the see. Clearly, some Catholics (not insignificantly, those who were among the rich and powerful) were happy to grant him due reverence because of his role. They perceived his role as more or less "safe"—he could have his cathedral, his preaching, his position as the head of the Church—because this role did nothing to really threaten their own power within the society. It was when he began siding with the poor, speaking to their yearnings for justice, that he became both dangerous to the powerful and authoritative among the weak. When Romero began to enter into solidarity with the poor, truly ministering to their needs and speaking to their concerns, he gained their respect and trust.

The Church must not be about maintaining that which is "safe." One of Romero's sermons points to this danger:

> A Church that suffers no persecution but enjoys the privileges and support of the things of the earth—beware!—is not the true Church of Jesus Christ. A preaching that does not point out sin is not the preaching of the gospel. A preaching that makes sinners feel good, so that they are secured in their sinful state, betrays the gospel's call.[43]

My greatest disappointment in the Church is that it often lacks courage. The problem is not simply the bishops, or the priests, or leaders in parishes, or catechists; it extends to all of us. To the extent that we continue to invest in companies that outsource to other companies practicing unjust labor policies, we lack courage to live according to the gospel. To the extent that we fail to discern the implications of a "gospel of life," as it affects our positions on poverty, abortion, warfare, capital punishment, social security, welfare, international trade, and so many other issues, we fail to think courageously. When our voting (when we actually do it) is often more based on our own economic desires than on issues of human rights and development, we avoid acting with courage. When we treat churchgoing or prayer as another event to fit into our already busy lives, we miss a chance to make a courageous decision. And when we believe that our work, our entertainment, our sexual relationships, our spending, our consumption are not the decisions that move us closer to or farther away from our ultimate good, toward which God invites us in every moment of our lives, we miss the opportunity to build our lives moment by moment on courage and hope.

We who represent the majority of the Church—the laity—are often the ones to lament poor leadership on the parts of priests and bishops. In an age when so many laity have graduate degrees in theology, law, sociology, psychology, business, education, health sciences, and so many other fields, we have the opportunity to take leadership roles in unprecedented ways, in order to be a community of persuasive life in the world. Bishops and priests do have important roles of leadership in the Church, but the Church's witness to the world is not limited to its ordained leaders. If the Church is to be a prophetic voice in American and world society, it will be the result of the combined work of men and women at every level, committed to the basic unfolding of the prophetic dimensions of divine love for humanity.

In the following chapter, we take a close look at those dimensions of the Church's theology that speak courageously to the hopes and fears of our age. Catholic Social Teaching, in particular, represents some of the best that this Church can offer as leaven in postmodern society, because it is rooted in a fundamental hope in God's care for each human being.

Chapter Two

Catholic Theology: Faith, Understanding, Action

I remember an occasion when a student came to my office to ask about the Introduction to Theology course for which she had just registered. "What is that course about?" she asked, trying to figure out if it was like the religious education she hated as a child. I tried to reassure her that it was a critical thinking course, in which students are challenged to think intelligently about basic questions about God, Jesus, the Church, and moral questions. "Good," she said, "because I thought theology was just about preaching, and I don't always believe what the priest says." After she left I had to smile—this was the kind of reaction I often get when I teach that course, and so inevitably I have to spend the first few classes trying to respond to students' protests. Over time, I'm happy to say, students for the most part find thinking about theology refreshing; it's why I enjoy teaching the introductory course. The reason, I think, is because everyone has questions about the things that theology is concerned with: Who is God? What has God done? Can we meet God? Can God meet us?

In this chapter, our aim is to ask about how Catholic theology can speak to the questions of our time. It first focuses on the cultural situation that Americans face in the twenty-first century. Since the Catholic Church has to a great extent functioned as a closed system over the centuries—meaning that it has developed its own language, practice, system of law, and relation to the outside world—its theology has to a great extent remained within that closed system. It makes sense to those within the system (though not always), but less often does it make sense to those outside it. In the twenty-first century, though, with its challenges of pluralism and authority, theology has been forced to move outside this closed system. It is not a surprise that to many, theology smacks of sectarian thinking; but the challenge for theologians today is to draw connections between the tradition of theological thinking, on the one hand, and the demands of the world, on the other. If Catholicism is to speak to the lives of ordinary Americans—let alone the rest of the world—then it must have a relevance for the day-to-day lives people lead in a complex, pluralistic world.

The second part of the chapter, then, focuses on a particular development within the tradition of Catholic theology: Catholic Social Teaching (CST). This body of teaching, we will see, represents a modern attempt—though not the first—to draw connections between theology and the world. CST has moved Catholic theology into conversation with economics, government, environmentalism, human rights discourse, and many other areas of contemporary thought, thereby challenging theologians to bring the concerns of ordinary human beings to bear on their attempts to discern the voice of God in human affairs. It represents an exciting frontier for the Church, and (I hope to show) a critical mode of engaging the younger generation of Catholics. The thesis of this chapter is that Catholic Social Teaching links authentic theology to lived experience in a way that can encourage young people in the process of spiritual and religious formation.

CATHOLIC THEOLOGY IN THE TWENTY-FIRST CENTURY

Catholic theology over the centuries has struggled to come to an understanding of its own claims to truth. On the one hand, it has arisen out of the reflection on a closed book—sacred scripture—such that one would expect a certain constancy in the way that Catholic theologians would engage in theological reflection. On the other hand, there has developed, especially over the last century, an awareness that our understanding of Jesus' teachings changes as our world changes.

The late Polish Nobel Laureate Czeslaw Milosz aptly describes the contemporary dilemma of Catholic theology in his poem "A Theological Treatise."[44]

> I am not, and I do not want to be, a possessor of the truth.
>
> Wandering on the outskirts of heresy is about right for me.
>
> In order to avoid what people call "the serenity of faith,"
> Which is, after all, merely self-satisfaction.
>
> My Polish compatriots have always liked the language of
>   ritual
> And disliked theology.
>
> Perhaps I was like a monk in a mid-forest monastery
> Who, seeing from his window a river in flood,
> Wrote a treatise in Latin, a language entirely incomprehensible
> To peasants in their sheepskin coats.

Milosz suggests much about the contemporary difficulty of the theologian, and of the reasons many find contemporary religion stifling. For if theologians are to be those who enable human beings to come to know God, many have sadly failed, producing scholarship accessible only to an intellectual elite. Similarly, many religious leaders seem to speak only to a religious intelligentsia, rather than help ordinary people grow in their faith.

His phrase "the serenity of faith" suggests how many religious people use their worldview as an excuse to avoid thinking deeply about the world. In my experience, the perception that many younger Catholics have about the Church is that it is filled with self-satisfied people. To more traditional Catholics, reactions against such self-satisfaction would appear, on the surface, to be faithless: apostasy or heresy. Yet the matter is not so simple. The reaction against self-satisfied religion is itself an act of deep faith, for it takes seriously the belief that religion is important. One does not mock something that is completely unimportant. My point is that in a period of the decline of cultural Catholicism, young adults have no consistent religious worldview through which to view reality. They have pieced together what they can—like children wandering through a trash heap—because no human being can live without a worldview.

Consider, against this backdrop, the observation that much contemporary pop culture is rife with irreverent religious imagery, often moving easily across lines of taste that once would have been considered sacrosanct. David Nantais describes Kevin Smith's film *Dogma* as one example, while Andrew Greeley cites the Madonna video *Like a Prayer* as another.[45] Vincent Miller explores the use of these kinds of religious "sampling," or bricolage, among postmoderns. Such bricolage, he asserts, is the response of those who have not the luxury of thorough, systematic construction of a religious worldview in the traditional manner. It is instead the attempt to use whatever tools are available to patch together a manageable framework for understanding the world.[46] Traditional theology has often been described using Saint Anselm's phrase "faith seeking understanding," which made sense when Christians undertook theology from a shared foundational commitment to the religious worldview formed through the centuries of Christian tradition. Today, however, the practice of bricolage is more akin to "understanding seeking faith"—in the sense that it involves people who are capable of articulating a rationally constructed worldview, but who are reaching out for various religious symbols to help them navigate those profound mysteries of human existence that elude simple answers.

I am attracted to Milosz's idea of "wandering on the outskirts of heresy," perhaps because that is precisely what Jesus did. Were not the Pharisees, in their own minds, possessors of the truth? Were not Jesus' followers sometimes deemed "heretical"? Those who feel like outsiders feel deeply the importance of religion, in ways that the insiders do not. The sense of being excluded is powerful—but perhaps more important, so is the simple antidote to exclusion: invitation. It is no surprise that Jesus' first steps in public ministry were invitations: "come, follow me." I am moved by the fact that Jesus did not go to those who were already insiders. Peter, in particular, has the kind of reaction one would expect from a person who is invited for the first time: "I'm not worthy!"

Seeds of Hope

There is great hope in recognizing that contemporary reactions against religion are themselves representative of the desire that religion be meaningful. The antithesis of piety is not heresy; it is apathy and cynicism. *Heresy* is a political term referring to those who, like the pious, share a passion for religion—but whom the pious deem dangerous. It is important to ask, though, about the origins of heresy. Today, it is very unlike the classic heresies—Nestorianism or Jansenism, for example—which arose from theological positions counter to those ultimately embraced by the leadership of the Church. Today, heresy among the young often amounts to a defective appropriation of doctrine. The onus lies upon all who have failed to form them in faith; but the opportunity is also ours to help them appreciate the beauty of it.

An example from my teaching may illustrate this point. A couple of years ago in my Introduction to Theology course I was about to lecture on the doctrine of the incarnation—a central theme in Christian theology. At the beginning of the class, after I had written the term on the board, one of my students asked, "Is that like reincarnation?" I was at once dumbstruck and encouraged: dumbstruck that she had heard of reincarnation, but not the incarnation; but also encouraged by the fact that she felt comfortable enough with me to raise that question in a public forum. The question led me to change the lecture I was about to give. Instead of dwelling on the history of the development of this doctrine from the biblical sources through the Christological councils of the fourth and fifth centuries, I spent time simply talking with the students about what the doctrine of the incarnation means for the way that Christians understand themselves in relation to God. Taking the creedal statement of the Council of Chalcedon (451 CE) as a point of departure, I offered that the doctrine of the incarnation means that there is no radical wall of separation between human beings and God. Turning to the Eastern theology of divinization—which suggests that, in the words of Saint Athanasius, God became human in order that the human might become God—I explained how this doctrine means that ordinary human beings manifest the face of God in the very fact of their existence. The doctrine of the incarnation, in short, means that ordinary human life is capable of manifesting God.

The discussion that day was lively, even though it became immediately evident to me that nearly all my students would have been declared heretics if they professed their views publicly in the fifth century. The experience of teaching that day has helped me to approach teaching in a new way—there must be an element of catechesis in the teaching of theology if it is to make any sense to those whose religious education has been inconsistent.[47]

To return to my metaphor of the broken city from chapter 1, let us observe that young people who practice religious bricolage—often crassly called "cafeteria Catholicism" by those whose religious formation was more systematic—are trying their best to piece together a coherent sense of meaning amid ruins. Instead of criticizing their inability to construct for themselves grand cathedrals, we ought to be praising their tenacity for trying to salvage symbols in the midst of the broken culture that lived Catholic tradition. In the contemporary religious landscape, they do not have to engage this tradition at all—they can choose from an array of religious symbols (and often do), but nevertheless they return to Catholic symbolism because there is something in it they find attractive. In contemporary consumer culture, religious symbols are easily divorced from the communities and traditions that make them meaningful, and become little more than artifacts to be exploited for their immediately perceived value. A recent example is the use of rosaries as fashion accessories among Japanese young adults[48] or of seated Buddhas as paperweights in the United States. Both the rosary and the seated Buddha are religious symbols, the meaning of which developed over time in the religious communities that used them; but in consumer culture, they are little more than free-floating objects for consumption.

Young people who have grown up in this kind of culture cannot be expected to have appropriated the fullness of Catholic wisdom unless they have been formed by people committed to passing it on. When they latch onto a Catholic symbol—perhaps a devotion to Mary, or an interest in gothic architecture, or a love of Latin—they do so for its immediate interest. It speaks to them in a unique way that opens for them a window of meaning they have not previously experienced. This is hopeful, even if they do not as a result continue to pursue an understanding of the big picture. This is the moment of opportunity, the teachable moment—the point that can provide the means of entry into the whole sacramental economy that is Catholic faith. For Catholicism is not merely a cluster of random symbols disconnected from one another; on the contrary, it is by its very nature systematic in its vision of the truth of Christ. One truth relates to all the others—or at least it should, and this unity of truth has always been the task of theologians.

Where theologians have missed the mark is in their overemphasis on exploring the systematic relationship of truths to each other, and their underemphasis on making them accessible and understandable to ordinary people. Milosz's image of the monk writing in Latin while a flood swirls round him is an apt metaphor. One might imagine that the monk was writing a critical treatise on the incarnation, but this topic is utterly irrelevant to the pressing needs of peasants struggling to rescue their loved ones from the deluge.

What the Church has to say about who God is and how God has self-revealed over human history is a fundamental question, to be sure, and intelligent treatments of Christology are important in helping Christians to understand their faith. A developed Christology, moreover, influences the devotions of everyday people of faith—when they consider how the story of Jesus makes them think differently about the world they live in. But in Milosz's metaphor, what comes to mind is the monk's disassociation with the immediate need of the world around him. Theology undergirds the way people live in the world, but it is not the world.

Theology is not always arcane and distant, though. The aim of Catholic theology as a whole is to show the interrelatedness of all the articles of faith in the unity of the truth revealed by God through Jesus of Nazareth. The monk may not have paid sufficient attention to the world around him—and theologians still make this mistake—but one can imagine that he was a person whose love of truth led him to cling tenaciously to that source of truth amid the vagaries of everyday life. In the end, one may wonder which of the regular crises we face in our lives will have significance when viewed from the perspective of the transcendence that theology seeks. In the contemporary Church, many U.S. theologians have learned much from feminists, Latinos, Asians, Africans, and others whose theologies have developed out of the lived experience of struggle with the communities that claim their fidelity. The title of Ada María Isasi-Díaz's book *En La Lucha* (In the Struggle),[49] which articulates a theology appropriate for Hispanic women, is especially suggestive of this new trend to connect theology with those people in "floods" of every sort.

The key for the Church in the twenty-first century is to find that balance between discerning ultimate truths (theology) and proclaiming the most basic good news about God (kerygma, from the Greek verb meaning "to proclaim"). On the one hand, there is always the danger of catering to an elite, those who are already formed in faith and whose desire to plumb the mysteries of faith lead them to seek ever more precise formulations of theological doctrines. The old critique of the medieval Scholastic theologians seeking to know how many angels could dance on the head of a pin is an example of this extreme. (As a footnote, no theologian ever wrote about this topic, but it captures the imagination.) On the other hand, there is the danger of dwelling on an oversimplified kerygma or proclamation about what God has done, a kerygma that lacks the sort of reflection that characterizes the life of serious thinking about what faith means. Without such reflection, minimally the Church runs the risk of devolving into a bland self-help organization, following whatever trendy mode of thinking prevails in a given cultural milieu. At the extreme, without good theology, kerygma can become a poisonous demagogy.

For the postmodern Church in the United States, such a balance is both critical and elusive. On the one hand, people in the Church must strive to avoid what the authors of *Habits of the Heart* describe as "Sheilaism," that is, a completely individualized spirituality pieced together as bricolage.[50] On the other hand, the Church must avoid the temptation of ecclesiolatry, the making of the Church itself into an idol. The Church is not God; it seeks to be the place of people's encounter with God. In the language of theology, the Church is the sacrament of God: the visible, tangible place of encounter with God. It is the community whose different elements challenge us to break out of our individualized idolatries (we all have them) to consider the radical call of God to become a new human being. Without the Church, there can be no authentic Christian spirituality. Isolated practitioners of spirituality will lose touch with that prophetic dimension of Christian faith, which always summons us out of our comfort zones into radical discipleship of love toward the hidden other. They need the discomfort of having to deal with other people.[51]

There must be a middle place between the extremes of abstract theological speculation and juvenile repetitions of the same catch phrases: "What would Jesus do?" "His pain, your gain," and other Christian T-shirt favorites. Later in Milosz's poem, he writes:

> There must be a middle place between abstraction and childishness
> where one can talk seriously about serious things.
>
> Catholic dogmas are few inches too high; we stand on our toes
> and for a moment it seems to us that we see.

This middle place, I suggest, is the area that demands the attention of those who preach, teach, and live among the Church's future. It is a place where the concerns of the everyday world encounter the living tradition of the Church, the place where, according to an image attributed to Reinhold Niebuhr, intelligent people have a Bible in one hand and a newspaper in the other. Locating that place will be the outcome of two clusters of activity. The first will be the lived experience of young people today; the second will be the body of theological and ethical reflection that is Catholic Social Teaching (CST).

THE NEED FOR CATHOLIC SOCIAL TEACHING

The reason young people's lived experience is so critical is because it is there that we will find the kind of theological literacy that eludes us if we quiz them on the *Catechism*. Young people have been shown to be poorly catechized, in comparison with the Vatican II and pre–Vatican II generations.[52] Yet they are arguably the most sophisticated cohort when it comes to their internalization of the most radical teachings of Vatican II: on the relationship between Catholicism and other religious traditions, on the nature of religious freedom, and on the dignity of the conscience, to name some examples. This observation is not to say that young Catholics can easily articulate what these teachings are, or that they came from the Council, or that there even was a notable Church council during the 1960s. It is, however, to suggest that at the level of lived experience, young adult Catholics have internalized what the Council wrote about. They recognize the truth in other religions, even if they are unaware of the Vatican II document *Nostra Aetate*. They believe in the freedom of religion, even if they have never read *Dignitatis Humanae*. They recognize the dignity of the conscience in making decisions, even if they have never heard of *Gaudium et Spes*. They may be only nominal Catholics; they may or may not go to church on a regular basis; they may or may not believe in all the teachings of the Church; but they have developed ways of looking at the world that will be enhanced, deepened through contact with those thinkers that have helped the Church to consider the implications of the gospel in the postmodern world.

Catholic Social Teaching represents the Church's sustained effort at making connections between the world people live in and what Jesus called "the kingdom of God." Because young people's experience of religion is filtered through their experience of the ordinary world, CST is an important resource that invites them to think more deeply about the ways the ordinary world is permeated with ultimate questions. Where the young person sees unjust labor practices in the sweatshops that produce athletic wear for U.S. teenagers, those formed in CST raise questions about the nature of consumer desire as an expression of fundamental freedom and the global economic forces that create wealth and dehumanize people as structures shot through with the realities of both sin and grace. Inviting young people to consider CST is an invitation to allow their passion for justice to bring them deeper into contemplation of Jesus' proclamation about the way God is dwelling in our midst.

CST is a response to the conditions of the late modern world, toward greater attention to the lived experience of ordinary people. Inasmuch as CST has drawn from the doctrinal tradition of the Church, it roots itself in a sound vision of the human being (a theological anthropology) that is more integrated than so many other visions that are prominent in the contemporary cultural landscape. In particular, CST challenges the truncated values of consumerism, and offers a lens through which to critique contemporary popular Catholic practice in the United States. CST critiques the current spirituality fad, moving us toward a more critical appreciation of why religion is a necessary complement to the development of any authentic Christian spirituality.

Before addressing these issues, it is important to confront a key difficulty facing not only the Catholic Church in the United States, but indeed all religious groups and other intentional communities such as the Sierra Club, the American Civil Liberties Union, or the Republican Party. The difficulty is this: the postmodern world is one in which all communities begin, in some sense, on a level playing field. The breakdown of traditional authority structures has meant that for many people there can be no such thing as self-evident truth, and that loyalty to a community can last only as long as it maintains fidelity to the values that attracted the person in the first place. In this world, the individual conscience becomes the locus of authority. And while Catholic tradition holds great reverence for the individual conscience—devoting a significant section of the Vatican II document *Gaudium et Spes* (Pastoral Constitution on the Church in the Modern World) to the dignity of conscience— still it has always seen conscience as fulfilling its dignity when it responds to the will of God.

I wish to suggest that when the Catholic Church is living up to its name, as both "catholic" or universal, and "church"—what the New Testament calls *ekklesia*, "those called out," that is, to be a community formed by God as leaven in society—it is radically different from other intentional communities such as those mentioned above. First, in its reaching for catholicity it must reject anything that smacks of parochialism. This is not to say that Catholicism must reject local culture in search of some abstract universality—this has been the error of colonialism, which several authors in the fields of ecclesiology and mission studies have aptly critiqued.[53] Instead, it is to say that its very attempt to be the community responding to the invitation of God makes it something different from a group simply doing what it enjoys doing with other like-minded individuals. Further, inasmuch as members of the Church are called out by God—regardless of how they understand what this actually means in their own lived experiences—they are acting not solely out of personal desire.

The reason these observations are important is because my thesis that young Catholics today need to better understand CST can be read as a kind of propaganda, a strategy for swelling the organization's ranks at the expense of other potential organizations. "Let's get the kids on our side!" might be the rallying cry. A great deal of evangelical fervor seems to be spent with the presupposition that the Church is competing for members, almost as if there were a cosmic NFL draft going on. In stating my thesis, then, I am not calling for a new strategy that will increase membership in the U.S. Catholic Church (though that might happen anyway). I am instead suggesting that there is a fundamental imperative today that has remained constant since the time of Jesus' commissioning the disciples to preach to all nations. It is an imperative with which Paul too was familiar: those called by God to be disciples become new human beings whose very lives ought to reflect what it means to be human. In sending the disciples to preach the gospel, Jesus was not telling them to make a powerful political body (Constantine notwithstanding). The size of the Church's population is a very poor indicator of its fidelity to the gospel. Instead, Jesus was telling them that the disciple is necessarily a public figure: a person who is allowing God to constantly re-create him or her in the divine image, such that all that person's actions testify to the work of grace. To be a follower of Jesus is to allow God to perform this work on a daily basis, and to further allow God to use oneself as a sign to others of what it means to be a human being participating in the upbuilding of the kingdom of God.

The implication of this theology is that authentic leadership in the Church must be about promoting the unfolding of what medieval theologians called "cooperating grace."[54] In other words, it means helping people to understand how God is working in their midst through their words and actions. It means creating structures in the community that enable people to come to deeper awareness of grace, and removing those structures in the community that hinder this awareness. More practically, it means helping young people to understand the already-present God in their lives, even if they have never set foot in a church, and encouraging them to deepen their understanding of the ways that God is working among them. Emphasis on Catholic Social Teaching is not just a clever marketing scheme designed to hook the younger set. It is instead the necessary response of the community of disciples in the postmodern world, a response that will enable people to discern God's presence in our complex world.

THE DEVELOPMENT OF CATHOLIC SOCIAL TEACHING

In order to understand further why CST is so important to the *postmodern* Church, we must recall something about the *modern* Church in which CST first took root. But since it can be difficult to imagine the world as it was over a century ago, I use a scene from contemporary China, where the economic conditions in many ways represent an accelerated version of those conditions in Europe and the United States at the end of the nineteenth century. Contemporary China is a study in the relevance of CST.

An Illustration: Contemporary China

In my most recent trip to the southern province of Guangxi, China, in the fall of 2003, I was on a bus ride from the center of the modestly populated city of Guilin toward the outskirts of the city and into the countryside. The ride was an experience of time travel. We were on a climate-controlled bus, having left a comfortable Western-style hotel. The farther we got from our starting point, the more the landscape changed. Elegant architecture gave way to more rudimentary brick dwellings, which in turn gave way to small huts and plots of farm. Eventually, as we left the city, the dwellings looked more and more ramshackle: corrugated metal and other refuse thrown together to form basic shelter from the elements. Later, aboard a tourist boat on the stunning Li River, we viewed small villages along the riverbanks that looked very much as they might have a hundred or a thousand years ago. Fishermen aboard bamboo boats continued to work as they have for centuries—even as our guides checked their voicemail on sleek cell phones.

A tour through China is a study in the development of the contemporary world. In August 2002, National Public Radio's Beijing correspondent Rob Gifford began a series of stories on the changes in modern China. He described how the world's most populous country is currently in the midst of what may be the most explosive economic growth in history, such that elements of premodernity, modernity, and postmodernity sometimes coexist within the same relatively small region. His audio portraits paralleled my own experiences there. Gifford's stories focused on the growing pains that China is experiencing as a result of rapid economic growth. One compelling story focused on the situation of a young migrant worker named Wu Dongmei, a twenty-something woman whose work has made her look older.[55] She left her home to travel some thousand miles to the boomtown of Shenzhen, just across the checkpoints that separate wealthy Hong Kong from mainland China. There she works in a clothing factory in conditions that Gifford calls "Dickensian."

Ms. Wu is conscious of the choices she must make to survive. Like millions of other workers who produce the countless "made in China" items that choke American department stores, she left a rural area because there was no money to be made there. She has chosen to work so that her younger brother might attend school and eventually earn more lucrative work. She lives in a dormitory with several other young women, but remarks that she is more fortunate than others in Shenzhen who are basically in slave conditions. She recognizes that she is being exploited in the factory, but comments, "What can I do? I need the money."

Shenzhen is a city that Deng Xiaopeng designated a Special Economic Zone in 1979 in order to encourage foreign investment in mainland China. At the time, it had little more than rice paddies—a stark contrast to the densely populated cosmopolitan Hong Kong, then under British rule. In a very short time, the city has undergone incredible growth, attracting both legal migrants as well as a very high number of illegal immigrants, both Chinese and foreign. The city is in many ways a showcase of Chinese economic power over the last couple of decades: bright, gleaming buildings rise from the all-new urban landscape; streams of young people—both Chinese and Western—throng dance clubs and restaurants.

Shenzhen has now become a tourist destination itself, when just several years ago it would scarcely have been a rest stop on the way from Hong Kong to the south China city of Guangzhou. There are, in a sense, two different Shenzhens: the one that one can view from a comfortable chair while surfing the Internet,[56] and the other that is hidden. It is the hidden side of Shenzhen today that closely resembles the kind of conditions that Charles Dickens described in his novel *Hard Times:* awful working conditions, child labor, and desperate poverty feeding an industrial machine benefiting a small minority.

What the Developing World Teaches Us about CST

Parts of contemporary China, like other nations of Asia, Africa, and Central and South America, are experiencing economic conditions similar to those that prevailed during the industrial revolution in Europe and North America in the late 1800s. Wealth and power have become concentrated in the hands of a few, while the majority of workers struggle daily to survive. Looking at contemporary China, one can imagine why figures like Pope Leo XIII began to turn their attention to economic conditions: they realized that it was necessary to understand the lives people were living if they hoped to share the gospel with them. Returning to Milosz's metaphor of the theologian in the flood, I am suggesting that the key significance of this movement is that it represented a concerted effort to watch the water rise—to use the resources in Catholic tradition to speak to basic human rights issues like the need for a fair wage.

It is therefore illustrative to look at a document issued by Pope Leo XIII in 1891, a document that has remarkable relevance today not only for China and the developing world, but also for those conditions in Europe and the United States that involve the exploitation of workers.[57] The encyclical *Rerum Novarum* (New Things, rendered in English as "On The Condition of Workers" or "On Capital and Labor") addressed the unfair labor practices that prevailed in many factories. While it was not the first papal document to address social concerns,[58] it nevertheless represented an important contribution to Catholic doctrine, both as a statement of what Catholics themselves believed about their faith and as a contribution from the

Catholic tradition to human society. One apt description of the impact of Leo's encyclical comes from Pope Pius XI's 1931 encyclical *Quadragesimo Anno* (Fortieth Year, referring to the anniversary of *Rerum Novarum*, but rendered "On the Reconstruction of the Social Order" in English):

> The Encyclical, On the Condition of Workers, compared with the rest had this special distinction that at a time when it was most opportune and actually necessary to do so, it laid down for all mankind the surest rules to solve aright that difficult problem of human relations called "the social question."
>
> For toward the close of the nineteenth century, the new kind of economic life that had arisen and the new developments of industry had gone to the point in most countries that human society was clearly becoming divided more and more into two classes. One class, very small in number, was enjoying almost all the advantages which modern inventions so abundantly provided; the other, embracing the huge multitude of working people, oppressed by wretched poverty, was vainly seeking escape from the straits wherein it stood.[59]

Rerum Novarum is usually named as the document that gave rise to the modern tradition of Catholic Social Teaching, in part because of its commemoration in later encyclicals that celebrated its fortieth, eightieth, and hundredth anniversaries. The reason it has achieved such prominence over the last 115 years is that unlike the majority of earlier papal encyclicals, which dealt with internal matters of the Church, *Rerum Novarum* was an extended attempt by the Church to address problems in the outside world. "The social question," as Pius XI put it, refers to what might once have been called "the secular realm," as distinct from "the sacred realm" of the Church itself. Consider that in 1864, just twenty-seven years before *Rerum Novarum*, Pope Pius IX issued a Syllabus of Errors, in which he wrote about the distinction between Church and society, a view rooted in Saint Augustine's fifth-century text *The City of God:*

church in relation to rest of the world

The faith teaches us and human reason demonstrates that a double order of things exists, and that we must therefore distinguish between the two earthly powers, the one of natural origin which provides for secular affairs and the tranquility of human society, the other of supernatural origin, which presides over the City of God, that is to say the Church of Christ, which has been divinely instituted for the sake of souls and of eternal salvation.[60]

This text points to a strong distinction between the Church and the world—a distinction that manifested itself in the image of the Church as a latter-day Noah's ark, saving the elect from the destruction of the world around them. *Rerum Novarum*, therefore, represents a change in the Church's posture toward the world. By drawing from the Church's theological heritage to address contemporary social concerns, Leo implicitly suggested that the Church is in some way responsible for the powers of both "natural origin" and "supernatural origin." Putting it more simply, Leo's encyclical suggests that the Church ought to seek not only its own good, but also that of the rest of the world.

There is an implicit theological perspective in this encyclical that developed over the next several decades, and reached its fruition in the documents of Vatican II (1962–65). The perspective has to do with the Church's self-understanding in relation to the rest of the world. If the Church seeks to serve the good of human society, then it does not see itself as radically separate from that larger society. And while it would be too simplistic to suggest that the Church had always held to such a view, it is nevertheless clear that in much of the nineteenth century, the Church was in a reactionary posture toward the world. The rise of science, the development of modern states, and the growth of biblical criticism were just a few of the factors that led to the waning of ecclesiastical authority that had prevailed during the Middle Ages. The Church, in short, was trying to hold onto the reins of power that it had once enjoyed, by distinguishing itself from the power "of natural origin," represented by the figure of Caesar. The Church was of

58

divine origin; Caesar was not. The Church, in short, was destined for heaven, while Caesar was merely a temporal authority.

Rerum Novarum thus represented a bridge between the two powers that Pius IX had described in his Syllabus of Errors. It was an attempt to bring out of Catholic tradition resources that might help men and women of the day to secure more livable working conditions. It was not, then, solely concerned with spiritual issues like salvation or eternal life; it dealt specifically with the daily reality of needing enough money. The encyclical begins with an observation about the ways that the world had been changing:

> That the spirit of revolutionary change, which has long been disturbing the nations of the world, should have passed beyond the sphere of politics and made its influence felt in the cognate sphere of practical economics is not surprising. The elements of the conflict now raging are unmistakable, in the vast expansion of industrial pursuits and the marvelous discoveries of science; in the changed relations between masters and workmen; in the enormous fortunes of some few individuals, and the utter poverty of the masses; the increased self reliance and closer mutual combination of the working classes; as also, finally, in the prevailing moral degeneracy.[61]

Leo discerned that the changes brought about by the industrial revolution might have a negative impact not only on the poor, but also on society as a whole if the different classes saw themselves at war with each other. He emphasized, in contrast to the doctrines of socialist thinkers like Marx and Engels, that there is an imperative to preserve the solidarity between the different classes. Unions among vulnerable workers were good, he indicated, but not to the extent that they should seek the revolutionary overthrow of the wealthy. Instead, he suggested, the aims of labor unions should be to seek the whole good of their members, both spiritual and physical. At the same time, he cautioned the wealthy about the dangers of exploiting workers, reminding them that Jesus often criticized the wealthy and blessed the poor. The danger for the wealthy, he suggested, is in seeing wealth as an end in itself, rather than as a gift from God to be used for the good of others.

In his encyclical, Leo called for solidarity among the different classes in light of their common origin and destiny in God. He thus articulated the beginnings of a theological economy—a vision of how human beings use the goods of the Earth in cooperation toward the building of the kingdom of God. Later treatments of social issues over the next century manifested a commitment to the development of this theological economy, and provided an important commentary on the conditions that we see in places like China and elsewhere. Later in this chapter, we examine in more detail the development of this theological economy and its meaning for the contemporary U.S. Catholic Church. In the next chapter, we inquire further into how it impacts the relationship between Americans and other people around the world.

CATHOLIC SOCIAL TEACHING AS CRITIQUE OF CULTURE

What is especially important for the unfolding of the U.S. Catholic Church in the twenty-first century, I suggest, is a commitment to drawing out and practicing the implications of such a theological economy. The reason is clear: the economy has become the preeminent lens through which most young people in the United States (and increasingly, around the globe) have come to understand themselves today. They are immersed in consumer society by what they wear; what they listen to and watch on TV and in movies; what games they play on the video screen; what degrees they seek for what careers they intend to pursue; whom they choose to become attracted to and (sometimes) marry. Returning to the question of the right balance of theology and kerygma, my point is that a theological economy draws from the Church's tradition of reflection on the gospel, in order to shed light on the emerging global marketplace. This marketplace is where people live: both those that purchase bobblehead dolls of their favorite sports stars, and those Chinese laborers who work in abusive conditions to produce them.[62] If the Church in this country is to preach the gospel, it must preach in the language of economics. The imperative is double-sided: it must reach young people who have become disillusioned by a rootless world in which all things have become items for consumption; and it must speak to a world market predicated on the misery of millions of people struggling to make enough money to survive.

The German philosopher Friedrich Nietzsche wrote that the history of the world is a history of the will to power.[63] And while this is not the place for a full evaluation of Nietzsche's philosophy, we can observe that in many ways this basic observation holds true even today. For it seems clear that much of the world's history can be read as the constant grasping for power on the part of different groups. In the West, one need only mention the names of Alexander the Great, Julius Caesar, Charlemagne, Napoleon, Hitler, and Stalin to observe that the thirst for power has shaped the cultural heritage of entire populations. Elsewhere, similar observations may be made of figures such as Qin Shi Huangdi in China, Genghis Khan in Mongolia, Suleyman the Magnificent in the Ottoman Empire, and Pol Pot in Cambodia. More recent history has demonstrated that the cooperation of economic and military power shapes worlds: fifteenth-century Spain has left its mark on the current societies of Central and South America; eighteenth- and nineteenth-century Great Britain affected the development of India, the United States, Hong Kong, and other colonies. Similar stories can be told of Portugal's influence in Brazil; France's effect on societies in Africa and Southeast Asia; the Netherlands' impact on South Africa; and the list continues. Today, the unmatched power of the United States affects nearly every corner of the globe, from the brand names that people wear to the foodstuffs that they consume to the entertainment they seek on television and at the movies. In this last case, though, this economic power is only obliquely connected to military force. For while the reorganization of global power following World War II did give economic advantage to the United States, at no time has it pursued a program of colonization like those of the European powers from the fifteenth through nineteenth centuries.[64]

The significance of this newer form of world dominance— through economics more than through military power—is that it is predicated in large part on individual choices to buy or not to buy. Whereas military power is truly coercive, economic power is more subtle, involving the psychologies of millions of individuals' self-interest. Political power once was directly related to military power, but today the situation is far more complex. To be sure, the United States has the most powerful army in the world. That it has the capacity to remove entire regimes from power—as in the case of the Taliban in Afghanistan and the Baath party in Iraq—is a stunning testimony that the age of military power is not past. Yet U.S. power in the world is not only a function of the political reordering of the world following World War II. It is also a result of those economic institutions that came into being during that same period—institutions like the World Bank, the International Monetary Fund, and the World Trade Organization—institutions whose leaderships are drawn from the major industrialized nations (most prominently, the United States), and whose policies have been critiqued for their negligence toward developing nations.[65] It is also a result of the fact that the U.S. economy was alone in the middle of the twentieth century in its ability to cultivate markets in every corner of the globe. Today, U.S. products are as common in the shadows of the pyramids in Egypt as in the snowy plains of Siberia as in the streets of Manhattan.

Beneath the layers of historical forces that have shaped the contemporary global order lie basic questions about the nature of the human condition. The common assumptions, it seems, have been that it is better to rule than to be ruled; the strong rather than the weak; the rich rather than the poor. If Nietzsche is correct, then world history is a history of dominance—and history itself is the record that the winners have written. Against this backdrop of cultural history, the legacy of Catholic reflection on the social teachings of Jesus stands in stark contrast. For the carpenter from Nazareth, like other keen observers of the human condition, recognized that such assumptions cannot go unchecked. Consider the way Luke the evangelist records Jesus' proclamations:

Blessed are you who are poor, for yours is the kingdom of God.

Blessed are you who are hungry now, for you will be filled.

Blessed are you who weep now, for you will laugh.

Blessed are you when people hate you, and when they exclude you, revile you, and defame you on account of the Son of Man.

Rejoice in that day and leap for joy, for surely your reward is great in heaven; for that is what their ancestors did to the prophets.

But woe to you who are rich, for you have received your consolation.

Woe to you who are full now, for you will be hungry.

Woe to you who are laughing now, for you will mourn and weep.

Woe to you when all speak well of you, for that is what their ancestors did to the false prophets. (Luke 6:20–26)

At first glance these statements seem paradoxical and counterintuitive. There is no obvious key to understanding exactly what Jesus meant by them, but an examination of the context in which he gave them gives a clue. In both Matthew's and Luke's accounts, they are part of a sermon Jesus gave to a crowd who had become interested in his public ministry. He had gathered attention due to both his charismatic preaching about what God's kingdom was like and his miraculous healings. Jesus' declarations about who is blessed, then, are references to the unfolding of God's kingdom. If our current use of the term *global order* makes reference to an emerging sociopolitical structure predicated on the changes set in motion during the early twenty-first century, then perhaps the term *divine order* might better represent a parallel claim that Jesus was making about the first-century world. The kingdom of God, or the divine order, had already been set in motion in history, with figures like Abraham, Moses, and the prophets; Jesus spoke about how this divine order challenged the existing conceptions of the world among his peers.

The divine order, in short, was not predicated on the use of power: Jesus' own solidarity with human beings, a solidarity poetically described in the mid-first-century "Philippians Hymn," was testimony.

> though he was in the form of God, [he] did not regard
>   equality with God as something to be exploited,
> but emptied himself, taking the form of a slave, being
>   born in human likeness.
> And being found in human form,
> he humbled himself and became obedient to the point of
>   death—even death on a cross. (Phil 2:6–8)

Jesus' words about the divine order, then, challenged the proclivity to see human liberation as a function of sociopolitical forces. Instead, Jesus' own life testified to seeking the will of God as the means of liberation. The poor are blessed because there are no priorities that prevent them from doing God's will. The rich are likely to want to protect what they have, thereby becoming more attached to things that are not God. The hungry must reach out desperately for the help of God; the filled are likely to be content with the status quo. Those who weep seek consolation in God; those who laugh are satisfied with themselves. Those who are insulted are not likely to embrace the values of their persecutors; while those who are esteemed are likely to be seduced by those values by which they are deemed important.

Looking at Jesus' words today against the backdrop of modern history, one can experience both despair and hope. On the one hand, it is painfully obvious that the way of power was the story of the twentieth century. On the other hand, it is clear that the way of peace found expression in the lives of many societies: Gandhi's India; Martin Luther King's United States; Desmond Tutu's South Africa. The fundamental sociopolitical struggle of the twenty-first century will be that between the way of power and the way of peace.

In our own more recent history we can see signs that the Church can represent the way of peace. Since the Catholic Church still remains the one truly national religious voice in the United States—unlike the other important religious voices in this country, which are limited in scope by geography (Southern Baptists), organizational structure (Evangelicals), or sheer numbers (other Protestant churches, Muslims, Jews, Orthodox Christians, and others)—it retains a presence in public affairs. In 1983 and 1986, respectively, the U.S. Catholic Bishops produced the documents "The Challenge of Peace" and "Economic Justice for All," both of which sought to address public issues from the standpoint of social justice teaching. The quadrennial publication of the United States Conference of Catholic Bishops (USCCB) "Faithful Citizenship" seeks to raise consciousness of voters in presidential elections, on the importance of applying a consistent ethic supportive of human life and society. Documents such as these have received national media attention, and are reminders that the Catholic Church has enjoyed—even in recent times, with its breakdown of authority—an influence on the way Americans think about their responsibilities to others.

On the grassroots level, the commitment of Catholics to the way of peace is profound. Organizations like the Catholic Worker, Pax Christi, Sojourners, Catholic Relief Services, and Catholic Charities involve thousands of people in works of justice and political action on behalf of those marginalized by society. In 2004, several of these organizations sought to respond to the initiatives of political parties to garner "the Catholic vote" by publishing articles in major news sources that suggested that no candidate could make a claim to fully support Church teaching on the range of issues from abortion to just war to poverty to immigration.[66]

An important consideration for leaders in the Catholic community is how to make connections between the justice initiatives already happening in the Church today, and those young people for whom the institutional Church is still suspect. For while many young people express a yearning for justice, and have engaged in service activities on college campuses and in service organizations, significantly fewer of them make the explicit connection between the demands of justice and the practice of religion. The reason may be simply that they do not see the Church as a socially just institution. Ironically, the Church's own tradition of social teaching offers a critique of its contemporary life—a critique that we do well to consider as we look forward to the Church comprised entirely of those born after Vatican II.

CATHOLIC SOCIAL TEACHING AS CRITIQUE OF RELIGION

It will without doubt sound odd to many who have grown up Catholic that the Church's own teachings critique the very life of the Church itself. Yet for others, this point is obvious. If the Church seeks to respond to the culture in which it resides, it must demonstrate in its own life that it seeks to be better.

The most pronounced shortcoming of the contemporary Catholic Church in the United States is not its leadership, its ordained ministers, its relationship to the Vatican, its feminists, its homosexuals, its theologians, its intransigent right or its heretical left. It is the entrenchment of attitudes formed in the wake of Vatican II that have poisoned the waters of the Church today, such that they are no longer life-giving. Young people who have no knowledge of liturgical reform, sexual ethics after *Humanae Vitae* (the 1968 papal encyclical condemning artificial birth control), the role of the laity, or other contentious issues have little foundation upon which to build their understanding of the current controversies alive in the Church today. They have become disillusioned by the fact that so much energy is spent trying to vilify the perceived enemy, rather than building a community founded in love seeking justice. In short, when they look at the Church they do not see much that reminds them of Jesus.

On various occasions I have spoken to audiences asking basic questions about why the composition of parishes does not reflect the fact that some 44 percent of Catholics in this country are under the age of forty. I have asked them to consider what the public face of Catholicism is today: How do people perceive the Church? Is the public image of the Church that of a community seeking through love and service to proclaim the good news that the divine order is upon us, and that we are called to be agents of the Holy Spirit in transforming the world into a more just and loving community? Or is it an image of a dysfunctional institution stumbling through various problematic issues? Inevitably the response of faithful Catholics—those that staff diocesan and parish level leadership positions—is sadness and even cynicism. They recognize that to an outsider, the Church does not always first appear as a privileged place of encounter with God's grace; on the contrary, they suggest, it often appears as a political party in decline. The point of my raising this issue is to encourage Church leaders to think about the way that young people answer the basic question, "Why should I be Catholic?" If the Church itself does not manifest the love it seeks to preach, it is not living up to Jesus' mandate to spread the good news.

What does this critique mean in practice? Does it lead to definitive answers on the contentious issues facing the Church today: on the role and ordination of women, the vocation to religious or lay life, the inclusion or exclusion of homosexuals, the practices of good liturgy and preaching? No—but what it does mean is that in a climate of pluralism among those who spend their lives caring about the Church, the prime emphasis must be on communion—that is, the gospel mandate of love for one's (perceived) enemies. In response to the charge that this critique leaves room for a bland truce that avoids the real problems in the Church, I offer the following illustration.

The state of reflection on controversial issues in the Church today is like a baseball game in which the opposing sides have come to argue about the rules. Let us imagine that each side is well convinced of its fidelity to the original intent of the game; further, that each side is passionate about ensuring the integrity of the game. The game continues, though every so often a brawl stops play and each side has to gather itself. The game is in a state of decline; spectators are tired of watching and so begin to leave, even as many others are showing up for the first time. Some, because of loyalties that their parents or grandparents established, side with one of the teams on the field and are ready to get involved in the fight. Others, because they are relatively new to the game, see only a bunch of pugilistic thugs and decide they'd rather go to a different park or even to a different sporting event altogether.

It is highly unlikely that a team or a Church will continue to draw people to what it is doing if its public image is characterized by infighting. To be specific—young people will not perceive the Church as a life-giving institution if their primary perceptions are those of controversies. At the heart of the Church's life is the simple kerygma that first energized the disciples of Jesus. He is risen! He is truly risen! This kerygma enlivened those who believed that God's work in the life of Jesus signified an unparalleled mediation in human affairs, a solidarity with those whom God created for God's own delight and whom God calls to eternal life. At the heart of the Church, in sum, is good news that must not be lost because of squabbles.

Paul understood the kind of stakes we are facing today. In his mediations with the church at Corinth, he recognized that there were factions—those following Paul, those following Apollos, and those following others—and even suggested that there was a proper time to expel those whose behavior was completely antithetical to what the Church was about (1 Cor 5:2), or to disassociate themselves from those Christians who acted immorally (1 Cor 5:9). His response—which must be ours—was to remind them of the most fundamental truths that they embraced as Christians. In his case, this reminder involved a meditation on the resurrection because he wished to demonstrate why their treatment of their earthly bodies had significance for eternal life. In our case, the emphasis must be on addressing the fundamental spiritual yearnings of the human heart in the twenty-first century. We must get back to basics.

To be a community of justice, we must practice love for each other that (minimally) sets a standard higher than those of opposing political forces in our society. We must listen to the marginalized among us, avoiding the temptation to let decisions that affect our churches be left to the powerful and well-connected. We must not fall prey to the hubris that persuades us that *our* ideas, *our* programs, *our* structures are those that will enable the Holy Spirit to work most efficiently. Perhaps instead we must be ready to change anything that does not lead us to authentic *latreia*.

We must remind ourselves of why we choose to embrace Christian faith, rather than any of the myriad other religious options out there. We must ask what it is about Catholic tradition that we find beautiful and sacred. We must call to mind why we choose to worship with other Catholics at Mass, and why we find joy in holding tightly to our faith even in the midst of turmoil. Ecclesiastes reminds us that there is a time for every purpose under heaven. In the years following Vatican II, it seemed right to tear down older structures in the hope of replacing them with better ones. Today, I suggest, is a time to rebuild—to refocus our energies as a Church community on the desperate needs of those who will be its future. Catholic Social Teaching addresses these needs inasmuch as it reminds us that authentic Christian spirituality can never be done in isolation from others.[67]

CATHOLIC SOCIAL TEACHING AS CRITIQUE OF SPIRITUALITY

The most common observation that young people make about their spiritual lives is that they consider themselves spiritual, but not religious.[68] For several years my response to students who made this claim was one of understanding, particularly since my own studies of young adult spirituality have in part focused on the positive dimension of this phenomenon. Now my response to the claim that one is spiritual but not religious is more simple: "no, you aren't."

The reason for my more pointed response is that any putative spirituality isolated from engagement with others is false. Of course, being a diplomatic person I try to honor their explanations about the necessity for finding meaning in life, seeking spiritual truths, praying to God privately because churches are boring and irrelevant, and so on. But I also am seeking to challenge them to consider whether any private expression of faith is really faith at all, or whether it is more properly called a kind of narcissism—a desire to feel more peaceful, a desire to have a belief in God that fits "me," a yearning for connectedness with what is beautiful, and so on. Much contemporary scholarship on spirituality seems to laud private practices, and for a time I could understand why. Now, however, I am convinced that people who really care about spirituality must take more seriously the challenges that arise from religious traditions. On the other hand, those who are members of religious traditions who care about authenticity must take more seriously the reasons spirituality in America has become more privatized.

I will speak of an ideal, since ideals can help us to imagine what needs to be done. The ideal is that churches will be places where people go to practice dying. Saint Augustine once preached a sermon in which he illustrated a metaphor that points to this ideal. He suggested that the Mass is the celebration in which we, like individual grains of wheat, come to be crushed and ground into bread. The metaphor is apt, since the central Catholic celebration of the Eucharist is a celebration of our communion with one another through the sharing of bread and wine. Augustine's sermon offers that it is precisely our dying as isolated individuals that enables us to more perfectly become part of the communion that is the Body of Christ on earth. And what we in the U.S. Catholic Church must take pains to recall is that those with whom we are called into communion are likely to be poorer than we are.

An authentic spirituality that ought to characterize the mission of the Church can be compared to military exercises. And while this metaphor may be offensive to the peacemakers among us, it is the metaphor used in one of the great spiritual classics in Christian history, the *Spiritual Exercises* of Saint Ignatius Loyola.[69] His observation that spiritual training ought on some level be like military training focuses on how both seek to break down a person's overemphasis on the self, in order to more perfectly conform one's will to that of the leader and in order to become a member of a cohesive unit. In Christian tradition, there is a consistent emphasis on learning gradually to conform one's own will to the will of God, thereby coming into greater and greater communion with others. The Church, according to this ideal, is the community of those seeking the will of God and manifesting it in the world.

Much of contemporary spirituality is really a truncated overemphasis on what Aristotle would call the "accidents," as opposed to the "essence" of the spiritual life. The essence of the spiritual life is practicing the will of God, in both senses of the word *practice*. It is about getting better, as in the examples of practicing playing the trumpet or practicing hitting a baseball. It is also about consistent effort, as in the examples of practicing medicine or law. In a consumer society, though, many become attracted to the practice because what they see are the accidents, and not the hard work that goes into producing them. Just as a young person might be drawn to practice medicine because he or she sees that doctors live well and achieve respect, many are drawn to spirituality because they perceive that it produces inner peace and a sense of meaning in life. The false conclusion in both examples is that the perception is the reality. Spirituality may produce equanimity and meaningfulness, but to seek those things as ends in themselves truncates what spirituality is really about. To practice authentic spirituality is to be ready to die, because it means seeking the will of a God who, Jesus tells us, enables us to find our life by losing it.

Catholic Social Teaching critiques our market-oriented notions of spirituality because it calls to mind the grim realities of the world. Is spirituality really authentic when we spend a couple hundred dollars going off on retreat rather than contributing to the mission that is hoping to build an orphanage for street orphans in Mexico City? Are we really seeking the will of God when we spend time perusing the spirituality sections of Borders or Barnes and Noble, rather than helping to build homes in the inner city with Habitat for Humanity? Do our lives become more holy if we fit in a meditation session or a visit to church before zipping across town in our gas-guzzling cars to watch overpaid athletes on a Sunday afternoon? Authentic Christian spirituality, I am arguing, cultivates the awareness that all our choices in everyday life challenge us with the basic question: is this God's will for me?

The implication of this ideal for the life of the Church, both in the United States and around the globe, is that to be a Catholic is to be a person on pilgrimage. Some are at the beginning; some farther along the way. Moreover, the practical implications of seeing Catholic faith as a commitment to the practice of authentic spirituality are diverse. Those at the early stages of this commitment, like those at the early stages of commitment to any practice, are often going to make mistakes. They will misunderstand the tradition, the language, the moral teachings, the social mores. This is to be expected, and ought not cause scandal. For example, during the contentious 2004 presidential election, in which the Catholic vote received more media attention than in previous years, there was much outcry on both the conservative and liberal sides of the Church: "how can one be Catholic and vote for _____?" The answer is simple: people express the political implications of their spirituality at a level commensurate with the degree to which they have been formed in faith. It is certainly important for Catholics to engage in mature discourse about the political implications of a mature faith, but to expect that every single Catholic will understand and express it at the same time is simply unrealistic. Moreover, because of the changing nature of authority today compared to earlier eras, it is not feasible to assume that the laity will automatically follow the direction of bishops on political issues. There is certainly an important role for bishops, theologians, and others to contribute to public dialogue, but today it is important that they do so in a way that does not alienate laypeople. Strong calls to obedience will fall on deaf ears, and will only further undercut the already tenuous claim to authority that bishops have among the youngest generations of the Church.

If today we are seeing a breakdown of the traditional connection between religion and spirituality, our response as a Church must be to try and repair that relationship. Young people must see the Church as the place where people seek to cultivate and express their spirituality. Catholic Social Teaching, I am suggesting, offers the opportunity to engage those issues with which young people are concerned—issues of justice and peace, economics and environment, rights and responsibilities, life and death—in such a way as to draw their attention to fundamental theological principles. The method of making this connection is simple: begin with the world, and show how consideration of the world leads to consideration of God's role in it. If we are concerned for poor people, is it not because Jesus instructed us to? And did not Jesus call the poor to our attention because of God's intimate care for them? And does not God care for the poor because he created them in the divine image and likeness? And don't all human beings share in the divine image and likeness from the moment of conception to the moment of death? And don't our considerations of image and likeness have implications for our approach to issues from abortion to euthanasia to capital punishment to stem cell research to adoption to marriage to family life to ecclesial life to the nature of the Eucharist to the celebration of the sacraments to discipleship to vocation to prayer to reflection on the Trinity to Christology to ecclesiology to eschatology and so on? In short, consideration of issues of justice in the world open us to further plumb the depth and breadth of Catholic theological reflection—and this is very good news, because the tradition of Catholic theology is a treasure for those who seek to understand themselves in the world.

CATHOLIC SOCIAL TEACHING AND THE GLOBAL VILLAGE

Catholic Social Teaching is the necessary theological response to the needs of the Catholic Church in the twenty-first century. It summons us out of our privatized notions of spirituality and into solidarity with the rest of the world. In chapter 1, we examined the two threads of the contemporary Catholic Church, paying attention to the issue of whether middle-class U.S. Catholics will choose to enter into solidarity with other Catholics around the world. This is indeed the key challenge of Catholics; but the dual hope of the Church in the twenty-first century is that there is both a body of theological resources that address this challenge, as well as a population of young people who have already internalized its most fundamental precepts.

What remains to be done for the formation of younger Catholics—not to mention the ongoing formation of older ones—is to draw together the implications of CST and the Church's doctrinal history. For younger people, it will mean making explicit connections between themes of justice and themes from theological doctrines. For older people, the move will be in the opposite direction: to make connections between the theological doctrines they learned in the *Baltimore Catechism* to themes of justice. Older Catholics know that the incarnation was God becoming a human being; the implication of this doctrine is that God has sanctified the dignity of the human estate, and that human beings must dismantle unjust social structures that assault this basic dignity. Younger Catholics know that sweatshop labor is fundamentally evil; they need an understanding of Catholic teaching on the incarnation in order to understand how the love of God is poured out both on the poor and on those who would minister to them.

Emphasizing CST as the link between the world and the Catholic theological tradition will help foster reflective awareness of the presence of God in human affairs. It is thus part of that same evangelical imperative that Jesus gave to the disciples at the end of his ministry: "go and make disciples of all nations." It must have a global orientation, but one that shows awareness of the sometimes unjust manifestations of Christian missionary activity in the past. U.S. Catholicism must exemplify the "catholicism" or universality of Christian faith. It will recognize the shortcomings of its missionary history, focusing on the most fundamental dynamic that continues to give rise to the evangelical imperative of Christian faith. This dynamic is the kerygma, the proclamation of the good news about God's presence in human affairs. Far from being a sectarian imposition on the rest of the world, it represents a service to the rest of the world. The U.S. Catholic Church, the single wealthiest religious body in the world, has an enormous responsibility to live out its salvation by offering its considerable resources in service to the world. The Church, in short, ministers to the world. Its ministry to its own members must thus be seen as a means to the greater end of serving the world.

There is an implicit ecclesiology—a statement about what the Church means today—in this position. The basic point is that it implies what the Indian theologian Michael Amaladoss has termed "regnocentrism"—literally, "centering on the kingdom [of God]"—meaning that what the Church should be bringing about is the divine order that was the heart of Jesus' preaching.[70] Younger and older Catholics alike hunger for spiritual integration, a harmony of their deepest desires as human beings, and this hunger cannot be satisfied in a Church that serves itself but ignores the rest of the world. For Catholics whose spirituality arises from the celebration of the God who has come to live among us, our joy is incomplete until our desire for God reaches out to embrace the communities in which we live, the nations in which we live, the entire world that we are called to transform.

Chapter Three

Ecumenism: Catholicity and Globalization

The term *ecumenism* comes from the Greek *oikoumene*, a word that in the ancient world referred to the entire populated part of the Earth. The verb *oikeo* meant "to live in," specifically a house. A person who dwelt within a home was described using the verb *oikeo*, and so by extension all people who made Earth their home were referred to using the term *oikumene*. Today, ecumenism refers to the attempt to reunite Christians of different churches, or by extension to bring together people of different faith traditions. It is the moral commitment to ensuring that all who share a dwelling place have what they need. To take this a step further, let us observe that our word *economy* uses the same root verb *oikeo* and the noun *nomos*, "law," and means "the law of the house." Economics is the law by which those who live together distribute those things proper to their shared dwelling place. Thus ecumenism and economics are related ideas.

In the previous chapter, I suggested that an unfolding of a theological economy is vital if Catholics are to draw together the implications of our faith for everyday life. Here I take that suggestion a step further. Attention to a theological economy is necessary for ecumenism, because all people in our own *oikoumene* are subject to a global economy. In this chapter, we explore how the movement toward a truly global vision will impact the Catholic Church in the United States, and what hope there is for the future of this Church by attending to ecumenical questions.

75

We begin with the Vatican II document *Unitatis Redintegratio* (Decree on Ecumenism) of 1964:

> The term "ecumenical movement" indicates the initiatives and activities planned and undertaken, according to the various needs of the Church and as opportunities offer, to promote Christian unity. (par. 4)

This rather straightforward definition of the term offers us a starting point for considering the efforts that the leadership of the Catholic Church has undertaken over the last several decades in order to pursue unity among Christians. The Decree on Ecumenism as a whole represents a stark contrast to the attitude that only Catholics could go to heaven—it recognizes that other churches can be places of grace and beauty.[71] The Council itself was significant for the insistence by Pope John XXIII that it include leaders from other Christian traditions as observers during the discussions that led to the Council documents. In short, what *Unitatis Redintegratio* articulates, and what the Council as a whole manifested, is an understanding of ecumenism as a task necessary for the full understanding and implementation of Christian life.

Later in that same document, the Council articulated its vision of how ecumenism is an integral part of the Church's own attempts at self-renewal:

> Every renewal of the Church is essentially grounded in an increase of fidelity to her own calling. Undoubtedly this is the basis of the movement toward unity.
>
> Christ summons the Church to continual reformation as she sojourns here on earth. The Church is always in need of this, in so far as she is an institution of men here on earth. Thus if, in various times and circumstances, there have been deficiencies in moral conduct or in church discipline, or even in the way that church teaching has been formulated—to be carefully distinguished from the deposit of faith itself—these can and should be set right at the opportune moment.

Church renewal has therefore notable ecumenical importance. (par. 6)

The thesis of this chapter is that ecumenism is a central task of all Catholics, but especially for us in the United States who live in a diverse society, because ecumenism encourages us to pay attention to the most foundational questions about our faith.

Thomas Ryan articulates several reasons this task is so central: the prayer of Jesus toward the end of his earthly ministry that there be unity among his followers (John 17:20–21); the teaching of the apostles ("Let there be no factions…Has Christ been divided into parts? [1 Cor 1:10]); the credibility of the gospel we preach, that we be reconciled to God and one another; God's own model of unity in diversity in the Trinity.[72] We must remember that the gospel is good news not because it enables us to withdraw into a closed society of a saved few—this is bad theology. Rather, the gospel enables us to think critically about the flourishing of all members of the global society, by attending to both their temporal needs and their ultimate spiritual well-being in the divine order. The gospel is, in short, a gift (*gratia*) of God to human beings, a gift that we as Catholics have the responsibility to pass on to all people: "Go, and make disciples of all nations" (Matt 28:19).

On an intuitive level, many are already aware that it is uncomfortable, and in some way not really "Christian," to marginalize people whose beliefs are in some ways the same, and in other ways different, from our own. Pope John Paul II demonstrated on a performative level how critical it is to move beyond a simple we/they distinction on the basis of beliefs.[73] Religious differences make us uncomfortable—and they should—because we want to think that we are able to find something more fundamental, more deeply rooted in human experience, than differences of belief. Ecumenism involves the attempt to find what is fundamental; and the process of making that attempt is important because it reminds us of those things that are (in the language of Aristotelian metaphysics) "essential" and those things that are "accidental" or peripheral to faith.

Today, U.S. Catholics are in profound need of returning to the essentials. As I have already suggested, part of this imperative has to do with reminding ourselves of why we choose to be Catholic, in order that younger Catholics might learn from us the value of their faith tradition. Yet there is a larger concern at stake as well: the insularity of U.S. Catholics from the rest of the world. As noted in chapter 1, U.S. Catholic history has involved the emergence of a kind of Catholic nationalism—think of John F. Kennedy, the Notre Dame football team, Thomas Merton, and Fulton Sheen.[74] Because Catholics were marginalized in U.S. society especially after the significant waves of European immigration changed America's cities (and workforce), many Catholics—hierarchy, the wider clergy, and laypeople—developed a ghetto mentality, and saw these figures as representative of their struggle within U.S. culture. To be sure, the fruits of Catholic culture during the late nineteenth and early- to mid-twentieth centuries are formidable, including such bastions of social justice work as the network of schools, hospitals, and charitable organizations that make the Catholic Church in the United States the largest provider of social services behind the federal government itself. It is worth remembering, however, that part of the impetus behind this expansion of Catholic culture was the need to minister to those marginalized by society: Catholics themselves. The emphasis today, I suggest, should be on reaching out to the marginalized, not on serving our own people exclusively. It was important that the Church minister to marginalized Catholics and thereby build a strong Catholic subculture within the mainstream (Protestant) U.S. culture. Today, however, many Catholics are as much part of the mainstream, and so a continued emphasis on building a strong Catholic subculture now seems like elitism. This is not to say that Catholics ought to abandon building a Catholic culture, a culture that many would argue is in dire need of recovery. Instead, it is to say that the energy of building a Catholic culture ought to be invested *ad extra*—in service to the world, rather than in service to itself. Catholic identity will flourish as a byproduct of our service to the nation and the world.

An economic metaphor will illustrate this point. A couple moves into their first new home (*oikos*), a small structure that holds great promise for them. The couple is new to the neighborhood, a bit shy, and yet hopeful that they can build a new life together there. They are poor, and already have several children, and so are prepared for the work of expanding the size of the house to accommodate the needs of their growing family. Over time, as each project is completed, the home becomes more livable for themselves and their children. The neighbors are a little put off by the fact that the outside of the house is not as well-maintained as are their own, and so keep their distance. But the happy couple keep working in the many ways that enable their children to be safe, comfortable, and happy. Over time, due to hard work and judicious investment, the couple achieve a certain measure of financial stability. Their house is now twice as large as it was when they first moved in. Their children have grown; some are already working as doctors, lawyers, and teachers; in short, the couple has achieved the American Dream.

In such a scenario, it would be self-centered of the couple to continue pouring all of their resources into their own home and family.[75] At a certain point, it is worth asking about their duties to the community and society of which they are a part. There is certainly propriety in attending to one's own, when one's own are in a state of need—as is the case, for example, of the new waves of Catholic immigrants from Central and South America, Africa, and Asia. However, it is an altogether different matter when many of one's own are now the privileged class. The U.S. Catholic Church of the early twenty-first century is not the U.S. Catholic Church of the early twentieth century. To be sure, there are certainly many Catholics whose economic situation is far from privileged—and attention to this fact is critical—but the story of U.S. Catholicism has been, for the most part, the story of the American Dream. Now that many Catholics have achieved it, what is our responsibility to the rest of the world?[76]

I am proposing that a theological economy is that responsibility. Catholic tradition, which is founded on Jesus' proclamation of the divine order and is carried through centuries of theological and spiritual insight, is a resource that contributes to a global conversation about the flourishing of human society. Later in this chapter, we take a look at a specific example of a global ethic: the United Nations' Universal Declaration of Human Rights. For now, however, I am suggesting that our primary energies as Catholics in the United States ought not be put into our own house. They ought to be put into addressing the question, "What can we offer the world?" In the economy of U.S. Catholic worship and teaching, most prominent should be the imperative to preach the good news, that God has created human beings for eternal well-being and that all dimensions of human society can work in harmony toward the dignity of all its members.[77]

The argument of this chapter is divided into three sections. The first section is a reflection on the nature of catholicity, and its implication that Christian faith, by definition, reaches out for inclusion of all those who follow Jesus. In more everyday language, the first section asks about unity among Catholics and with Christians from different churches. The more U.S. Catholics dwell on the questions that have historically divided different Christians from one another, the more likely they are to consider the foundations of Christian faith.

The second section looks more broadly at the relationship between Catholic Christianity and other religious traditions around the world. It takes its cue from two sources: the 1965 Vatican II document *Nostra Aetate* (The Declaration on the Relation of the Church to Non-Christian Religions) and the recent work of the Federation of Asian Bishops' Conferences, which has been at the forefront of dialogue between Catholics and people of faiths other than Christianity. What emerges from this section is the observation that the Catholic Church, as the only truly global religion, has a particular role to play in the cooperation of religious traditions in addressing issues of human development and rights. U.S. Catholics, in particular, can have a significant impact on this cooperation because of both their sheer numbers and their political and economic power.

The third section is broader than the first two, asking about the relationship between Catholics and other "people of good will." Recognizing that it is elusive to characterize people in terms of their religious affiliation, and that in the postmodern world religious belonging itself is hard to define, we observe that there is nevertheless a fundamental moral dimension to all of human living, and that perhaps the greatest contribution of any religious tradition is to call people to responsibility for others. Reflecting Paul's image in Romans 8:22 that all creation, including ourselves, is groaning in labor, it brings into conversation the UN Universal Declaration of Human Rights and the tradition of Catholic Social Teaching. Both represent attempts to articulate a global ethic, and both are founded upon a vision of the human condition. Understanding the Catholic vision, and particularly its resonances with the vision proposed by the United Nations, offers U.S. Catholics a hopeful model for a global ethic that can inform their local practices of faith.

UNITY AMONG CHRISTIANS: CATHOLICITY AND CATHOLICISM

Let us return to etymology, and observe that the word *catholic* comes from the Greek word *katholikos*, the root of which is the term *kata holos*, "according to the whole" or "universal." The term was used in a generic sense by Aristotle and others in the pre-Christian Greek world, but first appears in the Christian world (as far as we can tell) in a letter from Bishop Ignatius of Antioch in the early second century. His use of the term, which later writers followed, is illustrative of a point: an authentically "catholic" church is one that holds to right teaching, a teaching that is "universal" in its applicability. In other words, authentic catholicity meant that a church did not retreat into private beliefs and practices that separated it from the rest of the followers of Jesus around the *oikumene*. In the second century, catholicity was the antithesis of the movement known as Gnosticism, which held that the followers of Jesus possessed a secret knowledge, or gnosis, that made them an elite, a "chosen" or "saved" few. Originally, then, catholicity and ecumenism were flip sides of the same coin. The use of the term *Catholic* (capital *C*) as a particular name eventually took hold, in part due to the emphasis by later writers like Saint Augustine in the fifth century; and by the time of the Protestant Reformation in the sixteenth century, the particular name came to be associated almost exclusively with the Church centered in Rome around the figure of the pope.

It is helpful for us today to consider the early, non-particular meaning of the term *catholic*, which made its way into the early creeds of the Church: "I believe in one, holy, catholic, and apostolic Church." This non-particular meaning challenges us to think about the importance of the public dimension of Christian faith, that dimension that summons us out of our tendency to privatize faith. To claim belief in a catholic church is to claim that the gospel is necessarily a public announcement—literally, "good news" (*euangelion* in Greek)—and explicitly not a private communiqué between God and a select few. What this means for ordinary Christians is that the embrace of Christian faith does not thereby place us within a closed society, absolving us of our responsibility to the rest of the "unsaved" world. On the contrary, the life of faith is a summons to become a servant to the rest of the world, in the way that Jesus was a servant to those around him. "For the Son of man also came not to be served but to serve, and to give his life as a ransom for many" (Mark 10:45).

Today, the imperative of catholicity is more complicated, though no less urgent, than it was in the time of Ignatius of Antioch. Catholicism must strive for catholicity, in a manner alluded to by James Joyce: "catholic means here comes everybody." Yet at the same time, it must constantly wrestle with the thorny question of inclusion and exclusion, rejecting an oversimplified version of either. On one hand, Paul specifically counseled the Corinthian church to expel a member who engaged in illicit sexual behavior—a man living with his father's wife (1 Cor 5:1–2). More broadly, Paul counseled the Corinthians to expel from the church anyone who was guilty of immoral behavior (1 Cor 5:9–13). On the other hand, there are throughout the New Testament several suggestions that God wants to save sinners, and that Jesus himself came for sinners.

- Jesus came not for the righteous, but to call sinners (Matt 9:9–13; Mark 2:13–17; Luke 5:27–32).
- Jesus said there is joy in heaven over one sinner who repents (Luke 15:1–10).
- God shows his love for sinners, sending Christ to die for us (Rom 5:6–8).

What we find in the New Testament is a tension between the need to minister to sinners, as Christ did, and the need to keep sin from scandalizing the faithful.

The resolution to this tension is a recognition of the complementary dynamics of the Church *ad intra*, in its own life as a community gathered for a specific purpose; and *ad extra*, as a community sent in prophetic mission to the rest of the world. There is no doubt that Jesus commissioned the disciples to go out into the world (Matt 28:16–20), a world where there is sin. Further, there is no doubt that the implications of this commission were debated in the Council of Jerusalem, and that Paul and Barnabas helped persuade the disciples that God calls both Jew and Gentile (Acts 15). From these stories, together with the missionary activity of Christians in the first centuries of the Church, we can conclude that the Church's missionary work *ad extra* has involved the invitation to sinners to repent and follow Jesus in the community of the Church. Catholicity represents the imperative to offer this invitation to all people, regardless of what kinds of sinners they are. On the other hand, it is important to recognize that both Jesus and Paul reject the idea that sinners *as such* belong in the Church,[78] since the presence of notorious, unrepentant sinners within the Church might compromise the Church's broader mission of evangelization. Instead, what makes a sinner a member of the Church is his or her willingness to repent and believe the good news. The New Testament dynamic of the Church *ad intra* is a community of those who have undergone *metanoia*, a change of heart.[79] Catholicity, in other words, does not mean that the Church includes all people; this is impractical and unrealistic. It means instead that the prophetic mission of spreading the gospel includes an invitation to all people, even though some are not yet in a position in their lives to respond to the invitation. It means that the Church continually invites sinners (everyone) to repentance *(metanoia)* in order that they might share in the banquet of the Lord.

Let us observe, however, the danger of making sharp distinctions between the Church *ad intra* and *ad extra*. In an age when so many are nominally religious, when many have been baptized but have never attended a church as an adult, when many have left Church worship because of feeling abused by it, when many feel excluded from it because of its recalcitrance on tough issues—there are few easy distinctions between members and nonmembers. Do conservative Catholics have more in common with conservative Evangelicals or with liberal Catholics? Do liberal Catholics have more in common with mainline Protestants or with conservative Catholics? Are confessional boundaries the same today as they were in the seventeenth century, or are the issues that divide Christians from one another more based in differing political, rather than religious views?[80] More basically, who but God can judge *metanoia?*

What is called for is epistemological humility.[81] In his 2004 Catholic Common Ground Initiative Lecture, John L. Allen Jr. put it well:

> We have to re-learn the discipline of withholding final judgment, realizing that we may not always have the requisite data or reflection to draw definitive conclusions. This is not a plea for relativism; where reason shows something to be true, or scripture and tradition posit something as definitive, the mind should not hold back assent. But even in those cases, there may be implications or dimensions we have missed, and dialogue can reveal them to us. Dialogue is, in other words, an essential element of the search for truth, but only if we are open to being shaped by the experience.[82]

Good dialogue (dialogue)

Dialogue is a method for furthering the catholicity of Christian faith, not because it loosens the requirements or because it compromises the truth, but because it is a way to promote trust and learning.[83] Jesus knew this, and that is why he engaged in dialogue with the Samaritan woman (John 4:4–42). Paul knew this, and that is why at the Areopagus he engaged in dialogue with the philosophers (Acts 17:22-31). Good teachers know this, and this is why so many excellent classes involve the method of Socratic dialogue. It is simply more effective than lecturing to those who may or may not be listening. The imperative of catholicity means that Catholics are called to dialogue with each other, with those Christians who are not Catholic, and with people who are not Christian.[84] It also means that Catholics at every level attend to the structures within their families, their parishes, their dioceses, their hierarchies—making sure that these structures promote good dialogue.

The frequent objection to dialogue is that it is both unnecessary and unhelpful when one already has possession of the full truth.[85] An image from the domestic church can be informative: parents who know what is best for their children do not have the luxury of simply stating the truth and then expecting full compliance. Dialogue is not necessarily about questioning the truth; it can be about helping others to recognize that the truth exists. Imagine a parent telling a son or daughter that smoking is bad for one's health. The parent is in full possession of the truth, having studied the toxic effects of smoking and having lost a parent to lung cancer. If the parent should issue a simple command "you shall never smoke!" some children are likely to rebel simply because they don't like being told what to do. If, on the other hand, a parent should create a pattern of communication that enables a child to feel comfortable talking about what's going on at school, among friends, and so on, that child may be more likely to make the parent aware of factors that might lead to a desire to try smoking. Under such circumstances, is it not more likely that a parent's dialogue about smoking could prove to be persuasive to the child? And could not the parent, in engaging the child about the dangers of smoking, learn more about what is going on in the child's life?

The Catholic Church in the United States has undergone tremendous cultural shifts over the last half century. Once upon a time, laypeople were very much like children listening to their ecclesiastical parents: the Church was *mater et magistra*, mother and teacher, and most Catholics were content to obey. Today, however, laypeople especially have grown up in their faith, and resent being told what to think or do. In this, they are not unlike adolescents, who are old enough to know that they like independence, but not yet old enough to admit when they are wrong. Among my students, I recognize at the same time intellectual sophistication and theological illiteracy. They know how to think insightfully and creatively, but simply have not had the in-depth exposure to the heritage of Christian reflection. What is most important for our purposes, though, is a basic observation: they do not want to be told what to believe. They are more than ready to discover it for themselves, though, if someone would coach them how to do it. The classroom is a place of dialogue, a place where students can probe, discover, question, test, and reflect. Dialogue is thus the meeting point between what I have to teach and what they want to learn.

Most important, though, dialogue involves a posture of engagement with those whom we seek to understand. It is predicated on love for the other, even in the face of disagreement. The metaphor that most aptly speaks to the necessity of dialogue is one that moves us very close to the heart of Catholic worship: the family meal. Thinking about the way that a healthy family seeks communion at the dinner table offers us a way to consider further the relationship between catholicity and Catholicism.

Consider a family meal at Thanksgiving (an apt analogy, since *eucharisto* means "thanksgiving"). The family has been divided because of the last election; some are Republicans while others are Democrats. In the days leading up to the election, there were many heated debates among the brothers and sisters and their spouses; the father, too, was involved in heated exchanges with some of his children. Gone are the days when his ideas were considered sacrosanct. Some of the children have come to espouse the political views of their parents, but others—because of their own life experiences and education—now think about political issues very differently. Over the past year, the children with differing political views have called home less frequently and don't visit as often, deciding that they do not need the hassle of hearing their father's offhand remarks about politics. Yet their mother has summoned all the children to the table for Thanksgiving, and they lovingly oblige. A truce has been called; they collectively agree that there will be no talk of politics that day. The day is given to celebration and memory, looking backward with grateful hearts and looking forward with hope to the coming year.

In a world where we are witnessing polarization among political factions, religious groups, economic classes, and others, the family model can inform our relations with other Christians who have views different from our own. On the level of local communion, let us observe that Catholics of every kind are called together to the celebration of the Eucharist only after the Sign of Peace, the sign by which we are called to reconcile with others. The liturgical act of peacemaking should reflect an even larger, reality, though: our commitment as followers of Jesus to heal the wounds that keep us from breaking bread with those we are called to love and serve. Mary Ann Glendon puts it well:

> If over a billion Catholics, as members of a Church that transcends all national, racial, and ethnic boundaries, cannot act together in the struggle against violence, poverty, and religious persecution, it is hard to see from whence progress against mankind's old enemies might come.[86]

More broadly, however, the family model of communion can inform our relations with other Christians. The imperative of catholicity means, minimally, that Catholics should be profoundly discomforted at the reality of division among the followers of Christ. Pope John Paul II, for example, wrote and acted often on the necessity of the reunion of the churches of the East and West, suggesting that only with such reunion can the Church breathe with both lungs.[87]

I am not proposing a simplistic ignoring of difficult historical, theological, canonical, and practical problems that have arisen among different churches. Instead, what I am suggesting is that the imperative of catholicity must inform (and, in fact, deeply trouble) our sensibilities about what it means to be a church. One can certainly celebrate what is good about one's home—familial or ecclesial —but one cannot be complacent about the home when a significant part of the family is absent from it. Remaining vigilant about the passion for communion means focusing first on the most basic questions about what is absolutely essential to participation in family life—so much so, that there is little time for squabbles about what is peripheral.

UNITY AMONG RELIGIOUS PEOPLE: TRADITIONS OF WISDOM

In recent years we have witnessed not only the crossing of denominational boundaries by Christians seeking to build coalitions on social issues, but also the crossing of religious boundaries by people of faith seeking to articulate nuanced responses to issues of human rights, the environment, religious extremism, and others. Consider the following ways that Catholics have joined with people from other religious traditions to work toward the common good, most often around issues of social justice.

- World religious leaders meet regularly to discuss key social issues facing people of all faiths.[88]
- In Indonesia, Catholic students have worked with students from Hindu, Buddhist, and Muslim groups to urge elected leaders to promote economic and social conditions for constituents.[89]
- In Washington, D.C., Catholics joined with Jews, Muslims, Buddhists, Hindus-Jains, Sikhs, and others in prayer for the genocide in Darfur, Sudan. This effort was one of many in recent years that saw religious groups gathering together in response to a crisis.[90]
- In England, Cardinal Cormac Murphy-O'Connor reached out to members of the Muslim community, offering the cooperation of the Church on issues such as religious violence, the role of the family, hunger, and the friendship between Catholics and Muslims in English society.[91]
- Catholic Relief Services in the United States and the Catholic Agency for Overseas Development (CAFOD) in the United Kingdom work with local civic and religious organizations in many countries of Asia, Eastern Europe, Africa, and Central and South America on poverty, religious freedom, hunger, illness, and a host of other justice issues. Partners include the Asia Muslim Action Network, several Protestant churches, and a host of government and nongovernmental agencies.

Yet even with the many examples of religious traditions contributing to the common good on the local, national, and global levels, religion remains extremely controversial in the postmodern era. For many, the fundamental question is not "why seek religious truths?" but "why be part of an organized religion?" It is important to note that for many young people today, there is no easy answer to the latter question. On the contrary, it seems that a significant number of young people can find very little with which to answer the question positively. This is a typically postmodern phenomenon: the suspicion of metanarratives, as they are known, means a distrust of powerful institutions because of their propensity to shape history according to their vision of order.[92] Religion, in this philosophical context, can be seen as the preeminent violator of basic rights to freedom of belief and self-determination. The last 150 years have seen many philosophical challenges to the very possibility of religion as a benign force within human affairs,[93] and the violence erupting within and among religious groups seems to challenge the assertion that religion is a good thing at all. It is no surprise that in recent years there has been a burgeoning of books that deal with the theme of violence in the name of religion,[94] because for many this dark side of religious history outweighs any positive benefits these traditions offer.

Alexandr Solzhenitsyn once observed that the line between good and evil runs through the human heart.[95] Nowhere is this observation more relevant than in our ruminations about the ambivalence of religion; it has the capacity to cultivate holiness or to sanction violence. Yet in light of both human history and the complex entanglement of religions and cultures today, it is both implausible and irresponsible to suggest that we do away with religion altogether. The modern proposals to eliminate religion from human affairs[96] are predicated on a misplaced faith in human reason and progress, both of which have been shown in the last century to be finite and uncertain. Our goal must instead be to provide the social, economic, and political climate within which religious traditions can promote what is best within them. Contemporary studies of religion have shown, for example, that the contemporary phenomena of fundamentalisms—Christian, Muslim, and others— are a response to the forces of modernity that marginalized religious belief.[97] When some religious people perceive a division between faith and reason, they determine that faith trumps reason; and the implication is a truncated fideism ("faith-ism") without the moderating effect of good critical thinking.

The answer to religious fundamentalism, and to the violence that sometimes erupts from it, is a climate of trust between the forces traditionally associated with modernity (reason, scientific advancement, pluralistic politics) and the forces traditionally associated with religious traditions (scripture, prayer, community building). In any responsible religious system, these forces are not at odds with one another. Theodore Hesburgh once wrote that anyone who posits a conflict between theology and science is either a bad theologian or a bad scientist[98]—and his observation points to the kind of divisions we must overcome in the post-modern world. The enemy is not religion; it is bad religion. Catholic history, let us observe, is rife with examples of those who have used religion to justify terror, including its leaders and even its popes. And let us further observe that one can quickly and easily muster scriptural and historical support for violence: be it God's command to Moses to wipe out the Amalekites (Ex 17:16) or Saint Bernard's exhortation to wage the Second Crusade.

Catholic history, like the history of any ancient religious tradition, has been a shared history of violence and peacemaking. The reason for this dualism can be found in the very reality to which Solzhenitsyn pointed: the human heart. Yet what is truly great in the long Catholic tradition is the consistent call to conversion, both personal and institutional. John the Baptist, Jesus, and Paul all emphasized strongly the necessity of personal transformation, of willingness to allow God to pluck out our hearts of stone and replace them with hearts of flesh, to use the image from the prophet Ezekiel. This posture of humility before God is precisely the opposite of hubris, the manifestations of which have so frequently been violent attempts to assert private visions of putative religious truths. Even on the institutional level we can see evidence of conversion: the best recent examples are those of Pope John Paul II, asking forgiveness for the sins of the Church's past, in preparation for the millennium jubilee.[99]

The irreplaceable role that religions play in human affairs is that of calling individuals beyond their private notions of what constitutes the good life. In this era of privatized spirituality, it is critical to pay attention to this public dimension of religious belief and practice. Religion is indeed not the same as spirituality; many perceive that the latter is important for authentic living, while the former is only for those who do not think for themselves. This is a caricature, but it has arisen because of the propensity that many show for using religion as a crutch to avoid serious confrontation with the deepest mysteries of human living. We need spirituality, because each of us stands before God as a free and responsible creature. Yet we also need religion, because in our freedom we often avoid the responsibility to grow in the ways that are difficult by reaching out in solidarity toward others. Religion at its best encourages us in the process of conversion, of growing through both joy and suffering toward the more perfect practice of the will of God. If indeed Solzhenitsyn is correct, then we constantly face the tendency to cross over the lines in our hearts, to place ourselves before God. Religion is the practice of negotiating those lines, of developing habits in the community of those who seek to know God's presence through their public acts of worship. To worship publicly—to truly practice one's faith as a public profession—is to refuse to allow oneself to set limits on who God is.

Once it could be said that what divided people of different religions was the fact that they held different beliefs, undertook different practices, observed different laws and customs. Today, however, a different factor divides people: the willingness to publicly affirm and practice one's faith. It may be argued, for example, that a faithful Jew and a faithful Catholic have more in common than a devout Catholic and a non-practicing Catholic, or a devout Jew and a non-practicing Jew. Similarly, it may be argued that a devout Catholic has more in common with a devout Muslim, a devout Buddhist, or a devout Hindu than with a nominal Catholic. The reason is this: in the postmodern age, the most significant intellectual hurdle is the very possibility of religious belief and practice. To be a devout person is to make a double act of faith. The first act is the more traditional act associated with religion: I assent to the articles of faith, the creed. The second act, though, is more subtle: I assent to practicing my faith in a community with a history, with rules and laws, with quirks and foibles. There are many who make the first act, but not the second.

There is a false dualism, though, in avoiding the second act: a kind of postmodern Gnosticism.[100] This heresy posited a divide between the things of heaven and the things of Earth—the latter were tainted or corrupted, and so the spiritual seeker, it was thought, ought only be concerned with the things of heaven. The Gnostics believed that they could be saved by a secret knowledge, and so disdained the corporeal, the physical, the earthly. Those who posit that they wish to follow God or engage in a spiritual quest—but not be entrapped by the vicissitudes of religious belief and practice—are similarly guilty of disdaining what is human. In the early centuries of the Church, what emerged as the most nuanced response to dualism was the doctrine about Christ himself: he was fully human and fully divine, meaning that (among other things) Christ's divinity was by no means compromised by his full humanity. Humanity, in short, is not the opposite of divinity: it is the *oikos* of divinity. To dwell in a human world is to dwell in the place where we find God, and conversely to disdain the human world is to disdain the very place where we might find God. To be a spiritual seeker without engaging in religious practice is to make a god of one's own spiritual seeking. We need religion because we need to learn the hard lessons about practicing faith with other difficult people.

It is the very challenge of dealing with other people in a religious community that makes the devout Catholic have more in common with devout people of other religions than with nominal Catholics. Those who practice religion—those who (in short) put up with others and who go through the (sometimes) difficult calisthenics of ritual—make the choice that their spiritual growth must go through the reality of living in a complex, interdependent world. We need to be challenged to engage all dimensions of human living in our spirituality—not only those that strike us as being explicitly "spiritual," if by that term we mean some kind of exclusively personal otherworldly quest for meaning and peace. To be sure, there is something good and holy about the person (young or old) who decides one day to cultivate a spiritual life, and who conjures up visions of visiting holy hermits on mountaintops or of meditating regularly on the meaning of life. But these romanticized yearnings for spirituality are like the first blush of young love—beautiful and unrealistic. Mature spirituality, like mature love, confronts not only the beautiful and sublime, but also the ugly and mundane. Authentic spirituality is about not only the quiet prayer on the mountaintop; it is also about bringing groceries to the elderly woman, changing diapers, washing tables at the soup kitchen, and even worshipping at Mass with (other) hypocrites and with children screaming in the background. Our growth must involve learning to navigate hypocrisy and distraction.

mature spirituality

It is against the backdrop of the development of a mature spiritual life that we can approach the dialogues between Catholicism and other religious traditions. If dialogues are centered on doctrines, then the dialogues are destined to be short-lived. What Christians believe is simply not the same as what Buddhists believe, or what Hindus believe, and so on. Yet if our dialogues are centered on the ways that our different religious traditions help us to foster a reverence for the human condition, then there is much to discuss. *Nostra Aetate* observes, for example,

> Men expect from the various religions answers to the unsolved riddles of the human condition, which today, even as in former times, deeply stir the hearts of men: What is man? What is the meaning, the aim of our life? What is moral good, what sin? Whence suffering and what purpose does it serve? Which is the road to true happiness? What are death, judgment and retribution after death? What, finally, is that ultimate inexpressible mystery which encompasses our existence: whence do we come, and where are we going? (par. 1)

These and other questions are written into the very nature of human living, and as wisdom traditions the great religions address these questions in different ways over their respective histories. What is important for our purposes to recognize is the simple fact that what gives religious traditions their power is precisely their ability to address such questions in ways that move people to reverence for the sanctity of the human condition itself. And while it would be facile to suggest that all religions always foster this reverence equally well, or that all religions are ultimately the same (the "many paths up the mountain" approach), it is nevertheless helpful to observe that this reverence is certainly an outcome shared by people from different religious traditions. And it is because of those practitioners that we can observe that different religions can cooperate in the project of promoting the flourishing of human society in the new millennium.

Examples of how this cooperation has unfolded over the last several decades are in the churches of Asia. The Asian churches

Religions foster reverence

exist in places where the members are a distinct minority—in many countries, Christians constitute less than 5 percent of the population (with the exception of the Philippines, where Catholics are a large majority). And so by necessity, the Asian churches have had to reach out to other faith communities, working with them to address fundamental human rights issues such as hunger, workers' rights, slavery and human trafficking, and many others. Further, in the Federation of Asian Bishops' Conferences (FABC) we see a good deal of reflection on how the practice of Catholic faith has been enhanced by such dialogues.[101] There is much that the U.S. Catholic Church can learn from the experiences of the churches in Asia. We who have become so focused on our problems do well to remember that these problems do not discharge us from the duty of proclaiming the gospel by who we are and what we do.

There are three main themes that the U.S. Catholic Church can learn from the experience of Asian churches: dialogue with the poor, the culture, and other religions; Catholic identity in a pluralistic environment; and inculturation of Catholic faith. These themes have arisen from the Asian Catholic experience of being a small minority, needing to reach out to other religious groups both for safety and out of desire to make a positive impact on society. What makes these themes especially thought-provoking for U.S. Catholics is that they prompt us to consider what it would be like to live out a public faith, even when the public's understanding of that faith is limited. My experience around younger Catholics, and around young adults, is that there is widespread misunderstanding of Catholic tradition, even among those who are more likely to respect it. Consequently, the visible shows of power in the public square—those around abortion, gay marriage, stem cell research, and other hot-button moral issues—are not well received. What the lessons of the Asian churches can teach our Church is that there are ways to publicly preach the gospel that rely less on political power and more on cooperative engagement with those who suffer.

discuss this

See Next page Top

Dialogue with the Poor, the Culture, and Other Religions

The FABC has often articulated the necessity of this threefold dialogue. As minority groups, Catholic churches in Asia do not carry any tradition of political engagement like the U.S. bishops have shown in their publications. On the contrary, Asian Catholics are often marginalized, and are sometimes even the targets of violence. In a situation of marginalization, then, they must show a public face that emphasizes their benefit to society, in a manner analogous to what early Christian churches showed during the Roman persecutions before the time of Constantine. Instead of focusing on contentious moral and political issues in the public square—a focus that would be unlikely to persuade those who do not understand the philosophical and theological framework of Catholic reflection—they have tended to focus on obvious works of justice and mercy. Such a focus serves a dual purpose. First, it enables them to work cooperatively with other religious and political groups, thereby solidifying friendships and promoting positive perceptions of Catholics in their countries.[102] Second, it gives the Catholic faithful models of discipleship: the corporal works of mercy to the marginalized members of their societies. Catholics in many parts of Asia are recognized for their willingness to work on behalf of the poor, the sick, the orphaned, and many others in situations of need. Motivated by Catholic Social Teaching, they work with others to promote human dignity.

The reason this imperative of dialogue is informative for U.S. Catholics is because it reminds us to pay attention to the public, missionary role of the Church. In an age of mass advertising, image is important, and so cultivating a good public image (though liable to become an end in itself) can be seen as part of evangelization. What I suspect many older Catholics do not adequately understand is the extent to which young people's thinking has been shaped by postmodernity. Shows of political power are unpersuasive; appeals to universal truth are seen as political posturing. Natural Law theory, in particular—which undergirds much of Catholic reflection on moral issues—is foreign to many young people.[103] In such a climate, what persuades is what is most basic both in Jesus' preaching and in many other ethical systems, religious or not: the imperative of love. A church that is perceived as generous in love is the church that will draw those who hunger and thirst for justice. If U.S. Catholics were seen first as those who staff soup kitchens, run hospitals for AIDS patients, counsel women in difficult pregnancies, give money to those who experience disasters, adopt children in need of loving homes, teach inmates in prisons, run schools and hospitals in poor neighborhoods, teach English to immigrants from all parts of the world—then there would be little fuel to fire the kind of anti-Catholicism that exists in many sectors of U.S. society.[104] On the contrary, the Catholic Church would be perceived as the institutional structure in which unfolds the very basic message of Jesus to love others unconditionally.

Catholic Identity in a Pluralistic Environment

It is a matter of course for Catholics in Asia to deal regularly with those who have different religious beliefs. They have developed a level of comfort with this fact that, it seems, is still foreign to some Church leaders both in Rome and in the United States. In the preparations for the Synod of Asia in 1999, Vatican leaders sent preparatory notes, which focused on the issue of proclamation of Jesus as the one true Savior of humankind. The Asian bishops, in response, wrote that this issue was not central to their pastoral work. Instead, they suggested that it was more important to focus on the Asian way of being Christian, in cooperation with those who are not Christian. Their goal was nothing less than to proclaim a new way of being Christian—a way different from what had developed from the Eurocentric model, which had shaped so much in the first two millennia of the Church's life. Their point, it seems, is that Catholic identity (conceived as a unique set of beliefs) is less important than discipleship (conceived as a gift that Catholics give to the world). The FABC itself was formed not with a doctrinal purpose, but rather a pastoral one, in response to the need for cooperation among the bishops of Asia and with the leaders of other faith communities.

The history of Christianity in Asia is very different from its history in Europe or the Americas. The most poignant observations are that Christianity was from the beginning perceived as a Western religion (ironic, since its roots are Asian), and that Christianity remains a comparatively small religion in most of Asia. At no point, then, have Church leaders been in the position to wield political authority, as has been the case in Europe and North and South America. Nor has there developed on a wide scale the kind of "default Catholicism" that one finds in parts of Europe and the Americas—that marriage of Church and culture that means, in practice, that people are born and raised in cultures that are thoroughly Catholic. To be Asian and Catholic is, to a great extent, an intentional choice based on a person's experience of positive encounters with other Catholics. And very often those encounters are related to works of social justice: schools, hospitals, and other ministries.

It would be a generalization to say that there are no tensions between Catholics and people of other religious traditions. Yet on the other hand, we can observe that the presence of other religious traditions makes Catholics careful about making nuanced claims about the nature of Christian faith. It is possible to proclaim Christ as the Savior of humankind while working with Buddhists and Muslims on programs that aid the poor. It is possible to have faith in the real presence of Christ in the Eucharist while working with Sikhs or Taoists in the areas of homelessness or drug use. It is possible to profess the creed, sing Marian hymns, and baptize one's children, while at the same time comforting a dying Muslim.[105] What U.S. Catholics can learn from Asian Catholics is that pluralism does not itself compromise or threaten faith; on the contrary, it can provide the milieu within which faith can be expressed as love and justice. This was certainly the case in the Hellenic world where Paul preached; it is the case today in Asia; and it can certainly also be the case in the United States.

Negotiating the relationship between the Catholic Church and the other great religious traditions is not without difficulty, as is evident in the Vatican responses to theologians Roger Haight and Jacques Dupuis.[106] Both have sought to articulate new theologies that reflect the pluralistic environment in which we live today, and both were investigated for ideas that were perceived as contrary to the deposit of faith. Their situations remind us that negotiating the challenges of ecumenism is still new to Catholics, and that we have much to learn. For the great majority of Catholics, though, there need be no controversy in recognizing the value of cooperation with people who profess their faith in other communities.

Inculturation of Catholic Faith: The Local and the Universal

There is a divide between those older U.S. Catholics who have some experience of Catholic culture, and those younger Catholics who do not. For the younger Catholics, then, appeals to the remnants of Catholic culture—whether it be abstinence from meat on Fridays of Lent or the recitation of prayers remembered from parochial school days—will seem like quaint reminiscences of days gone by, rather than vibrant practices of a Church engaged with the society. Younger Catholics do not know what it is like to express and practice an inculturated faith. Older Catholics, on the contrary, often do not recognize the extent to which their practice of Catholic faith is inculturated according to their comfort levels. Their recognition of this fact may be elicited (for example) by a critique of music in Church that sounds too modern to them.

For Asian Catholics, the issue of inculturation has been significant from the very beginning. One need look no further than the examples of the Jesuit missions to India and the Far East in the sixteenth and seventeenth centuries to see this tension. Christians were perceived as Westerners, and therefore different. Figures like Matteo Ricci in China and Roberto de Nobili in India spent many years living and dialoguing with people around them in order to learn how they might ultimately spread the gospel.[107] They came to similar conclusions: one must understand and practice the customs of the host culture, if one wishes to authentically share one's Christian faith.

The experiences of missionaries across the world have led scholars to consider the relationship between culture and faith, and more broadly the relationship between the local Church and the universal Church. At one extreme, we can recognize that it is not possible to expect a singular, uniform practice of Catholic faith across the globe. Even when Latin Mass was the same in England, France, Germany, Italy, and every other part of the former Roman Empire, there were still inculturated manifestations of the faith in the apostolic churches of Greece, Egypt, Ethiopia, Syria, India, Armenia, and other places. Christian history has never seen a uniform practice of faith.

At the other extreme, however, we can recognize that there must be some thread that unites Catholics around the world, in order to preserve the catholicity of the Church. Asian churches have wrestled with this question; the Asian bishops in particular expressed in their 1999 Synod that they valued their relationship with the universal Church in communion with Rome. Yet they also highlighted the fact that the very experience of being Asian means that the practice of Christian faith must take on an Asian face. There is no such thing as a pure or non-inculturated Catholic faith—every culture understands and practices its faith in ways that reflect the culture.

For our purposes, it is important to consider the various factors in the inculturation of U.S. Catholicism, not the least of which involves generational differences. The experiences of the Asian churches can inform our discussions of inculturation, because they have wrestled with their status as a minority group without political power; their need to work with other faith traditions; and their practice of a fully Asian, non-European faith. For young adult Catholics in the United States, there are similar dynamics at work. They do see themselves as a minority group, because they are accustomed to living in a world in which religion is marginalized. They have come to recognize the value that other faith traditions offer, and do not believe that any religious tradition can claim exclusive understanding of divine mysteries. And they too wrestle with the question of how to belong to a Church that is not their own, but their parents' and grandparents'.

If the Asian churches are in some ways a model for the U.S. Church, then there is reason for hope. Thomas Fox's book on the churches of Asia is aptly named *Pentecost in Asia* because of the parallels he sees between those churches and the newly formed Church of the apostles at Pentecost. They, like the apostles, are moved with hopefulness by the good news of Christ, even in a world that sees a good deal of religious discord. What we learn from their experiences, like those of the apostles, is that ultimately the Church is not the work of human beings, but of the Holy Spirit. There is a foundational principle of sacramental theology that says that God's grace moves freely among human beings as long as we do not put up any barriers.

> For as the rain and the snow come down from heaven,
> and do not return there until they have watered the earth,
> making it bring forth and sprout,
> giving seed to the sower and bread to the eater,
> so shall my word be that goes forth from my mouth;
> it shall not return to me empty,
> but it shall accomplish that which I purpose,
> and succeed in the thing for which I sent it. (Is 55:10–11)

The early missionaries in Asia came to the conclusion only after much reflection that it was European culture, not Christian faith itself, that was a barrier to the Asian appropriation of the gospel message. Today, I am suggesting, it is the attitudes of those formed before and during Vatican II that are the barriers that prevent younger Catholics from coming to know God's grace. Political battles, hot-button issues, arcane liturgical squabbles, uncharitable rhetoric—these are the elements of the culture of the Vatican II generation that must be dispensed with, if the Church is to be a place where young Catholics encounter God's grace. Practically speaking, this will mean an attentive listening to younger Catholics, as well as learning from those who study their patterns of belief and behavior in society, on campuses, in workplaces. As more priests, lay ministers, teachers, and Church leaders come from the ranks of those born after Vatican II, it is more likely that inculturated churches will develop, following the models of those missionary churches that developed by stages until they were led by people native to the region in which they minister.

UNITY AMONG PEOPLE OF GOOD WILL: A GLOBAL ETHIC

The very difficult lessons of the twentieth century have brought into sharp relief the stakes involved in the human struggle for life on the planet. What have emerged as the major factors in the global economy of the twenty-first century are in many cases the effects of the rebuilding after World War II. In particular, we might note the institutions that emerged out of the gathering of leaders at Bretton Woods, Vermont, in 1944: today they are known as the World Bank, the International Monetary Fund, and the World Trade Organization.[108] These institutions, while deeply flawed, developed out of the perceived need for structures that operated not on national levels, but on truly global ones. The war itself, leaders recognized, highlighted the fact that the survival of humanity could be achieved only through the cooperative efforts of all peoples. The United Nations itself emerged as an organization that sought to address the issues that face people of all nations: the need for food, shelter, security, and all the other elements that make up ordinary human existence.

More recently, we have seen numerous examples of cooperation among different nations around the world. In addition to the United Nations, there are nongovernmental organizations like Doctors Without Borders, the Red Cross/Red Crescent, Amnesty International, Oxfam, and others that are forging a kind of secular ecumenical movement. These groups, organized around issues of justice and peace, promote human development across the globe by appealing to basic principles of human flourishing. Catholic organizations, including those formed under the auspices of Catholic dioceses around the world and those sponsored by various groups of religious or lay Catholics, cooperate with literally thousands of these secular organizations on issues across the spectrum. The United States–based organizations Catholic Relief Services and Catholic Charities, for example, have partnered with many civic organizations to address justice issues. Such partnerships are examples of the kinds of trust that have developed between religious groups and nonreligious groups to address shared areas of human concern.

Consider the outpouring of international support that came in the wake of the December 2004 earthquake and tsunami that hit Southeast Asia. Catholic organizations like the Jesuit Refugee Service and Catholic Relief Services were among the first to respond, since they had staff in the immediate areas affected by the catastrophe. They, together with dozens of other religious and non-religious organizations, worked together to address what was an obvious threat to human well-being. That the different organizations had different foundational beliefs was, under those circumstances, beside the point: what mattered was their ability to respond to the crisis.

Estimates of the death toll rose to over 150,000 human beings within a couple of weeks after the event. This was a tragedy, the latest in a constant stream of tragedies that regularly afflict human society. Famines, the AIDS pandemic, malaria, genocide, and any number of other human tragedies are a regular part of the global picture, and equally deserving of international attention and support. Catholic institutions have an important role to play in the unfolding of a more just global order, in part because of the catholicity of the Church's concern. The opening line of *Gaudium et Spes* puts it well:

> The joys and the hopes, the griefs and the anxieties of the men of this age, especially those who are poor or in any way afflicted, these are the joys and hopes, the griefs and anxieties of the followers of Christ.

Inasmuch as there is *always* some issue that demands global concern, the Church must be part of the public, international voice of that concern. Further, Catholics themselves, called into solidarity with the poor whom Jesus loved, must be people committed to redressing those concerns by practicing just living; sharing economic, political, and social burdens; and praying together for the courage to serve those in need.

The fact that so many organizations around the world can come together to address basic problems like poverty is itself a hopeful sign. For U.S. Catholics, this kind of cooperation has a particular significance. For as we are witnessing the emergence of global ethics, and of global commitments to human development as an integral part of civilized societies, we can celebrate the role that Catholic Social Teaching has played and will continue to play. A significant reason there is a hopeful future for the Catholic Church in the United States is because this Church can play a pivotal role in the unfolding of a more just global economy. U.S. Catholics are uniquely positioned to support the poor and marginalized of the world against forces (corporate, governmental) that might otherwise crush them under the wheels of an impersonal globalization. The stakes are incredibly high; already we are seeing the dark sides of globalization in the trafficking of persons, in the slave-like conditions that prevail in some factories of Southeast Asia, in the levels of consumption among the wealthiest minorities of the developed world. On the other hand, we are witnessing a renewed interest in the religious traditions of the world, reflecting the observation that only religions have the social currency to bring wisdom to bear on this season of human progress. In my view, a factor that will impact many young people's embrace of religious traditions is their perception that while flawed, these traditions are *NEED* necessary for responding on a large scale to the darker implications of a globalized world. In short, people will see the need for religion, because only religion has the social power to make people think about the world in ways not governed by market forces.

As observed earlier, the Catholic Church is the only truly global religion—and even though its various dioceses around the world vary in size and political power, still as a whole this Church is comprised of hundreds of local churches with direct experience of human struggles of every sort. In short, the Catholic Church has a catholic understanding of human suffering and hope. With access to such vast resources, local churches in the United States are faced with tremendous responsibility: How do wealthy churches in the United States manifest their communion with the suffering around the world? How should local churches use their resources, both for the benefit of their own members and for the benefit of others around the world? What can local churches do to show their solidarity with others, and how can they manifest a concern for human dignity?

These kinds of questions are at the root of an emerging global ethic. This ethic has crystallized around the theme of human rights—a theme that suggests that all human beings share a fundamental nature and ought, then, to be accorded the freedom to secure what is necessary for their lives. In 1948, the United Nations promulgated the first truly international political statement on human rights, a statement that drew heavily from both the Western liberal tradition and, interestingly, Catholic Social Teaching. The very development of the Universal Declaration of Human Rights indicates the parallels between this emerging global ethic and the fundamental principles of CST. The impetus behind the emerging global ethic is the recognition that in a truly global society, it is difficult to identify universal moral principles. The differences among various cultural mores, religious beliefs, and systems of law mean that what is perceived to be true in one culture may not be perceived to be true in another. At the extreme, some would hold that the very plurality of beliefs means that there is no such thing as any universal truth. Yet in light of twentieth-century history, many came to recognize that the logical implication of such an extreme view is that there is no basis by which people can judge right from wrong, justice from atrocity. The UN Declaration represents an effort to situate global moral issues by appealing to a kind of faith in the goodness of human nature.

Catholic Social Teaching can inform and deepen appreciation for this secular faith, because CST is based on centuries of reflection on the very question of what makes us most fully human. Philosophically, the UN Declaration can be described as a kind of positivism: a "positing" that human beings deserve rights, without tracing back farther why this should be the case. On an intuitive level, we know the reason: if the nations of the world held any other opinion, there could be no hope for international laws that protect human beings from the evils they unleash on each other. Without a faith in human rights, any form of ethnic cleansing, genocide, economic imperialism, or slavery could be written off as politically expedient to whomever holds power. In short, there is a pragmatic—even utilitarian—aim in the positing of faith in universal human rights: it is the foundational principle upon which nations and international organizations can be held responsible for making the world safe and fair for all human beings.

Yet Catholic tradition points to an even more foundational claim, shared with other religious traditions, that has given rise to a faith in human dignity: that God is the author of all creation, and that human beings are created in the image and likeness of God. This claim is at the root of CST, and the implications of this claim are what fill many volumes of theological, political, and moral reflection. Historically, Catholic thinking on human dignity has made use of Natural Law theory, which can be described broadly (using the philosophy of Saint Thomas Aquinas) as the way human beings are able to discern the order in the universe created by God. Ironically, the most compelling international writings on Natural Law are those that do not explicitly name it as such. I am thinking in particular of the judgments at the Nuremburg war crime trials after World War II[109] and, not surprisingly, the UN Declaration. Both rest upon the belief that there is a discernible moral order, or at least some standard by which it is possible for nations to recognize the difference between law and crime. Even without making reference to God, they both articulate a clear recognition of the necessity of right thinking that leads to right moral conclusions.

It is important to observe that the formation of the UN Declaration was influenced by Catholic Social Teaching. In her 2001 Marianist Award Lecture at the University of Dayton, Mary Ann Glendon outlined this influence.[110] In 1941, Pope Pius XII gave a radio address in which he called for an international bill to address human rights. This same concern was brought forward by the several Latin American nations that were charter members of the UN, and as a result the Human Rights Commission was formed. They surveyed a number of prominent thinkers from East and West, and determined that there were shared principles among the different religious traditions. The UN Declaration itself draws proximately from political documents of the twentieth century; but those documents—especially from Latin America—were ultimately influenced heavily by such documents as *Rerum Novarum* and *Quadragesimo Anno.*

Yet the influence was not one-sided. In 1948 in Paris, the French member of the Human Rights Commission, René Cassin (a self-described secular Jew), was encouraged by the papal nuncio in Paris, Angelo Roncalli, the future Pope John XXIII. Glendon writes that Roncalli's later work manifested the influence of the UN Commission. Indeed, the mention of the Universal Declaration of Human Rights in *Pacem in Terris* (sec. 143) shows his recognition of the document's importance. More fundamentally, however, the pope uses the term *rights* no fewer than seventy-seven times in the document—a noteworthy fact when one considers that prior to *Mater et Magistra*, much of Catholic reflection on the human condition focused much more strongly on the Natural Law tradition and its emphasis on obedience to the will of God. (By contrast, *Quadragesimo Anno* has nearly twice as many references to duties as to rights.) Pope John XXIII—that figure who summoned the Church to greater involvement in the wider world and to greater engagement with the other religious traditions of the world—was influenced, it seems, by the international deliberations on human rights that emerged from World War II. Those deliberations, further, were enhanced by the contributions of Catholic Social Teaching.

This recent chapter of global and Catholic history is a model for the kind of healthy dialectic that can unfold between an ecumenically minded Church and the world's political leaders. It is different from the triumphalistic call for a renewed "Christendom," reminiscent of the high Catholic culture of Europe during the Middle Ages. For while that culture demonstrated a flourishing of art, music, philosophy, literature, theology, and other manifestations of developed culture, it arose from historical factors that would be impossible to re-create today. Instead, the relationship between Church and world is better understood in terms of mission: Christ has called his followers to be servants to the world, to offer it all the resources of a gospel that calls human beings to realize their status as creatures created in the image of God.

A final word on evangelization is relevant to this argument. In the past, missionary activity was sometimes badly understood as the attempt to baptize as many people as possible, thereby saving them from eternal damnation. It is little wonder that this benign (if naïve) desire to help people was misunderstood as a kind of imperialism, for many indigenous peoples perceived only a foreign power coming into their land (often at the heels of vicious economic or military powers) and demanding conversion to their foreign religion. Today, any missionary activity—any type of evangelization—carries with it this historical baggage. In the United States, in particular, where there are so many religious traditions, evangelization can be perceived as backwards and irritating. In light of this history, can there be an authentic evangelization in the twenty-first century?

Yes, but in many ways different from the past. Evangelization in the twenty-first century will involve what Paul Lakeland called "persuasive life in the world," as noted in chapter 1. Saint Francis is credited with the exhortation "Preach the gospel at all times. If necessary, use words." This is a helpful image in a postmodern context, when rhetoric is perceived as masking larger, unnamed agendas. Persuasive life in the world is about doing the will of God in all things. It is about discerning the implications of one's vocation, and embracing the responsibility of that vocation, from the most dull to the most stressful to the most exhilarating. Those whose faith drives them to undertake great things, as well as those whose faith drives them to undertake ordinary things with beauty and grace, preach the gospel to a cynical world. Their very lives are statements of the *euangelion*—the good news—that Christ has called us into relationship with God, and that our lives made meaningful by virtue of the fact that God creates us to do the good.

Beyond the witness of the everyday saints around us, there need only be invitation, in the manner that Jesus extended to the disciples of John who were curious about what made Jesus tick: "Where do you live?" "Come and see" (John 1:38–39). God invites people to deeper relationship, and we need only be ready to welcome them when they come. Mindful of this, we need not see any contradiction between ecumenism and evangelization. Ecumenism is an attitude of shared responsibility with the other members of our global family. Evangelization is an attitude that welcomes those who freely come to us in order to know the truths by which we live. And if those truths lead us to service toward the other members of our global family, then evangelization can be seen as a way to draw others into further sharing that gift. Pope Benedict XVI articulated this balance between sensitivity to ecumenical concerns on the one hand, and evangelization on the other: "A Christian knows when it is time to speak of God and when it is better to say nothing and let love alone speak."[111]

107

Chapter Four

Liturgy: The Mystagogy of Communion

Christianity began as a persecuted religion in the Roman Empire; and it was during this period that the Latin writer Tertullian observed that the blood of the martyrs is the seed of the Church. Martyrdom gives witness to the radical implications of Catholic faith, and in liturgy we find the consummate expression of that faith. Even today, Catholics are persecuted in different parts of the world,[112] and their examples lead us to ask a basic question: why die for this faith?

To celebrate the Eucharist is to give thanks for God's presence in human affairs. It is to be willing to die, for in the Eucharist we profess our willingness to be transformed into the Body of Christ. It commits us to the poor, for by sharing in the same bread we enter into solidarity with those whom Christ loves.[113] We become what we eat: we become Christ for the world. In so doing, we come to look at the rest of the world through the lens of the gospel. We become critical of those tendencies in human societies to dehumanize others, and of those doctrines that lead people away from knowledge of God and creation. We gather in the presence of the Holy Spirit, who burns away in us everything that keeps us from being able to love as Christ loved. We become more fully human by becoming more fully divine. In short, when we Catholics gather in liturgy we come more and more to achieve the end for which God created us: the praise, reverence, and service of God our Lord in the very concrete circumstances of our lives.

From this perspective, it would seem that all of us should be thrilled by the very opportunity to pray together. To be in the presence of the risen Christ ought to generate in us the same response of the disciples on the road to Emmaus when they realized that Christ was with them: "weren't our hearts burning within us!" Yet our response is more often like that of the disciples before this moment of recognition: we are distracted, inattentive, caught up in the latest news of the day.

YOUNG CATHOLICS AND LITURGY

Today among the youngest generation of Catholics, regular attendance at Mass is more the exception than the norm. Why is it that many young people perceive the Mass—as well as the panoply of sacramentals that constitute the world of Catholic devotion—as irrelevant? Why is it that many young Catholics will at once claim membership in the Church, while at the same time expressing that it is possible to be Catholic and not participate in the Mass? Why, after decades of liturgical renewal aimed at fostering greater participation of laypeople, do so many find liturgy out of touch with the realities of their lives?

Before we take a look at the challenges for liturgy in the Church of the twenty-first century, let us observe two things. First, young Catholics consider their faith tradition important to them even if they do not practice it regularly.[114] Second, young people live in worlds in which symbol and ritual figure prominently. Indeed, the most meaningful moments of their lives—from concerts to sporting events to graduations to parties to weddings—are rife with symbols and rituals. What these observations suggest is that there is great promise and opportunity if the Church could make compelling connections between Catholic worldview, identity, and practice. Liturgy that helps young people to understand and be critical of their own lived experience has the possibility of transforming the way that they look at the world.

Young Catholics' experience of liturgy is conditioned by a recent history of which they are almost completely unaware. Some may have learned that their parents or grandparents used to go to

Latin Mass, or used to go to confession often—but their experiences of liturgy are based primarily on what they have experienced. They do not have a deep understanding of the liturgical movement of the twentieth century, which involved greater attention to the experiences of laypeople in the Eucharistic assembly. Hence they cannot see liturgy as a contrast to something earlier: the sense that "this is so much better than when I was a child" does not apply to them. In short, their only knowledge of liturgy is its face value: the actions of people involved, the songs, the worship space, and so on.

This is a critical observation if we are to imagine the possibilities for liturgy today. Unlike their parents or grandparents who grew up in a more or less enclosed Church community, young people today grow up in a complex, multipolar world, and view Church membership as an option that makes sense only to the extent that it sheds light on the rest of the world they live in. Liturgy is not self-evident: its internal coherence is of a lesser value to them than its coherence with the larger state of human affairs. The question of female acolytes (altar servers) and extraordinary ministers is an example of this difference in perspective. For an older generation, the question of the propriety of females in these roles was answered, in large part, by an appeal to the integrity of the Church itself: Is the extension of these roles consistent with the gospel? With the Church's tradition? With canon law? (Note, by the way, that these questions can be answered in either the positive or the negative, and one's answer suggests something of where one falls on the conservative/liberal divide.) By contrast, younger Catholics are, in my estimation, less concerned with whether such a position is continuous with the Church's tradition. They are more concerned with whether the position is continuous with the world they live in. The questions they ask are not about the Church, but rather about the world: Is it right that the actors in Catholic liturgy are all male? What does the Church's assignment of liturgical roles suggest about its relationship to other institutions? In this particular example, there is a rather common hermeneutic of suspicion, that extends to the question of the priesthood of women—the Church's practice seems so unlike what they see in other institutions that it appears at first glance suspect.

Underneath this and similar examples is a fundamental theological question that has been with the Church since its inception: the relationships between Church and world, nature and grace. What does it mean to be an authentic disciple of Jesus Christ? How does one manifest that discipleship in worship? What does it mean for one's life? There is a continuity between our wrestling with these kinds of questions today and our predecessors' wrestling with similar questions. We must begin, then, with the understanding that wrestling with difficult questions about how to be a Catholic Christian is by no means antithetical to faith—in many ways, it is a manifestation of faith. To put it differently, the fact that young people stay away from Mass is not in itself a sign that they do not take faith seriously; it is perhaps rather a sign that they expect more from us who comprise the community of faith.

WORLD AND CHURCH

Young people live in a world of technology: of instant messaging, of cell phones, of video games, of the Internet. Theirs is a world of fractured relationships: of divorce, of "hooking up" (casual sexual relationships with friends), of scandal within the government and the Church. Theirs is too a world of violence: of images on TV, of misogynist music lyrics, of reports on the news of bloodshed. And theirs is a world of yearning for a better world: for reaching out to the poor, for solving the AIDS pandemic, for treating their friends who have abused drugs.

When young people look at the Church from the perspective of the world in which they live, it is not surprising that they often perceive it to be a closed system. Why, they wonder, do people even bother? Why get dressed up in order to go sing some songs, say some words, participate in a ritual that has little to do with the real problems in the world? Isn't it just a way of comforting ourselves and convincing ourselves that we're headed for heaven?

It is imperative that we resist the temptations to treat liturgy solely as a duty to be discharged, or a remembrance of Jesus, or a chance to think about God, or a place to meet like-minded people. It may have elements of all these; but if we are to practice a faith that reflects Jesus' prophetic description of the kingdom of God, then our commitment in liturgy must fundamentally be about solidarity with the rest of the world. Liturgy, this chapter argues, must be a schooling in solidarity: a mystagogy of communion. At the parish level, this commitment begins with hospitality. The reason this commitment becomes so central today is simple: previous generations were at home in the Church. This one is not, and so they must be welcomed.

On a practical level, we must observe that it is precisely the lack of welcome that seems to dissuade young adults from becoming more fully engaged in the liturgical life of the Church. Kristeen Bruun suggests that among twenty-somethings, hospitality, more than any other factor, affects their measure of satisfaction with the liturgy.[115] Hospitality can be described as a virtue that, like Shakespeare's description of mercy, blesses both the giver and the receiver. Catholics need to practice hospitality not only because it will impact the way young people perceive the liturgy, but also because it will give life to the way Church communities pray with one another.

An early reference to the imperative of hospitality appears in Paul's letter to the Romans. He addresses a mixed community, describing both the "strong" and "weak in faith," specifically directing the former to welcome the latter (14:1; 15:7). Elsewhere he writes of the need for hospitality (12:13) as part of the duties of Christians within a community, if the community is to thrive. In general, we see Paul concerned for the welfare of the Roman Church, focusing on the theme of the Body, which is the heart of his eloquent description of Church life in his first letter to the Corinthians. The basic point seems to be this: if the Church is a community that Christ has called to himself, then their spiritual growth is as a Body of which Christ is the Head. Hospitality and welcome are thus the practical responses of those different members of the Body, who recognize the various roles that the different members play.

A hospitable Church is an evangelical Church: it recognizes that people come to know the gospel by degrees, and it seeks to nurture the faith of the entire community. It further understands that if the Church is indeed the Body of Christ, then the health of

Welcome

the entire Body is compromised when parts of it are not adequately nourished. Practically: when parents see that their children don't go to church, it can be painful. When spouses can't celebrate their faith together, their marriage suffers. When young people earnestly desire to deepen their spiritual lives, but perceive the local Catholic church as a harsh place, they seek elsewhere, even if what they find does not help them. And the Catholic community as a whole suffers, because it loses the chance to be challenged, invigorated, edified, and changed by the presence of those who feel excluded. We do not need to revise the liturgy—we need to revise our manifestation of welcome. For in becoming a Church that welcomes, we will at the same time become a Church that practices solidarity—with those who are growing in faith, with those who are developing faith, and even with those who have no faith.

Since this is a book about hope, let us observe what is hopeful as we consider the state of the liturgy today: even in a post–Catholic-ghetto society, many people (including young adults) still participate in liturgy because they think it is important and obligatory to do so. Moreover, the experience of Catholic liturgy leaves a mark on young people, even those for whom Mass attendance is a distant memory. They still consider themselves Catholics, and their religious imaginations are deeply affected by their experience of liturgy.

The thesis of this chapter is simple: the objective of Catholic liturgy today is to foster and deepen the communion between God and people (the so-called vertical dimension of liturgy), and among people: Catholics, other Christians, and the rest of the world (the horizontal dimension). On one level, this objective is no different from what has prevailed since the time of the apostles, whose *agape* (love) celebrations, the prototypical Eucharistic liturgies, reflected a desire to practice the same self-giving love that Jesus showed in his ministry. The new challenge, the challenge for the postmodern era, is that liturgy be a mystagogy of communion. The term *mystagogy* comes from the Greek meaning "leading into the mystery"—it is suggestive of what happens when an experienced Christian coaches a new Christian on how to lead a holy life. What makes a mystagogy of communion such a challenge today is the fact that the postmodern world is characterized by fractured and truncated relationships

113

among people, to the extent that real communion seems to many impossible. Violence and casual sex are two symptoms of the same cause: failure to see all human beings as bearing the image of God. Right worship—"orthodoxy" in the etymological sense of the term—will therefore involve a transformative experience of communion with God through communion with others. Further, this challenge is not solely for bishops and priests to address: in order to be a Church that makes possible a mystagogy of communion, ordinary Catholics in the pews must be willing to practice welcome every time they set foot in a church.

In this chapter, we explore what a focus on mystagogy of communion means for the practice of Catholic liturgy. Our first look is at the relationship between liturgy and solidarity: specifically, how meaningful liturgy must involve not only words but also symbolic actions that manifest the reality about which we are speaking in the liturgy. From there, we will go on to consider a specific type of ritual behavior, one which (I argue) can help us to pay close attention to why liturgy is still vitally important even for younger Catholics who stay away from Mass. I am referring to sexual behavior— which will surprise many—but which, I hope to show, represents a kind of basic human ritual from which we can learn a great deal for our ruminations on liturgy. The basic reason is this: sexual behavior is a universal human ritual activity, and as such it challenges each human being to discover the relationship between ritual and communion with another. It involves its own kind of mystagogical process; and if done well, it can lead partners into a deepening of communion analogous to the deepening of communion between God and the human being. Moreover, this analogy between sex and liturgy is founded on a long biblical history, from the prophets Hosea and Jeremiah to the Song of Songs to Paul. And it is an area in the lives of many young people that most clearly manifests the need for a mystagogy of communion—a need, in short, for good liturgy. Good liturgy, I argue, must be a schooling in what it means to love other people, and thereby to love God.

LITURGY AND SOLIDARITY

—The church is a community of human beings. The key word to me is "human." Therefore if the church is to be successful, its image should resemble that of a person— alive, feeling, thinking, acting. Too often young adults view the church as either nonexistent in their lives or as a powerful and sometimes unapproachable organization without feeling and without a face. If it desires a better relationship with its younger people, it must come alive and become human in their eyes.

—We need to feel wanted and welcomed. We want to participate, but many times we need to be asked. We need to be given the opportunity to explore how we can fit into this thing called parish.

—To reach out to young adults, the parish must first and foremost foster a sense of community.[116]

The above comments by young adults show that the *way we celebrate the liturgy* is more important than the *content of the liturgy itself.* This is not to minimize the content of liturgy, for it is important. Rather, it recognizes that post–Vatican II liturgical theology is sufficiently developed that we need not place our primary energies on ensuring perfection in content. Our primary energies are better spent on the pastoral question of how to encourage Catholics to do the "work of the people"—a phrase that translates the Greek roots of the term *liturgy.* The focus must be on the practice of liturgy as an act of solidarity: in other words, liturgy is an individual and corporate decision to be transformed into the Body of Christ.

Some examples will illustrate this point. There is a difference between talking about being a welcoming person and actually welcoming someone into your home. There is a difference between saying you love someone and actually performing an act of love for that someone. There is a difference between a Church whose liturgy speaks of the paschal mystery and a Church that itself lives the paschal mystery by the very way it comes together. Churches— and by this, I mean both individual Catholics as well as structures

115

at the parish and diocesan levels—must manifest a commitment to solidarity. There is both a theological dimension and a practical dimension to this imperative.

The theological dimension of solidarity is simple: it reflects the ministry of Christ, whose incarnation was itself an act of divine solidarity. God calls human beings into communion, and the incarnation of Christ manifested the fullest expression of this communion. Those who seek to follow Christ must, then, practice a commitment to solidarity with others, in order to share with them the good news that Christ's life enables human lives to be transformed through communion with the coauthor of our lives. Discipleship is not a distant, theoretical commitment to solidarity as a nice idea. It is fundamentally a decision—sometimes wrenching—to be for others and not only for oneself.

Many of us in the United States, particularly those of us who are materially comfortable, have lost touch with this most basic dimension of the demand of liturgy. We find it easy to listen to the readings, say the creed, exchange a perfunctory handshake of peace, and get in line for communion in time to head out to the parking lot. We can tolerate the Mass because we're used to it, and because it doesn't place too many demands upon us.

But if the liturgy is to be a celebration of the ministry of Jesus, it must be demanding. The language that is so prominent during the Easter season, when we recall our baptismal commitment to Christ, is suggestive of this demand: we who die with Christ also share in Christ's resurrection. Liturgy is an imaginative summons to our own death, a death of everything in us that prevents us from more fully doing the will of God in our lives. To celebrate the Eucharist is to invite God to transform us into the Body of Christ. The demand is staggering. It is very easy to talk about laying down one's life for a friend; it is altogether a different thing to actually do it. Going through the motions of liturgy without actually allowing ourselves to become what it speaks about is the contemporary version of Gnosticism.

How can a church manifest a commitment to solidarity in its liturgy? Following are a number of examples. What is important to underscore here is the observation that each community—each parish, prayer group, or organization—must discern the specific ways that people can manifest this commitment.[117]

1. The community itself. In very few organizations do people from different socioeconomic, racial, and generational backgrounds have the opportunity to interact as peers. A good church is one that is diverse: old and young; rich and poor; single, married, divorced, and widowed; black, white, and brown all come together for the purpose of worshipping God. Of course, there are practical questions that only individual churches or dioceses can answer, like whether the makeup of congregations is an adequate representation of the population in a given area. Here, people at the local level need to be friendly with sociologists, to determine whether parishes are providing the kind of place where all members of the Catholic community feel welcome. If, for example, a parish has a median age of over fifty, then it is time to ask whether that is because the area simply has a high number of retirees, or whether the parish itself has failed to welcome younger members. Similarly, if all the cars in the parking lot are valued at over $30,000, it is time to ask whether the parish has adequately reached out to lower-income families. The key point is this: if a church is to be a place of welcome, it must know whom it is seeking to invite. It must learn about the community of which it is a part.

2. The greetings at Mass. An important question that parishes must ask—especially those in urban or suburban areas where there is frequent residential turnover—is what people with no prior experience of the parish will encounter upon first coming to Mass. Other questions: Will they feel welcome? Will someone help them find a place to sit? Will they know what is going on, if this is their first time in a Catholic church (or the first time in many years)? Will they be made to feel inferior if they are alone, without a family? Will they feel shamed if they come late? Common sense should help dictate how to respond: teach ushers to make everyone feel welcome; make sure latecomers are seated somewhere; and so on.

There is a larger issue, though: catechesis in solidarity. For many, Mass going is a duty, an obligation, one that is to be treated with solemnity. For them, people who are improperly dressed, or late, or unfamiliar with the Mass are guilty of irreverence toward God and the Church. It is likely that lifelong Catholics, or those raised in cultures with deep roots in the Church, will retain such views because they have been taught that the Church is the human presence of God. Instead of dismissing such attitudes, it is important to respect that they arise from a commitment to the Church itself. Yet it is nevertheless important within the context of liturgy to also focus (for example) on Jesus' critiques of the Pharisees, whose absolutist positions on liturgical propriety often obscured the more fundamental commandment of love. Good liturgy must help Catholics discern the proper balance between reverence and duty, on the one hand, and openness and welcome, on the other.

3. The religious imagination. The many uses of symbol throughout the Church's liturgy serve to cultivate a religious imagination. During Advent, we wait expectantly for the coming of the Messiah like the Israelites waited for generations. During Lent, we retreat into a period of self-examination and purification like Christ in the desert. The different colors, the changes of scenery around the altar and the rest of the Church, the use of flowers and holy water—all these are to cultivate our imaginative entrance into sacred mysteries. Catholic tradition shows many examples of such imaginative connections to the stories of the Bible and Christian history: from stained-glass windows to statues to prayer cards to rosaries and so on. The presupposition is that the more a person of faith can imagine himself or herself as participating in the unfolding story of God's relationship to the world, the more he or she will be able to participate in the Church's worship of God.

There is, however, another way to cultivate a religious imagination, one that is well suited to the postmodern era. While the more traditional methods of religious imagination are good, they demand a fair amount of understanding of biblical and Church history; and this understanding is, according to the studies of the post–Vatican II cohorts, sadly lacking. It is little wonder that younger people fail to connect with the symbolism in much of the Church's liturgy; they haven't had the opportunity to really learn it. Instead, cultivation of religious imagination in the postmodern era should take its cue from Jesus himself: parables. The genius of

Jesus' parables is that they presuppose little or no knowledge of religion. Instead, they provide images from the culture in which the listeners lived, and then illustrate a God whose ways are more compassionate, more loving, more prodigal in mercy than those of ordinary people. Jesus' own actions, and his life as a whole, were parabolic: they testified to the stories that Jesus told. The Church community must aim to reproduce this example. It must not only tell parables in the lingua franca of the twenty-first century; it must act in ways that are more compassionate, more loving, more prodigal in mercy than the ways of the rest of society. Where society judges on the basis of money and appearance, Catholics must love each person as being in the image of God. Where society involves polarization between liberals and conservatives, Catholics must practice agapic love for those who think differently. Where society invites us to overindulge in everything that does not nourish us, Catholics must come together around the Eucharistic table.

4. The response to popular culture. Today the Church is immersed in popular culture because popular culture strongly affects the imaginative worlds of people in the Church. In theory, the liturgy represents an entrance into a different world: the architecture of the Church and the flow of the liturgy itself can be seen as a foretaste of the heavenly Jerusalem.[118] Practically, however, the people who come to celebrate the liturgy spend most of their time immersed in popular culture; and this is especially true of the young. Thus the way that churches respond to, and participate in, popular culture is important.

The most profound show of emotion I've ever witnessed in a church was on September 12, 2001—the day following the destruction of the World Trade Center towers. The church was in western Pennsylvania, a relatively short drive from Shanksville, where the third plane had crashed. It was an ordinary weekday communion service (there was no priest present); but not surprisingly many, many people attended who normally would not be present at a weekday liturgy. People came to share their grief in the company of other Catholics; like many across the nation, they sought to make sense of the tragedies. On that day, however, there was not enough Eucharistic bread for everyone—some who had lined up for communion had to return to their seats, unfed and irate. How, their expressions seemed to suggest, could the church be so unprepared to respond to such an emotionally charged day?

The experience highlighted for me how much more people are affected by what is going on in the world in which they live, in comparison to the world of the Church's liturgical life. It is difficult to imagine similar emotion erupting from a congregation's participation in the imaginative recollections that constitute a Good Friday service.

The Church has its own special celebrations that instill a rhythm in our sharing of the biblical stories. These celebrations are good, and tie us to the long history of Christian practice. But Americans who go to church also remember Mother's Day, the Fourth of July, and September 11; and a church that does not pay attention to these celebrations will seem out of touch with the lives of its congregants. Let us take this observation a step further: a church must also pay attention to events that touch the lives of its members, from the deaths of beloved entertainers to news events at schools and workplaces to book or film releases that capture people's attention. The liturgy may be a foretaste of the heavenly Jerusalem, but it is also a celebration of the incarnation of Christ: an incarnation whose implication is solidarity with the ordinary day-to-day lives of ordinary people. (The largest portion of the liturgical year, it may be observed, is aptly named "ordinary time.") A church that practices solidarity is a church with deep roots in the lives of its members.

5. The language. One of the more contentious liturgical issues in recent years involves language: both the language used to render the biblical stories and the language used in prayer. Should lectors render the inclusive "brothers and sisters" when Paul explicitly uses the term *adelphoi*, "brothers"? Should we say "for the praise and glory of *God's* name" rather than "of *his* name"?

The liturgy is a catechesis, a drama, and a mystagogy. As catechesis, it seeks to teach people about the ministry of Christ, and it does so by faithfully and accurately representing the teaching of Christ. From this perspective, it would seem wrong to change the words of scripture to suit our purposes. Further, changing the words of scripture might obscure the fact that the cultures that produced these texts were different from our own, more patriarchal and dismissive of the gifts that women bring to the liturgical life of the Church. Perhaps retaining the original language would highlight the need for good preaching to emphasize (for example) that Paul's directives to the early Christians now apply to both men and women.

On the other hand, liturgy is also a dramatic anamnesis. Our participation in liturgy is a participation in the unfolding story of salvation history, meaning that our objective in liturgy is to render worship to God in our way, just as people of previous times and places have rendered worship to God in their way. From this perspective, use of inclusive language would seem to be more appropriate, since we want to honor the gifts that women bring to the Church. And since our society is neither a first-century Palestinian one, nor a medieval European one, our language must be inclusive in order to more fully enable all Catholics to assume their proper roles in the liturgical celebration.

Finally, liturgy is a mystagogy of communion, meaning that those who participate in it will deepen their understanding of how to love each other. Inasmuch as many find non-inclusive language hurtful, it would seem that the use of it is antithetical to the objective of communion. Because mystagogy is such an important need today, my sense is that inclusive language ought to be used frequently.[119] Practicing with our language an attitude of solidarity is more important than being precise in our use of traditional turns of phrase.

6. The participants at the altar. There is no easy solution to how our Church can heal the division over ordination of women. For while some are quick to point out that male-only ordination is firmly established in both the scriptures and tradition, the difficult point that other Catholics highlight is that this doctrine means that no woman will ever preside at a Eucharistic liturgy. Since the question of ordination is beyond the scope of this book, let us instead recognize that the people in visible liturgical roles do have an important impact on people's perception of what is going on. Therefore, leaving aside for now the question of ordination, let us observe that it is critical for churches to ensure that both men and women, both girls and boys, both old and young, both ordained

and lay take roles in the liturgy. The actors in the liturgical drama must symbolize that all people are invited into the full participation in worship. The people involved in the liturgy ought to be representative of the community, and not merely a chosen few.

Let us also observe that a key factor in the current tension over women's ordination is not only the content of the teaching ("women can't be priests"), but also the manner in which the community of faith deals with it ("Rome has spoken; the matter is closed"). Is it possible that the Church can use this issue as an opportunity to manifest what it means to be a loving community, one that seeks to know and practice what Jesus taught us? What might it look like for those who agree with the current teaching to reach out to those who do not? Conversely, how might those who disagree with the teaching demonstrate that its modification will enable the Church to practice Christ's teachings more faithfully?

7. The celebrations of family life and single life.

> Most parishes, whether city or suburb, are populated by families (young and old). The messages I have heard in these churches have been related to having a family…All the announcements relate to married life and children.[120]

Many parishes are still practicing the model of parish life common in the middle to late twentieth century focused on family and parish school. Few, save those with significant numbers of young adults, have adapted to a basic datum that makes the post–Vatican II generations different from their predecessors: they marry later in life. Until parishes learn to welcome single people, many of whom are discerning a vocation to single life, they will fail to attract and retain a vibrant young adult membership. In addition to celebrations of baptisms, Mother's and Father's Days, first communions, and the like, parishes can celebrate graduations, first jobs or job changes (e.g., a Labor Day blessing), new homes, and so on. Further, because the young adult population is growing (and now constitutes the largest group among Catholics in the United States), dioceses must make a priority of establishing an office for young adult ministry if they have not already done so. The examples in dioceses like Chicago and Atlanta can serve as guides to those dioceses that have not yet established such offices. The United States Conference of Catholic Bishops, too, have established an office for young adult ministry under their Secretariat for Family, Laity, Women and Youth.[121]

Many parishes have long-established mechanisms for welcoming those in married life, largely because of the natural connections with the sacraments of marriage, baptism, reconciliation, Eucharist, and confirmation. All these serve as rites of passage through the (more traditional) stages of young adult life. They served well, when people married in their late teens and early twenties. Today, however, these celebrations must be complemented with others that minister to people who stay single into their thirties or later. It is easy for these Catholics to feel like second-class citizens in their own parishes, because there are no celebrations specifically for them. Churches will do well to consider what ways they can invite single people into fuller celebration of liturgical life.

8. The collection of money. Once upon a time, a church could pass around a basket, and people would put money in it simply because the church asked for it. Today, however, in the era of diocesan bankruptcies, closings of parishes and schools, calls for transparency in financial reporting, and so on, there is a need for a church to be very upfront about what it does with its money. Ideally, the collection of money during a liturgy symbolizes the community's offering of gifts for the common good, in a manner reflective of the apostolic community's sharing of all things.

A church that is willing to be upfront about its finances is a church that will instill trust in its members. People give money when they believe it will contribute to a greater good, and a church can easily show how it does that simply by publishing a financial report. Clarifying the nature of the collection in the liturgy, and even publishing in the bulletin a link to the parish's financial report, will help parishioners know that their offerings are enabling the Church as a whole to practice good stewardship.

9. The announcements. Related to the example above, many announcements at Mass are for those who easily plug into established structures of social and devotional life in the parish. Announcements, too, are symbolic: they symbolize the Church's implicit approval of what's described in the announcement. The

absence of announcement of events can similarly serve a symbolic function. Good announcements will issue open invitations to all sectors of the parish, not only conveying information to a select few.

10. The invitation to new members. What happens at the parish office can make or break a newcomer's feelings toward not only the specific parish, but to the Catholic Church as a whole. Postmodernity is the age of spiritual consumerism, church shopping, and whether this is good or bad, it has a significant impact on the way people approach the Church for the first time, or the first time in a while. If the answer to the comment, "I'm thinking about joining this church," is "OK, fill out this form and the donation envelopes will be mailed to you," then the neophyte may be unlikely to feel welcomed.

Consider the following illustration as a way to understand the importance of what happens at the parish office. A young person has had some nominal involvement in the Church since his youth; his parents wanted him to choose his own religion and so didn't force any religion on him. During college, he stopped going to church, and hasn't had any significant prayer life in the meantime. But the years have passed, and he was seriously involved with a girl he wanted to marry. But during their engagement, she suddenly called it off, and he's devastated. He can't believe that God would do this to him, and yet he feels that he desperately needs God. His friend, seeing his pain, suggests he accompany him to church one week; and without any better idea, he consents. During the week that follows, he decides he wants to stop in to talk to the priest, in a somewhat desperate attempt to get a handle on what he's missed since he last set foot in a church ten years ago. He says to the receptionist at the parish office, "I'm thinking about joining this church."

What the receptionist is presented with is not, as many would assume, a request to simply be added to the mailing list. It is nothing less than a *kairos* moment,[122] an opportunity for God's grace to permeate deep into a person. People at every level of the life of the Catholic Church today must learn to read these signs of the times. For they are manifested to not only priests and nuns; in fact, it is much more likely today that they will be manifested to ordinary people. And we must learn to recognize them. The proper response to the opportunity of a *kairos* moment is openness: "Do you want to talk about it?" "How can I help?" "Tell me more."

Yet there is a further demand implicit in our invitation to new members: the imperative of evangelization. We simply cannot expect that people will come knocking at our church doors anymore. We must be, like the apostles of Jesus, those "sent out" *(apostolein)* into the world to preach the good news by the way we live. To invite new members means more than posting a sign, having an open house, or sponsoring an event. It means being in the world where people live and manifesting what it means to be part of a Church. It is not proselytizing, "hard-selling" Christianity because of a backwards eschatology. Rather, it is patiently and humbly affirming that one's own life is rendered meaningful because of one's ability to practice and share faith within the context of a Church community, and sharing with others an invitation and welcome to be part of it.[123]

11. Partnering with churches in other parts of the city and world. Wealthy suburban parishes can partner with poorer inner-city parishes; ethnic parishes can partner with parishes in a country of origin; parishes with racially homogeneous congregations can partner with parishes with different ethnic makeup. The opportunity is for people to reach beyond their comfort zones that so often lead to ennui in the liturgy. Crossing racial or ethnic boundaries to celebrate in parishes where the majority are different from those in one's home parish can be exciting and challenging. Further, such partnering is more likely to keep focus on people, rather than on the liturgy itself. In theological language, what we celebrate in liturgy is not the liturgy itself—the *res et sacramentum* or symbolism of the rite—rather, we celebrate the grace of God, the *res tantum*, poured out and manifested in people, who bear the image and likeness of God. Partnering will always be a challenge; it simply is not easy to encourage border-crossing when there are many factors in U.S. culture that make it difficult. Yet it is a fruitful challenge if it enables people to practice greater solidarity with others whom they might otherwise know only from the local news.

12. Organizations that meet at the church. A church that hosts different organizations on its property is likely to be a church that practices solidarity. In addition to the older communities like

St. Vincent de Paul, the Legion of Mary, the pro-life group, and others, churches can invite recovery groups like Alcoholics Anonymous or Narcotics Anonymous, support groups of various sorts, social clubs, advocacy organizations, and so on. The more that a church is perceived as a place that seeks to foster community, the more likely it is to draw people into its liturgy. Conversely, the more that it is perceived as a place for a theological elite, the less likely it is to be perceived as a welcoming place.

13. Outreach to the community. A church whose members are actively engaged in good work in the community will be a place that practices and manifests the paschal mystery. For many, celebration of the Eucharist is little more than a ritual act with little meaning. For those who regularly give of themselves for the good of others, though, the Eucharist is a profound source of comfort. Those who can say with Jesus, "this is my body given up for you"— those who regularly engage in self-sacrificial acts of compassion for others—come to celebrate the liturgy with greater intensity and purpose.

The example of Mother Teresa's Missionaries of Charity is challenging. Mother Teresa herself was quick to point out that the reason she and her sisters were able to undertake the great and painful work they did every day was because of a profound Eucharistic devotion. They who sought out and comforted the dying poor of Calcutta every day did so because of the deep-seated belief that everything they did was for Jesus.

We in the United States who struggle to answer young people who ask why church is necessary do well to consider the implications of the Missionaries of Charity's belief. They need the Eucharist because it strengthens them to do the work of God. Are we any different? If we can point to our participation in the Eucharist as that act that enables us to make the difficult choices in our lives, about money, sex, and power, will not others ask why? If our lives testify to the presence of God, will not our celebration of the Church's liturgy emerge as the obvious source of this testimony? Will not young people, whose lives are starving for meaning and purpose, be moved by the example of those whose love transforms cynicism into hope, and inquire further into what exactly it is about this Catholic thing that enables them to do that?

14. Shared liturgies with other churches and communities of faith. While full communion among the followers of Jesus is still a hope and not a reality, we can nevertheless share with other Christians prayers for the good of society. At public events, at weddings, at special occasions, Catholics can join together with other Christians in prayer for the good of the world. Similarly, Catholics can reach across confessional boundaries during times that call for prayer: times of great suffering or great joy.

15. The key question: who is left out? In all their liturgies, churches ought to be sensitive to the question "who is left out?" For every liturgy involves symbolism, and symbolism is by its very nature multivalent—meaning that we cannot control the way people will perceive the symbols. Even the most joyful liturgical celebrations have their darker sides. The celebration of communion is at the same time a manifestation of our failures at communion: with non-Catholics who might be present, with divorced and remarried Catholics, with those who consider themselves too sinful to communicate. The celebration of marriage, too, is a joyful event with a dark side, for those who are unmarried yet desiring marriage or for those recently divorced. Sensitivity to the dark side of liturgical symbolism is a critical need in this age, especially since many who participate in the liturgy have not had adequate catechesis to understand it. The face-value symbolism is therefore important: What do people first see and hear? What are the different ways these things can be interpreted?

Liturgy is not an end in itself; it is a medium through which the community of faith prays together. The only true end of Catholic liturgy is God—the God whom we worship in liturgy and the God whose image we more fully achieve when we pray together as a communion. To the extent that the liturgy enables us to practice orthodoxy, right glorification of God, it is good. But if we use the liturgy as an excuse to avoid the hard demands of compassion, it is idolatry. To achieve the proper end of liturgy in this postmodern world, we must practice solidarity—a solidarity that young people desperately need, because so often their experiences in the rest of their lives are of fragmentation. A liturgy that demands of them the honesty to acknowledge their own humanity, the humanity of those around them in the pews, the humanity of others outside the doors and around the world is a liturgy that they will learn to celebrate with great joy. They will see that the liturgy is real in a way that much of their world is not real: in the language of older sacramental theology, it will "effect what it signifies"—real communion among people, a communion that manifests in human flesh the reality of a loving God.

SEXUALITY AS A KEY TO UNDERSTANDING LITURGY

Perhaps the most provocative analysis of the postmodern world and its effects on young people is through the lens of sexuality, and it is through this lens that we can view the importance of liturgy as a mystagogy of communion. Ours is a consumer society, one in which nearly all elements of human experience are subject to market forces. Among these elements, sexuality is the most prevalent. Aside from being a product in its own right—with Web sites, magazines, stores, and other media promoting its consumption—sexuality is also used as a "hook" to interest the consumer in purchasing everything from shampoo to automobiles. Manipulation of sexuality is ubiquitous in the world of young people, whose vocabulary is so often based on sound bytes from the entertainment and advertising industries. Sexuality, they perceive, is about power: the power to persuade others to respond to their consumer desires.

Sexual mores among many young adults today are in large part the result of socialization in this consumer society. When human beings, like products, are perceived as objects for consumption, sexual mores become more juridical than symbolic. What emerge as the predominant mores are thus minimal, contractual obligations: sex must be consensual, and not harmful; sex brings no permanent commitment, but rather temporary pleasure. And like other objects for consumption today, sex becomes a throw-away object, one that can be easily acquired again at a later date.

What is interesting and hopeful to observe among young people today is their reaction against this generalization. The above sketch of sexuality in postmodern society does not represent the common practice of a majority—rather, it represents that against which many young people measure their actual sexual practices. Against such a backdrop, it is easy then to rationalize that a string of monogamous relationships is actually a strong moral commitment: "I don't want sex to be meaningless. I want to be in love with the person I have sex with." There is a strong sense that random sexual consumption—while not necessarily morally wrong—is nevertheless somehow a bit selfish, not unlike someone who shops too much. When pressed to describe when sex is moral, many will respond that it ought to be predicated on love (whatever that may be!). This inchoate sense that sex and love ought to go hand in hand is a clue to why there is a place for liturgy in the lives of young people today. They know at a deep level that the absence of a spiritual foundation for their moral lives can lead to the uncoupling of sex and love; and at the same time they find themselves unwilling to live out the consequences of this uncoupling. They need liturgy to be the place where they learn—or better, relearn—what it means to love.

Young people crave good liturgy because it offers them an experience not available in the market-driven world. When done well, liturgy invites them to

- immerse themselves in a world not governed by market forces, but by love
- experience mystery, which opens them to know a God of love
- participate in a tradition of those seeking to love as Jesus did
- encounter other human beings as human beings worthy of love
- consider human living in the face of eternity

We examine each of these invitations below. If liturgy is to thrive in the twenty-first century, it must be suffused with love. It must draw young people to become constructively self-critical so that their experiences of sexuality can be understood against the backdrop of a theological anthropology, one that emphasizes the human being as God's beloved.

Liturgy as Immersion in a World Not Governed by Market Forces, but by Love

Observe that at Sunday liturgies, many of the small number of young people present dress according to their habits of everyday life. There are a few who still wear their "Sunday best" out of habit or duty; but more often than not, young people will wear the fashions that would look equally appropriate at school, hanging out with friends, or at a coffeehouse. Long gone are the days when modesty was the expectation! For many, encounter with the dress habits of young people at Mass brings out prudish attitudes: "That's not appropriate! I can't believe she's wearing that!"

It is little surprise that young people will bring their cultural sensibilities with them into church. We ought to celebrate the fact that they do, rather than either (a) bringing a false self to church, one that is sanitized for the sake of not offending anyone; or (b) avoiding church altogether. (Both options do happen, nonetheless.) On the other hand, these cultural sensibilities ought to give us pause: many young women (especially) dress the way they do because they have come to perceive it as a cultural necessity. For many years, I taught at a college in which three-quarters of the students were women; and over the years I came to lament the fact that dress habits in class often seemed to me inappropriate. I do not exaggerate when I observe that on occasions, young women came into class dressed in apparel that would have easily fit into a Victoria's Secret catalogue. Over the years, I came to know many of my students: some were single mothers in their late teens; others were victims of abuse; others were divorced from cheating husbands. I came to understand how captive many of these women were to the market forces of fashion: they dressed the way they did because they had to, in order to be perceived as young or as "eligible."

Young people live in a world governed by market forces. They understand that they must compete on every level, and that they are measured by their market power. Much of that measuring is at the level of their sexuality: if they are attractive, they believe, they will be happy. Yet what is unfortunate is that much of their self-image is appropriated at a preconscious level—they are not even aware of the extent to which they think of themselves according to these market forces. Those who perceived themselves as over-weight or ugly did not expect to be treated well by a professor; those who believed they were good-looking expected good rapport and eventually good grades. Too often their experiences of "love" were rather experiences (or lack thereof) of attention from young men, ranging from simple dialogue to sexual activity to abuse. In short, for them love was another market force.

When sexual experience is impersonal, when it fails to sym-bolize a deep interpersonal love (as can happen only over a lifetime), it tends to persuade young people that all human relationships are governed by market forces. What this means is that they come to believe that love—experienced as (at least) temporary experiences of being consumed by/with another—is no different from other trans-actions of supply and demand. Sex, in short, can be bought and sold, and therefore people's lives can be bought and sold.

Young people need liturgy because they need an encounter with other human beings in real attempts at communion. No church is perfect; all communities fall short of communion. But they must try! Young people need experiences of love that are not governed by market forces: to be loved not because of attractive-ness, but because they are created in the image and likeness of God.

The first lesson that every Catholic liturgy ought to foster is that each person (present and absent) is beloved by God. This is the most fundamental element in a mystagogy of communion: to be human is to be loved by God. The kind of love that is celebrated in liturgy has nothing to do with market forces: good looks, wealth, political power, talent. It is no surprise that in the early Church there were many on the margins of society; those on the margins are quick to embrace this view of love. It can be more challenging to those who succeed in the world of the market, because it can be difficult to relinquish the esteem one has worked hard to achieve. Yet if we are a Church that believes Jesus' counsel that we must lose our lives in order to find them, we must be prepared to practice and celebrate the love of God that defies market imperatives.

There is a prophetic dimension to this element of good liturgy. A church that celebrates non-market-driven love will reach out to those to whom the market is violent:

- women who are treated as objects for consumption
- men whose self-worth is measured by machismo or sexual prowess
- children who are objects of aggressive marketing
- girls suffering from eating disorders because they have internalized cultural standards of beauty
- boys abusing steroids because they have internalized cultural pressures about male strength
- women who are beyond the average age of Hollywood's leading ladies, who are driven to various therapies to stay young-looking at all costs
- men who are addicted to pornography because of constant stimulation from advertising and entertainment

In short, a liturgy that celebrates the mystery of divine love by what it practices will be a force for healing for those who suffer from the effects of market-created desire. Good liturgy will draw people to celebrate the reality of love in contrast to what they experience in the market-driven world.

Liturgy as Experience of Mystery

Perhaps the element of young adult spirituality that most confounds older Catholics is their attraction to older forms of devotion such as the Latin Mass, Eucharistic adoration, or the rosary. Many see these devotions as throwbacks—conservative responses to the post–Vatican II liturgy. Far from being throwbacks, however, these practices are for many young people discoveries: they are counter-cultural responses to both a secular society and a jejune liturgical practice among many Catholics.

A colleague once told the story of her conversion back to the Catholic faith of her youth. It took place over the course of her travels through Italy during college—frequent visits to cathedrals and art galleries immersed her in the religious history of that country. Eventually, she came to appreciate the grandness of a cathedral Mass in a place like Santa Maria Maggiore in Rome; for her, it was like entering a whole different reality. Over time, she came to critique

Cardinal Law's church!

what she had been taught as a child about her faith: her question was, "Why was I never taught about this?"

The postmodern world has eroded a sense of mystery; the celebration of it in liturgy can be refreshing. Modern science challenged the older reserves of theological truth-claims, rendering theology to a great extent obsolete; it could not explain the origins of the universe, the origins of humankind, the makeup of the physical world, and so on. And so theological thinking retreated into a more discreet corner of the university, while various sciences grew to assume the places in which it once held pride of place. In the popular world, too, language about God slowly was replaced with language about physics, biology, psychology, sociology, and so on—everything could be explained by appeal to some body of experts. God was a projection of the psyche; miracles could be explained by medical or physical science; sexuality was biological and psychological; Jesus was a historical figure who had some interesting teachings.

One casualty of the modern world was the sense of wonder. The postmodern world that young people have inherited is thus a world in which nothing is really mysterious anymore. There are some things that have not yet been properly funded for study, but eventually human ingenuity will understand everything.

The issue is that the explanations the experts have given them are no longer satisfactory. Like water, they are finding the leaks in the experts' reasoning and recognizing that these leaks suggest a more fundamental structural problem. They have been told that the big bang can explain everything in the material world up to nanoseconds after the explosion, and they ask, "What about before that?" They have been told that religion represents a stage in a culture's growth, and that eventually more enlightened models of thinking replace it; and yet they find themselves still hoping that there is a God who loves them. They have been told that events like Columbine and September 11 shatter any belief in a good God, and yet they still find themselves reaching out to God and hoping that God is listening.

Good liturgy must cultivate a sense of mystery because it persuades them that the way the world works cannot be easily explained, and that therefore there is still reason for hope. Perhaps the worst mistake we Catholics can make today is to demonstrate that we already have all the answers. Our answers will not hold up against those of other experts—at least not for those who have no grounding in faith, and they will only serve to convince young people that we are caught up in an intellectually indefensible, medieval model of authority. Instead, we must cultivate a sense of awe in the face of the great mysteries of God, divine love, human existence, and hope. Primarily, good liturgy will celebrate and imitate the mystery of divine love, echoing the attitude of Peter upon witnessing Jesus' transfiguration: "how good it is to be here!" A world of mystery is a world in which God may be acting; and such a world is ripe for discovery.

The liturgy will thrive to the extent that it allows time and space for imagination. When the former archbishop of Milan, Carlo Maria Martini, celebrated Mass for young people in the beautiful cathedral, radio broadcasters of these Masses had to find ways to fill the "dead air" that occurred during periods of silence in the Mass. Ironically, some expressed to the broadcasters their desire that the periods of silence be left silent on the radio! The image of a radio listener enjoying the silence of a broadcast Mass gives a clue about the state of liturgy today: perhaps it is too programmed, too much a product to be delivered and not enough a *kairos* in which a community comes to discover the God who has pitched a tent among us.[124]

Fundamentally, the experience of mystery in Catholic liturgy can challenge young people to reevaluate their sense that sexuality is little more than a commodity to be exchanged. While their sexuality is not the only measure of self-identity, it is a preeminent one: and to the extent that they can consider their sexuality as an integral part in a much deeper mystery about themselves, they will find in the liturgy a fundamental challenge. What you see is not what you get; what you see (and hear, and smell, and feel, and taste) in liturgy is the symbolic manifestation of a far deeper, inexhaustible mystery of a God who loves in ways we can never understand. Liturgy, in this perspective, is an initiation into a new way of considering the world: through symbolism. How can bread be the Body of Christ? How can sitting in this odd building be an experience of communion? How can what I sense be an invitation to consider a deeper reality? Every element of liturgy must ultimately symbolize the love of God: from the physical space to the choice of actions to the ways that people treat each other. This immersion in symbolism is the beginning of the mystagogy of communion: everything ought to encourage people to contemplate the love of God, and over time this immersion ought to bear fruit in people's concrete lives. For young people, the connection between mystery, liturgy, and sexuality is this: good liturgy will cultivate a sense of the mystery of human life, persuading us that what we experience in the flesh is only one manifestation of a much deeper reality we have yet to fully comprehend. More basically: good *NICE* liturgy will help young people to understand that people are more than their bodies, and that sexuality is a gift that can enable us to encounter the mystery of another human being in a profound way. Good liturgy will cultivate a sense of mystery, which young people will carry into their relationships with others.

Liturgy as Participation in a Tradition of Those Seeking to Love as Jesus Did

Tradition is one of those thorny elements of contemporary Catholicism; responses to it tend to polarize different members of the Church. On the one hand, tradition is an indispensable element of Catholic faith, inasmuch as it ties us through the ages to the ministry of the apostles sent by Jesus into the world. On the other hand, excessive clinging to tradition can sometimes hamstring authentic development in the Church, as Cardinal Newman tried to highlight in the nineteenth century.[125] Most fundamentally, however, the benefit of tradition is that it connects us to others in the past who have wrestled with the same kinds of questions that we face today.

There is a formative effect of tradition, especially on young people. Those who see themselves as part of a tradition feel part of something greater than themselves, and consequently are more likely to consider their choices as somehow related to that tradition. My friend whose tour through Italy spurred her growth in faith was affected by the symbols of tradition she encountered, for they reminded her that there was a long history of those whose lives were deeply touched by their Christian faith. In a world where real authority is difficult to discern, tradition lends credence—it says, "many have believed this and have profited by it."

More specifically, tradition reminds us that living memory is ephemeral. What "everybody" thinks today may be forgotten tomorrow—whether it be about the important news item, the compelling film, or the current controversy. Church tradition, in particular, ties people to an ancient tradition, one that in so many ways challenges the way we think about the postmodern world. Witness the coverage of the 2005 papal funeral and conclave—the world's attention was focused on the Church's celebration of tradition, even while many either misunderstood or openly disagreed with what it represented. The attractiveness of tradition is that it reminds us that our understanding of the world is limited.

It is quaint today to speak of tradition when speaking about sexuality; our age has been so deeply affected by the sexual revolution of the late twentieth century that it is difficult for many to imagine young people reserving sexual expression for marriage. Yet one strength of liturgy is that it does not live at the level of discursive thought, but rather at the level of symbol and ritual. What one cannot say in discourse without sounding archaic—sex is best reserved for marriage—one can nevertheless celebrate in liturgy. We do not bless serial monogamy or promiscuity, but rather committed marriage.[126] At a symbolic level, this liturgical celebration says "marriage is a sacrament, a place where husband and wife manifest to each other the love that Christ shows for the Church." And when it says this, it implicitly rejects that the same can be said of other kinds of interpersonal relationships. Tradition, conveyed through symbolism, serves as cultural critique: it highlights that what the Church has done in its past is different from what many people do today. And while the multivalence of symbol makes it unlikely that young people will automatically understand and agree with what the liturgy symbolizes, nevertheless there is likely to be an effect on young people's imagination. ("Why is marriage such a big deal, anyway?")

Yet if good liturgy as a whole offers a mystagogy of communion, then its importance is not limited to wedding traditions. All the dimensions of liturgy, I am suggesting, ought to symbolize the love of God (the *res tantum* of medieval sacramental theology), thereby enabling a person to come to greater and greater understanding of what real love demands. If the liturgy is the human response to the love of God, then it is a transformative experience through which we become more and more like Christ. We come to love as Christ loved; we see human beings as the precious creations that God fashioned. We come to know that their desire to be loved is like our own; we come to treat them as moral and spiritual peers. Our sexuality—the outward manifestation of who we are as beings capable of relationship with others—becomes one poignant expression of our love to others as male or female. And thus, in the process of this mystagogy, we come to regard our sexuality as a gift that enables us to love others in particularly profound ways. More precisely, we come to appreciate our potential to use sexuality as a unique gift to another.

Social mores are powerful; we need tradition because it carries a currency that uniquely has the power to critique social mores. Contemporary sexual attitudes and practices are toxic to young people, even though many are not aware of it. Good liturgy has the potential to help young people discover and imagine alternative responses to their sexuality, responses that will be based on the fundamental question, "How can I use this to celebrate the love of God?"

Liturgy as Encounter with Other Human Beings as Human Beings Worthy of Love

When human persons are reduced to objects for consumption, they are no longer seen as capable of love. On reality TV shows, they are objects for approval or disapproval; in advertising, they are consumers whose dollars are sought; in entertainment, they are "eye candy" (fun to look at) or targets of violence; in video games they are virtual realities; on the Internet they are images on a screen. Yet even through these media, people have the ability to be touched by the humanity of people: we can feel for the player just voted off the show; we can resist being treated only as a source of corporate income; we can sympathize with entertainment figures even when we don't fully know them; we can remind our children that there is a difference between video games and reality; we can

VIRTUAL WORLD

reach out to other people using the Internet as a tool for communication. Ours is in many ways a virtual world, in which our encounters with people are through various media, and so truly seeing the "face" of the other often takes effort. Without this effort, it can be difficult to see others as "other selves"—that is, as individuals who, like us, need to love and be loved.

The virtual world in which so many young Americans live is their response to loneliness: it is an attempt to connect with the larger world, to feel included in the excitement of what people are doing. The virtual world is attractive because it is broad: it allows us to know (or think we know) a little of everything. Yet knowledge in the virtual world is deceptive. One comes to know a little about many things without necessarily coming to know much about anything. More specifically: the relationships that one forms in the virtual world—from attraction to popular figures to acquaintances in chat rooms to online dating relationships—tend to lack depth. The burgeoning interest in online dating services over the last several years is an interesting case. They have moved from more-or-less free ranges for conversation, in which people could pretend to be whomever they chose (thereby providing the situation for predatory practices), to very structured third-party organizations in which a tightly controlled policy of disclosure protects party A from party B until both assent to the sharing of personal information. This development in online dating gives a clue to why the virtual world remains different from the real world: there are different levels of symbolism and privacy. In the virtual world, it is easy to restrain one's self-disclosure, and even lie about oneself. In the real world, people meet literally face to face. Our bodies immediately disclose a great deal about our identity: we are male or female; we have a certain age; we have a certain appearance. From the face-to-face encounter, people will make assumptions about our lifestyles: ethnicity, economic background, education level, marital status, and interests. People will discern in the overt symbolism of our physical appearance much about us even before we speak.

The extent of young people's immersion in the virtual world is difficult to gauge; but ask them to fast from anything involving electricity and one can get a sense of their dependence on it. An "electricity fast" would involve temporary relinquishing of TV, cell

fast

phones, video games, computers, CD/MP3 players, and so on. In short, it would feel to many like giving up a lifeline to their world. It is likely that many would be unable to undertake such a fast for long, simply because they would find it hard to fill their days with anything else! Of course, like any fast, an electricity fast would not be about what one gives up, but rather about what one is supposed to gain as a result. In this case, the objective would be to loosen dependence on the virtual world, in order to live more fully in the real world of real people.

Perhaps one reason many young people can treat sexuality flippantly is because they have lived in a virtual world, and have thus lost the sensibility that the body is an irreplaceable symbol of ourselves. Paul's advice about the body would seem archaic:

> Do you not know that your bodies are members of Christ? Should I therefore take the members of Christ and make them the members of a prostitute? Never! Do you not know that whoever is united to a prostitute becomes one body with her? For it is said, "The two shall be one flesh." But anyone united to the Lord becomes one spirit with him. Shun fornication! Every sin that a person commits is outside the body; but the fornicator sins against the body itself. Or do you not know that your body is a temple of the Holy Spirit within you, which you have from God, and that you are not your own? For you were bought with a price; therefore glorify God in your body. (1 Cor 6:15–20)

Regrettably, within Christian tradition this honoring of the body has sometimes devolved into a fear of the body, and so many young people do not regard Church teaching on sexuality to be either positive or helpful. Yet what we see in Paul's letter to the Christians of Corinth is a sensibility that the body is something unique in human experience—it alone manifests or symbolizes who we are. The body, according to Paul, is not merely a tool to be used however we please. My body is me: or better, the way I show myself to the world, and so the way I choose to use it is the way I choose to be as a human person.

In the virtual world, our humanity is located primarily in the head: we are titillated by images on a screen or by sounds in headphones, and respond with images or sounds we produce. In the real world, though, humanity is bodily. We move our bodies around doing things, going places; we meet other people via their bodies; we interact with the world around us by means of our bodies. Liturgy must be located in the real world of human bodies. This is not to say that it ought to avoid the virtual world altogether—on the contrary, it can be enhanced by judicious use of the virtual world.[127] But it must be rooted in the real encounter of human beings with one another if it is to be a mystagogy of communion.[128]

The liturgy places all persons before God as equals. Fundamentally, then, the experience of liturgy can engender a sense that all persons share an innate dignity as children of God. Real persons with real bodies are, then, what Paul calls "temples of the Holy Spirit," meaning that bodies are privileged places of disclosure of the sacred. An appropriation of this liturgical reality would thus lead young people to a deeper appreciation of sexuality as capable of a unique kind of disclosure of the sacred. In lay terms, this means that people who pray the liturgy will come to view others' bodies as sacred, and make moral choices that reflect this view. If God has given me the gift of my body to use to God's glory, and if God has similarly given others the gifts of their bodies to use to God's glory, then our sexuality is part of this giftedness. And thus God has given us the gift of sexuality to use to God's glory. We have the opportunity to use our sexuality to love others; we also have the capacity to use our sexuality to hurt others. The liturgy can help us to learn how to love in all things, and it will have repercussions for the way we imagine using our sexuality to love.

Liturgy as Fostering a Sensibility of Human Living in the Face of Eternity

In its Constitution on the Sacred Liturgy *Sacrosanctum Concilium* (8), the bishops of Vatican II described the liturgy in colorful, imaginative language:

> In the earthly liturgy we take part in a foretaste of that heavenly liturgy which is celebrated in the holy city of Jerusalem toward which we journey as pilgrims, where Christ is sitting at the right hand of God, a minister of the holies and of the true tabernacle; we sing a hymn to the Lord's glory with all the warriors of the heavenly army; venerating the memory of the saints, we hope for some part and fellowship with them; we eagerly await the Saviour, Our Lord Jesus Christ, until He, our life, shall appear and we too will appear with Him in glory.

The liturgy derives its efficacy from the power of ritual and symbol, both of which enable people to create imaginative worlds which, in turn, challenge us to see the real world in a new way. Two people can emerge from a church having shared the same experience: one might say, "I have taken part in a foretaste of the heavenly liturgy as a pilgrim, journeying to the heavenly city of Jerusalem!" while the other might say, "I spent the hour thinking about everything I have to do this week." What the bishops articulated was an ideal: an illustration of what we are aiming to do as Christians when we undertake liturgy. As an ideal, it functions at the level of imagination: the imaginative world provides a *telos*, an end or goal, of our actions. We are not just singing; we are joining the choirs of angels and saints as we proclaim God's glory. We are not just reading from an old book; we are listening to the Word of God revealed to the writers of scripture. We are not just getting in line for bread and wine; we are sharing in the Eucharistic banquet for the remission of sins and the salvation of humanity.

The symbolism of Catholic liturgy serves as a consistent reminder that our lives are unfolding in the face of eternity: the God who is eternal has created us to share eternal joy with God. At the Easter Vigil, which serves as a kind of focal point for the entire liturgical calendar of the Church, the liturgy of the word involves a broad sweep of the entire unfolding story of salvation history, from creation through the call of Abraham, the exodus of the Israelites from Egypt, the rise and decline of the Israelite nation, the writings of the prophets, and the coming of the Messiah and genesis of the Church. These are powerful stories for those who are claimed by them—those that see themselves as being part of the Church. For others, though, who do not have the same sense of identification with the Church, these stories are foreign, as is the notion that their lives are unfolding in the face of eternity. Participation in the liturgy in a meaningful way means appropriating its symbolism, and this takes time. Children, for example, are not expected to participate in the liturgy before a certain age; they will not get it before they are able to pay sustained attention to a person speaking or reading in front of a crowd. Similarly, one who has never been to Mass before will more likely feel like a spectator than a participant, simply because he or she has not had the chance to learn what is going on.

Many young people are more like spectators than participants because they have not been taught how to understand the symbolism. They have no conceptual apparatus with which to make sense of the imaginative world that the liturgy creates in the minds of participants. They need catechesis—some of which can take place in the liturgy itself, and some of which is better reserved for other situations. One important element of this catechesis will address how Christian faith transforms the way the faithful consider the nature and scope of human life. This is more than a cursory point. It confronts very basic assumptions that prevail in much of postmodern culture: that there are no universal truths, and that appearances of truth itself are always relative and conditioned.

At the heart of Catholic liturgy is a basic truth-claim: God loves us, and in the liturgy we are publicly and communally returning that love. It would be extremely difficult to defend such a truth-claim in the philosophical language of postmodernism. Nevertheless, what Catholics do in liturgy is not first an intellectual act: it is an imaginative act of surrender to the mystery of God. In many ways, it is a courageous decision to de-center the intellect: to believe that God has lived among us; to believe that bread can become the Body of Christ; to believe that hope will prevail over despair. Catholic faith, then, is predicated on an act of hope. To be sure, we affirm the truth-claims of Christian faith (e.g., the kinds of things one finds in the *Catechism*); yet there must be a more fundamental act of hope in what Jesus taught us. We hope that our faith is true.

Well said

Earlier I suggested that one casualty of the modern world is the sense of wonder. One casualty of the postmodern world, then, is the sense of hope. For in a world in which everything can be explained, but in which there are no universal truths, there is little to hope for, least of all in the eternal sense. There may be small victories: the kinds of hope that emerge when a good person is elected to office, or when a war is ended, or even when a medical breakthrough promises to save millions of people. But there is no hope that echoes the closing words of Julian of Norwich, reflecting on God's revelations of love:

> And these words: You will not be overcome, were said very insistently and strongly, for certainty and strength against every tribulation which may come. He did not say: You will not be troubled, you will not be belaboured, you will not be disquieted; but he said: You will not be overcome. God wants us to pay attention to these words, and always to be strong in faithful trust, in well-being and in woe, for he loves us and delights in us, and so he wishes us to love him and delight in him and trust greatly in him, and all will be well.[129]

Julian does not deny that faith in God will involve tempest, travail, and affliction; but God tells her that in the end all will be well. This hope is an eternal one.

The courage to treat human beings as sacred manifestations of divine love; the courage to pray in hope that God is listening; the courage to make hard moral choices in the hope that they will bear fruit—all follow from the conviction that our actions, and the people that we become through them, are made for eternity. A liturgical mystagogy of communion will help young people to look at others as persons on pilgrimage toward eternity. They will begin to see each other not primarily in terms of their attractiveness, but rather in terms of their fragility, their weakness, their hopefulness—in short, in terms of their humanity before an eternal God. In the face of eternity, sexuality becomes less a tool for pleasure and more a gift for sanctification—of both self and other. These of course are ideals; but ideals can thrive in the imaginative world that unfolds when one embraces the possibility (even with doubt) that God has created us for eternal happiness.

Young people need the liturgy because they need to see themselves and others in the face of eternity. They need to be persuaded that their choices around sexuality have consequences for themselves and others—not strictly in the negative sense (which they perceive us church folk to be talking about in a way that diminishes our authority), but rather in the very positive sense that sexuality is a great gift that can transform lives. They need the witness of older couples who have lived faithful lives for decades. They need the witness of younger couples who have acted on hope by choosing the sacrament of marriage. They need the witness of other singles who are struggling with the same hard choices they are. They need the witness of courageous religious women and men, who choose to serve others by forgoing married life and embracing a community of need. Most of all, they need a church community that hopes in God's grace by choosing to live in solidarity with others.

The liturgical renewal of the twentieth century focused on the content of the liturgy: what we do. The liturgical renewal of the twenty-first century must focus on the participants in the liturgy: who we are. The world is too needy for us to treat the liturgy as an arcane ritual exercise, a "magic show" as a friend once put it. It must become a mystagogy of communion because it must reflect the mystery of the God who became incarnate among us in order to love us to our salvation. We who pray the liturgy must commit ourselves to become more and more like the one we worship, in order that this same God might then use us to contribute to the well-being of the rest of the world.

Chapter Five

Spirituality and the Critique of Consumerism

Many older Catholics will recognize that there has been a kind of spiritual revolution in the Church—a changing of attitudes about prayer and the life of discipleship. In the twentieth century, especially in the years following World War II, there was a flowering of lay spiritual movements, which encouraged ordinary Catholics to draw from the long tradition of Catholic reflection on the spiritual life. More laypeople began reading the works by and about Benedict and Scholastica, Francis and Clare, John of the Cross and Teresa of Avila, Catherine of Siena, Ignatius of Loyola, Hildegard of Bingen, Julian of Norwich, Dominic, Therese of Lisieux, and many others. In the middle of the twentieth century, a surprising bestseller was Thomas Merton's *Seven Storey Mountain*, the autobiography of an atheist-turned-Catholic who later became a Trappist monk. In the wake of Vatican II, too, many laypeople appropriated the Council's emphasis on the common discipleship of all the baptized to learn more about their tradition's spiritual riches. For many, learning the practice of spirituality outside the walls of a seminary became a lifelong search for meaning.

In the wider U.S. culture, the notion of a spiritual search gathered momentum in the same period that saw the change and even decline of religious institutions. It was during this period that the traditional linkage of religion and spirituality started to uncouple, such that many Americans could proclaim themselves committed to the spiritual life, without the strictures of any religious tradition telling them how to pray.[130] The very term *religion*, has, over the years, become for many synonymous with "restrictive." Where religion is about following rules, spirituality is about a meaningful life; where religion is about obedience to authority, spirituality is about freedom of conscience; where religion is about dusty traditions and stifling rituals, spirituality is about living the truth creatively. These are unhappy caricatures, both of religion and of spirituality.

It is understandable that during the periods of cultural breakdown of the twentieth century, people sought out new forms of piety that honored what they perceived as the kernel of Christian faith. (I do not even address the wider spiritual searches that led many beyond the Christian tradition of spirituality.) What has emerged, though, is a shortsighted understanding of religious tradition, one that does not attend to the reality that Jesus himself was both engaged in, and thoughtfully critical of, religious practices of the community in which he was raised. Today, the challenge is to reconnect religion and spirituality; what is interesting is that many young people are discovering for themselves that they need them both.[131]

If Christian spirituality is modeled after Christ, then it is not about *us*—it is about *God*. Contemporary treatments of spirituality invite us to consider how we can make our lives better: by focusing on prayer, by learning to meditate, by disciplining our desires through various means, and so on. Yet all these invitations to do new things, think new ways, consider the world and its inhabitants more profoundly overlook the fact that spirituality is not a technique or a practice, and so no technique or practice can replace the invitation of God to participate in the life of God. For younger Catholics, who feel no strong connections to the Church and its traditions, the suggestion that spirituality is about a search for meaning leads many to conclude that they are on their own in the marketplace of ideas, wandering around with no way to judge what is good. They have not learned the necessity of religion, a necessity that many older Catholics have taken for granted and have thus ignored. Older Catholics were taught how to pray; and while many recall with fondness their memories of parochial school or CCD classes, others recall only that the environment was stifling. Younger Catholics have, in large part, not been taught how to pray; and so when they find themselves in need of God (as all of us do,

church draws us into a relationship w/ God + Others

sooner or later) they very often discover that they have no idea what to do. An important dimension of the mystagogy that young Catholics need is prayer, following the example of the disciples' request to Jesus: "Lord, teach us how to pray." And what quickly emerges from any authentic discipline of prayer is the recognition that God's will is not the same as our will, and that God calls us into a community where we learn to serve others. Religion is fundamentally about ordering such a community—and so if spirituality is honest, it depends upon religion.

The difficulty, of course, is that reality often differs from the ideal. It is one thing to suggest that authentic spirituality ought to be practiced in the context of a religion; it is another thing to recognize that many of the structures of the Catholic Church are in disrepair. In the wake of the sexual abuse crisis, many diocesan ministries are underfunded. Because of the growing shortage of priests, many parishes lack good leadership, particularly of young people. And because we live in an age when the roles of lay ministers are still in many places poorly defined, often those with skills that could be of service to the Church are left wondering what they ought to do.[132] An important challenge for the Catholic community in the twenty-first century is to develop new structures that draw young people to cultivate their spiritual lives in the wider context of the Church community, helping them to appropriate the role that good religion can play in the development of a faith community. We must not let what is wrong with the Church distract us from proclaiming what is most right about the Church; and what is most right is that it draws us into relationship with God and others. And it does so in ways that a private practice of spirituality cannot.

There is an intimate relationship between authentic spirituality and organized religion. It is simply not possible to treat spirituality as a private matter, because it summons from us demands that must be addressed by the entire Body of Christ. Conversely, the Church today desperately needs from its members a deepening of authentic spirituality. Each of us is part of the entire Church, and so our desire must constantly be to deepen our faith lives both as individuals in relationship with God and as members of the Body in relationship with God and one another. To illustrate my thesis that authentic spirituality demands institutional religion, consider the following dilemmas facing us today. These dilemmas under-score how the private practice of spirituality cannot suffice if we take seriously the responsibility to address these dilemmas.

1. The human tendencies toward sin and greed are visited most upon the poor and vulnerable. Unless Christians rooted in Jesus' commands to reach out to the poor[133] develop structures that can converse with and sometimes challenge the extremes of market-centered (rather than person-centered) economics, their individ-ual acts of charity will not suffice to create a more just global order.

2. The most profound contributions of the Christian faith tradition to practices of personal spirituality—reading scripture, praying the Lord's Prayer, imitating the good Samaritan, and so on—are part of the contemporary spiritual landscape precisely because there have been people committed to the handing on *(traditio)* of their religion. Without religious institutions, there can be no traditions.

3. The large moral issues of the day—war and peace, abortion, stem cell research, euthanasia, the death penalty, and many others—involve reflections from religious traditions. Without such reflections, the cultural dialogue on these issues is impov-erished. Religious institutions like the Church are necessary to preserve, highlight, and advance thinking on the most funda-mental questions of human existence.

4. Environmental concerns and human rights issues are increas-ingly global in scope, meaning that even national-level discourse has become inadequate to address basic questions about the flourishing of our world. As a global body, the Church has the capacity to transcend national interests and focus on very basic human concerns.

These four dilemmas give us a glimpse of why the call to respond to the invitation of God cannot remain private. The com-mand to love God and neighbor involves a spirituality of both per-sonal commitment and ecclesial membership. Clearly, it is important to practice those things that many would agree are the hallmarks of an authentic spirituality: generosity in love; openness to growth; tenacity in the face of suffering; awe in the presence of beauty; sympathy amid suffering. But it is equally important to bring these gifts into the community of those seeking to praise, reverence, and serve God, in order that the community itself begins to manifest the sacramental presence of God in the world.

In order to cultivate a healthy ecclesial spirituality—a spirituality of being called to participate in the community of the Church—let us now focus on five points:

- Catholic spirituality is rooted in a true story.
- It is "catholic," or universal, not parochial.
- It is thus a call to solidarity, especially with marginalized people.
- It is a call to worship, according to what Jesus has revealed to us.
- It is realistic, meaning that it calls us not to avoid the world, but to be ready to confront it in all its ambiguity.

CATHOLIC SPIRITUALITY IS ROOTED IN A TRUE STORY

Catholic spirituality is founded on the life and ministry of Jesus: his obedience to the will of the Father, even to the cross; his proclamation of the kingdom of God; his reaching out to the outcasts of society. Yet it is also founded on the beliefs formulated in doctrines by the early Church: Jesus' divine and human natures; his identity as the Son of God, the second person of the Holy Trinity, the Word made flesh, the Messiah. To encounter the faith of those who follow Jesus is to encounter a living, kerygmatic tradition, meaning (among other things) that the only way to know Jesus is to encounter the community that proclaims who Jesus was.[134] The opening lines of Luke's Gospel suggest something of the responsibility of the religious community:

Since many have undertaken to set down an orderly account of the events that have been fulfilled among us, just as they were handed on to us by those who from the beginning were eyewitnesses and servants of the word, I too decided, after investigating everything carefully from the very first, to write an orderly account for you, most excellent Theophilus, so that you may know the truth concerning the things about which you have been instructed.

Luke's desire to instruct Theophilus about the reality of Jesus' life is what all Christians ought to desire. Fundamentally, Christian spirituality is predicated on the story of Jesus: it is about living one's life in light of the reality of God among us. What the beginning of Luke's Gospel spells out is the important need for the followers of Jesus to have the whole truth. It is not enough, Luke seems to suggest, to have strong feelings about justice or love or mercy or meaning or compassion or sin or corruption or evil—one must wed these feelings to a right understanding of what God has revealed to us in the story of Jesus.

The Catholic religion—by which I mean somewhat broadly the practices that Catholics undertake as Catholics—is rooted in a story that we believe is true: God has lived among us as a human being, and remains with us in the presence of the faithful, the Church. Catholics are, almost by definition, conservative: we conserve that which we hold most dear, our identity as it has been shaped through our practice of following Jesus. Paradoxically—at least for those who look at the world through a political lens—our conservatism is liberal, in the sense that we believe that our faith points to God's liberation of human beings from the bondage of sin to the fullness of life. The disciplines of religion are thus like the disciplines of military or academic life; they exist in order to promote a specific model of growth that liberates the person from false desires.[135]

The "political hermeneutic"—that perspective on the public life of the Church that presumes that everyone can be easily labeled "conservative" or "liberal"—is poisonous. From the perspective of the New Testament writers, there was no liberal or conservative reading of the story of Jesus; there were rather the attempts "to compile a narrative of the events that have been fulfilled among us." Some did it well, others did it badly—and in the latter category were authors like "Thomas" and "Peter" and others whose eponymous gospels were judged by early Christians to be inadequate or misleading. But what is perhaps most surprising—a fact that

Catholics today ignore with great ease—is the fact that early Christianity was characterized by a certain humility in truth-telling. There are four Gospels, not one, and this fact alone means that Christians had to become comfortable with the fact that different authors told the story of Jesus differently. Far from enshrining a kind of early relativism, however, they determined that authentic discipleship, authentic spirituality, was predicated on both knowledge of the story of Jesus and humility that one's understanding of the story was limited.

I suggest, then, that an authentic Catholic spirituality today moves in two directions: first, it involves coming to greater knowledge and understanding of the true story of God's revelation to the world; and second, as a consequence of the first, it involves the liberation of the human being. That liberation consists in a person becoming conformed to the image of Christ, and thereby expanding his or her heart in courageous love of God and others. These movements are not in tension, but rather in harmony. One grows in knowledge of God when one loves; but similarly one grows in love of God when one knows what God has done.

Reread

CATHOLIC SPIRITUALITY IS CATHOLIC

In chapter 1, we began to consider how the story of twentieth-century U.S. Catholicism was about the development of a kind of Catholic nationalism—a conflation of the progress of the Church and of Catholic Americans. To be a good Catholic was to be a good American: thus the election of a Catholic president represented a high point in our history.

Today, however, it is important that we bring a critical reflection to the narrative of U.S. Catholic nationalism. It is poignant to consider, for example, how the terms *American Catholic* or *Catholic American* are misleading: they could encompass not only those Catholics in the United States (a significant number of whom are of Latino/a descent), but also Catholics in Canada and Central and South America. The narrative of truly "American" Catholicism is a much grander narrative of the encounters between colonial empires and native peoples; of both racist conquerors and saintly missionaries; of churches that crossed the linguistic boundaries of not only France, Spain, England, and the Netherlands, but also of the Aztecs, the Mayans, the Guahibo, and the Guaraní. The recent history of Catholicism in the United States has not been characterized by a strong awareness of these other American Catholic communities, and our shortsightedness represents a serious deficiency in our call to communion with other followers of Jesus.

A recent example of a positive attempt to overcome this conflation of nationalism and Catholicism came from Cardinal Roger Mahony of Los Angeles, who spoke boldly against a bill that would make it a felony to assist any illegal immigrants. Los Angeles, of course, has a large population of Mexican and other Central and South American Catholics, many of whom have entered the United States illegally. The cardinal rightly observed that the Church's role is spiritual and pastoral, and that it could not observe any law that forbade priests, for example, to administer the sacraments to illegal immigrants.[136] It could not, in short, privilege the national interests of the U.S. government over the mandate to undertake the corporal and spiritual works of mercy for illegal immigrants.

U.S. Catholic nationalism isolates us not only from other Americans; it isolates us from the rest of the world. To be a follower of the crucified one is to be part of a narrative in which the poor, the isolated, the disenfranchised, the subjugated, and the outcast assume central roles. Jesus himself was a victim of torture and murder under a brutal imperial government: our most potent religious symbol—even in the midst of kitschy overuse and iconoclastic mockery—is that of the crucifix. To meditate on this symbol ought to draw us into consideration of its implications, one of which is that to seek the will of God is to be ready for death.

The United States is a global superpower. Like the Roman Empire that crucified Jesus, it has the capacity to extend its authority over many lands and peoples, because there is no one who has the power to stop it. And like the Roman Empire, it produces many good fruits: then, there were roads, aqueducts, sanitation, and the rule of law; today, there are the promotion of democracy, trade laws that allow the global movement of resources, funds for the rebuilding of broken societies, and others. Yet we are naïve if we believe that in the global community—then or now—the superpower's influence was/is always good. Jesus surely walked Roman roads, participated in a society governed by Roman law, and bought goods made possible through Roman trade policies. Yet he was also deeply critical of Rome; his distinction between what is rendered to Caesar and what is rendered to God suggests something of this critical eye. Our posture toward our government, any government, must similarly reflect an attempt to read its policies through the interpretive lens of God's will.

To begin with, let us observe that we Americans—or, perhaps better, *estadounidenses*[137]—consume a gross disproportion of the world's resources. We are the ones with two blankets whom Jesus exhorts to share with those who have none. Luke describes the earliest Christian communities as gatherings of people who held everything in common (Acts 2:44; 4:32); their desire to be in communion with each other meant that the imperative toward communion trumped every existing social barrier. It is extremely difficult to imagine a catholic (small *c*) communion in which some have a great deal, while others have nothing. To be a catholic church, the Catholic Church in the United States must model a thirst for global communion that (minimally) represents a challenge to other global bodies. If we Catholics cannot model what it means to be in communion with others around the globe, who else has the global reach to accomplish this?

A catholic spirituality, I am suggesting, must begin by bringing a critical eye to the habits that we develop in a consumer society.[138] It must represent a constant vigilance to weigh choices around money and time against the fundamental call to love God and neighbor with our whole selves. Practically, it will mean different things for different people. While some may follow the examples of saints such as Francis of Assisi to live a radical life of solidarity with the poor, for others it may mean raising children in a safe middle-class neighborhood. At the local level, however, the imperative toward a catholic spirituality will mean primarily cultivating a radical vocation to communion with the world. It will involve constant calls toward the sharing of time and money with those in need, thereby transforming the liturgy into a time of burden-sharing. A catholic spirituality will find its home in the Mass as an act of sacrifice: both a memorial to the sacrifice of Jesus and a rededication of those gathered to sacrifice themselves, like Eucharistic bread, for the upbuilding of the Body of Christ. To be a Catholic is to be a global citizen, one who is brother or sister not only to those of similar socioeconomic circumstances, but also to those many nameless people whose faces stare back at us from the pages and Web sites of relief organizations. A truly catholic spirituality will draw us out of where we feel comfortable and place us next to those whose sufferings Jesus asks us to share.

The beauty of this call is that such a catholic spirituality is what all of us desperately need in our own times of crisis. Far from being a noblesse oblige, it represents a willingness to allow the poor to minister to us, to call us from our slumbers of economic or social comfort, to a reminder that God has called us to something grand and majestic. We *estadounidenses* are prone to isolation and all the pathologies that result from it; yet God needs us to transform a broken world. Whether we minister to seniors in a nursing home, adopt orphaned children from poor areas, work in inner-city soup kitchens, help teachers in the local school, or dedicate our time to contemplative prayer for others, we become the Body of Christ for the world. No one who has such vocations will ultimately fall prey to the ennui that results from loss of meaning in one's life.

The fact that many young people choose to volunteer out of a concern for social justice ought to give us hope. What many young people lack in reflective knowledge of Catholic doctrine they make up for in performative knowledge: they perform the corporal works of mercy, very often side by side with people of good will from other religious traditions. Many pray, using the language they have at their disposal. Many have a deep sensibility about the dignity of the human person, whether in Africa or Central America or Asia or the inner cities in the United States, and are motivated to make their lives make a difference.

The youngest generations of Catholics are more likely than their parents and grandparents to see themselves as part of narratives very different from that of Catholic nationalism. They are more likely to find convergences of belief with Evangelicals and others whose choices to belong within a religious tradition are often countercultural.[139] Many young people most serious about the convergence of spirituality and religious practice are also deeply interested in global issues.[140] Perhaps what we are witnessing is the emergence of a narrative of intentional Catholicism predicated on an apostolic vision of the *euangelion*, the good news of Christ's incarnation and its ramifications for people of all nations. Such a narrative, I would argue, is the logical consequence of the coming-of-age of Catholics in the United States: they no longer worry about making their place in U.S. society, and can now be free to turn their gaze outward to the rest of the world. Instead of "Catholic nationalism," I would call this narrative "Catholic mission," predicated on an apostolic connotation of the latter term. Jesus' mission (Greek *apostolein*, to send out) to the apostles was simple: tell my story. In a highly technologized, globalized, networked planet struggling toward sustainable transnational civilization, Catholic mission represents the attempt to allow one's life to tell the story of Jesus in a nonviolent way.

Catholic mission is rooted in the story of the genesis of the Church at Pentecost, when Jesus' closest friends reached across ethnic boundaries to begin their task of telling Jesus' story. It is no surprise that the first serious controversy in this early period of the Church's life was that of the relationship between Jesus' and the disciples' Jewish faith and the faith of the Gentiles. In following Paul's exhortation to reach out across the ethnic divide, the early Church made a conscious decision not to let national boundaries determine the shape of the Church's kerygma. The story is remarkably relevant for us today, as are the many missionary journeys of Paul: to live the gospel, these stories tell us, is to take on the task of reaching across national boundaries to tell the story of Jesus. Paul himself did so courageously, but also nonviolently; he was not accused of being imperialistic because he did not persuade from a position of power. On the contrary: his effectiveness was precisely a result of his willingness to operate from a position of equality with his interlocutors. Western Christians in the post-Constantinian churches have, in many cases over history, failed to observe this fundamental element of Paul's mission.

Today, however, Catholic mission is possible because Catholics less frequently operate from a position of power. As noted earlier, the dynamics in the churches of Asia are instructive: when one lives in a Christian minority, one's evangelization can hardly be called imperialistic. To share one's faith when one carries no power is not proselytizing: it is simply allowing one's life to testify to the narrative of Jesus' life. In the United States, young people have grown up in a context in which the Church is no longer in a position of power: on the contrary, it is more often perceived as a liminal institution, on the fringes of the cultures in which young adults live. Making the choice to publicly profess Christian faith can often be a choice to marginalize oneself: to assume a position that can be easily ridiculed. Such a position is possible precisely because of the culture of pluralism—a culture that in many ways resembles that of the Hellenistic world in which Paul preached. His public profession of Christian faith was similarly subject to ridicule; and yet it was this public profession that made possible his witness *(martyrion)* to Christ.

Inasmuch as Catholic mission is predicated on a narrative different from that of Catholic nationalism, it is more likely to take a critical eye toward U.S. society. It is more likely to think from a global perspective, asking hard questions about the ways that Catholics in the United States practice communion with Catholics around the globe. For example: How do U.S. practices of consumption of the world's goods—energy, food, and others— affect others around the globe? How do the practices of U.S. corporations affect our relationships with developing countries, especially those that provide unskilled labor? How do the priorities of U.S. Catholic bishops reflect on the issues that affect poor Catholics in other parts of the world? How do American beliefs around life issues (abortion, the death penalty, stem cell research, assisted suicide, warfare, poverty) compare with the beliefs of other Catholics around the world? How do American attitudes toward other contentious moral issues (homosexuality, the future of the priesthood, birth control, the roles of politicians) compare to those of the Vatican, or of Catholics in Africa, Asia, and Latin America?

Cultivating a catholic spirituality presents U.S. Catholics with challenges not unlike those of the earliest apostles: crossing the boundaries of a faith narrative. For Jesus' earliest followers, that narrative was about the people of Israel, whose hope for a messiah, they believed, had reached its climax in the person of Jesus. For them, the challenges were great: the messiah was to restore the kingdom of David, not die as a criminal. He was to overthrow Rome. He was to fulfill the prophecies of the coming of the kingdom of God. Jesus, though, did not provide the ending to the story that they believed they were living through—he challenged them to see themselves in an altogether different story, one that read the prophets and the Law through a different interpretive lens. That lens, they came to understand only very slowly, was one that involved restructuring their hopes for what "the kingdom of God" meant. Like the disciples on the road to Emmaus, they had to listen carefully to the way that Jesus told the story before they could understand what his sacrifice meant.

U.S. Catholics are on the road to a new Emmaus; they are in the process of learning a new story of faith that will help them to understand the gospel anew. And like the earlier disciples, they will come to understand the meaning of sacrifice in a more profound way. For us, that sacrifice will entail nothing short of an ethic opposite of one predominant American ethos: instead of espousing the "upward mobility" so written into American mythology, we Catholics will be challenged to espouse a "downward mobility" of solidarity with the world's poor.[141] Our Catholic spirituality will be the food that nourishes our passion to bring about a world that more closely reflects the divine order.

CATHOLIC SPIRITUALITY IS A CALL TO SOLIDARITY

As a correlate of the observation that Catholic spirituality is catholic is the implication that it is a call to solidarity. Pope John Paul II used the term *solidarity* frequently in his writings:[142] it represents a summons toward a healthy globalization and a critique of the destructive tendencies of some economic and social practices. Consider the following excerpt from *Sollicitudo Rei Socialis* (On Social Concerns, 1987):

in a world divided and beset by every type of conflict, the conviction is growing of a radical interdependence and consequently of the need for a solidarity which will take up interdependence and transfer it to the moral plane. Today perhaps more than in the past, people are realizing that they are linked together by a common destiny, which is to be constructed together, if catastrophe for all is to be avoided. (par. 26)

Written during the closing years of the Cold War, the encyclical points to what was then an emerging global order. Such an order, the pope perceived, had profoundly moral dimensions; and so like his predecessors who authored social encyclicals, John Paul II called upon people of good will to highlight human concerns, particularly those of the poor. Later, in his apostolic letter *Novo Millennio Ineunte* (At the Beginning of the New Millennium, 2001) he returned to this same theme. Referring to the Church's jubilee year, he wrote:

That Jubilee gathering also gave me the opportunity to voice a strong call to correct the economic and social imbalances present in the world of work and to make decisive efforts to ensure that the processes of economic globalization give due attention to solidarity and the respect owed to every human person.

What is fascinating about the pope's call for an authentic solidarity is that while rooted in the gospel, it attends to the social and political movements in the world. It is an attempt to understand the structures that govern human interactions: those constructs such as language, trade rules, political theories, government powers, and so on that create divisions among people; it is also a plea that the fundamental respect for the sanctity of the human condition supersede these divisions.

What makes Catholic spirituality a call to solidarity is its rootedness in the narrative of salvation history. Unlike certain theologies that have arisen over the Church's history that suggest that God's salvation is for those who meet certain criteria, the Catholic theological tradition has emphasized a universal call to holiness.[143] This universal call to holiness is predicated on core beliefs: the dignity of the human person created in the image and likeness of God; the human dependence on God's grace for salvation from sin; the moral imperative to love God and neighbor; the responsibility to reach out in love toward the poor and disenfranchised. As a Eucharistic people, Catholics are committed to the poor.[144] The very center of Catholic worship is an act in which rich and poor gather at a table to manifest what they claim to be: the living Body of Christ.

It is precisely this "corporal" or "corporate" metaphor that Paul uses to illustrate what it means to be a people of solidarity. In suggesting that the Christian community is a body (1 Cor 12), he suggests that the diverse roles that people play in the world ought to work together in a harmonious relationship. It is ironic that today we speak of transnational corporations in reference to global conglomerates that make profits on such things as oil, agricultural products, business machines, and retail items. For many, these transnational corporations are targets of criticism because of their tendencies to dehumanize workers for the sake of profit. The Church could be described as the first transnational corporation, following Paul's metaphor: the difference, of course, is that instead of profit what it should be seeking is the divine order, the kingdom of God.

CATHOLIC SPIRITUALITY IS A CALL TO WORSHIP

The disconnect that many young adults perceive between spirituality and organized worship is troubling, because it truncates the full expression of Catholic faith. To become part of the story of Jesus' mission in the world is to participate in the life of the Church—and at the heart of this life is the call to worship. We revisit a recurring theme in this book: if young people no longer feel the strong obligation to attend Mass, what compelling vision of Catholic worship can we offer? Why, in short, ought they to be part of it?

From a theological standpoint, the question is relatively easy to answer. The language of the Vatican II Dogmatic Constitution on the Church *(Lumen Gentium)* expresses it straightforwardly:

159

> Incorporated in the Church through baptism, the faithful are destined by the baptismal character for the worship of the Christian religion; reborn as sons of God they must confess before men the faith which they have received from God through the Church. (par. 11)

Catholics are called to worship because in baptism they are joined to the Body of Christ, the Church, in whose assembly they profess their common faith. From a more practical standpoint, it is equally easy to recognize that anyone who belongs to a group ought to do what the group does; and as a religious group, Catholics ought to pray together.

Yet the question of why young people ought to worship in the Church today is not so simple. We must observe, for example, that while Catholic theology holds that baptism represents a sacramental incorporation into the Body of Christ, there is nevertheless a very large number of baptized people who have no intention of ever practicing their faith in a meaningful way. We cannot, therefore, assign to baptism a kind of magical power, as though God mysteriously moves the heart of every baptized person to do what God wills. At the root of all the Church's sacramental theology is a recognition of the freedom of the person, a freedom that is not overridden in the person's participation in the sacramental life of the Church. Those who worship, in short, are not compelled by God to do so—they must choose freely, which means that their choice to worship must be guided by judgments that they make as human beings.

Here, then, lies our difficulty and our opportunity: if people make decisions whether to worship, then it is possible to provide them with compelling evidence in order that they make judicious choices. What will persuade young people that Catholic worship is a valuable investment of their time and energy? In what follows, we explore a number of points. What is important to underscore, however, is that there is no greater witness to the importance of worship than worshipping people. The kerygma of one's own life is invaluable. Saint Monica, the mother of Saint Augustine, is perhaps the most compelling example. In his *Confessions*, Augustine described her tireless hope that her son might come to the Church;

and after many years of prayer her hopes were rewarded, when a mature Augustine chose to be baptized. There are many Catholics today who are concerned that their children no longer attend Mass—these many latter-day Monicas may have hope in a Church that is growing, and has the richness from which to draw in order to gather its younger, more skeptical, members.

1. We need Sabbath. The rich biblical term *Sabbath* involves recognition of our limits as human beings. Usually meaning "rest," the term is different from the kind of rest that one engages in during a weekend off work. Weekends, as we know them in the West, are the product of post–industrial revolution labor movements that recognized that workers needed time off for health and safety reasons. The forty-hour work week, weekends, vacation time, and so on are social constructs designed to enhance the lifestyles of many workers. These constructs do not presently exist, for example, in certain Asian factories.

Sabbath too is a social construct, though a very ancient one, predicated not on the physical limits that people experience in their labor, but rather on spiritual limits that people experience by simply being alive. We need Sabbath because we need the chance to take stock of our lives on a regular basis—weekly—to ensure that the lives we are leading reflect the purpose for which God created us. In the first creation story in Genesis, God's resting on the seventh day was God's chance to see all of creation, and appreciate its goodness. For us, Sabbath is the necessary time to appreciate who God has made us to be, and to discern whether our life choices are enabling us to grow toward our fulfillment. The practice of Sabbath is an exercise of freedom—the kind of freedom one most fully understands only when one takes a step back from the normal vicissitudes of daily life. It is a chance to step off the treadmill and ask why one is usually on it in the first place.

The conversion story of Inigo Lopez is a compelling illustration of why Sabbath is necessary. This sixteenth-century knight was badly injured and forced to convalesce in a place where his only reading material was a story about the life of Christ and a book about the saints. His period of convalescence—of forced Sabbath—gave him time to imagine himself in the stories he was reading.

Eventually he realized that the feelings he experienced during these imaginations gave him greater joy than he had experienced as a knight, and so he decided to devote his life to God. It was precisely because he was forced to rest, in other words, that he had the fertile time to take stock of his life. It was a remarkable life—we know him today as Saint Ignatius of Loyola. His later work *The Spiritual Exercises* is a guide on how to use periods of rest from labor for the purpose of spiritual growth, by imagining oneself as part of the Gospel stories. (Perhaps it would not be unattractive to suggest to young people that we invite them to come to Church in order to daydream.)

2. We need to connect with other people around issues beyond everyday life. Many people would argue that it is possible to practice Sabbath with friends, out in nature, reading a good book, and so on. I do not disagree. Yet I would add that there is something especially necessary about public worship because of our tendencies toward myopia. Encountering people of different age groups, different ethnicities, different economic backgrounds, and different educational levels is important for us to gain perspective on our lives. There are few communities that gather regularly that can include such diversity; this fact alone makes churches interesting sociological studies.

Yet there is more. Catholic worship is more than a diverse group gathering together in a single room. It is an act of communion. There is something profound about a diverse group of people all coming together for the sake of worshipping God, even when that worship involves the usual distractions inherent in any event. We may be looking around at other people; we may be trying to get children to behave; we may be thinking about work or football; we may be stewing about so-and-so on the other side of the room; we may completely miss the readings and recite the prayers mindlessly. Yet when we do these things in a church community gathered to worship God, we are nonetheless participating in the sacramental life of the Church. And this observation rests upon a fundamental Catholic belief: that it is precisely in the looking around, the negotiations with children, the distracted thinking, the stewing, the mindlessness that God is nonetheless present to us.

3. We need to be held responsible for our prayer lives. The success of support groups or organizations like Jenny Craig and L.A. Weightloss Centers is in the fact that people need the support of others to face significant challenges in their lives. They need to be held accountable for what they are trying to do, because it helps them through the difficult times.

On a larger scale, participation in the worship of the Church holds us responsible for our prayer lives. It is certainly true that a person can encounter God alone in prayer, but this observation misses the point. What we need in public worship is the constant reminder and support of others in the same room who have faced the same questions that we face.

The Church's worship, its sacramental life, is oriented around three key movements: initiation, healing, and vocation. Our initiation into the life of worship proceeds through the sacraments of baptism, confirmation, and Eucharist. The first two are one-time-only rites of passage, while the third is the regular sacrament of our communion in the Church. The healing sacraments of reconciliation and anointing of the sick remind us of our frailty and invite us into greater understanding of God's presence to us in our suffering. The sacraments of vocation, marriage, and holy orders invite us to discern what God calls us to do in the community of the faithful. All of these sacraments have a necessarily public character, which have the cumulative effect of reminding us that we participate in a community throughout our lives. In an era that is characterized by fragmentation, isolation, and the breakdown of community structures, many individuals develop feelings of isolation from the rest of the world. The public character of Catholic worship represents for many an invitation by God to be forever at home in the community of the faithful around the world.

4. We need a communal experience of sacred scripture. It is easy to forget in this age of communication that the scriptures were originally used as texts read aloud in the assembly. We who live in mostly literate cultures can have a hard time imagining what it's like to rely on others to spread news. We forget that before widespread literacy, catechesis was in stories read aloud, pictures etched into stained glass or painted onto walls and canvases, and words drilled into children's memories by parents and

elders. There is a strong difference between reading a text privately and hearing it proclaimed publicly. Biblical texts were not written for private reading; even those ancient monks who learned to read privately did so mindful of the primary encounter with the scripture in the assembly.

In China today, newspapers are posted on public bulletin boards. It is not uncommon to see crowds gathering around them, engaged in heated discussion. There is something about learning news in the midst of a crowd that enables discussion. Our closest example of this phenomenon today is the water-cooler discussion, which people who work together will engage in the day after some newsworthy event. People need to have ways to digest what they are thinking, and this observation holds true for scripture as well. Thinking through the meaning of scripture with others brings it alive and makes it take root in a person's life—it helps the person to avoid the temptation to distraction by the hundreds of other things going on.

5. We need rituals. A visit to any sporting event illustrates how much people like participating in rituals, because of the ways that they enable us to encounter meaning in ways that ordinary day-to-day living does not. Church rituals have evolved over millennia, meaning that the symbols that they employ are invitations to deeper understanding of how they manifest the community's faith in the ministry of Christ.[145]

There is no easy way to persuade someone of the importance of rituals, particularly if he or she is unaccustomed to being part of the community that celebrates them. This observation is critical today, since for many young people it is precisely their previous experiences of the meaninglessness of Church rituals that keeps them away from churches. We must remind ourselves that the significance of a ritual is usually not self-evident—a person must be taught about it in order for it to break open to him or her a world of new meaning. A person from Africa will not understand the rituals at a baseball game unless someone instructs her; a young person with little experience of the Church will feel lost in the Mass unless there are some guides to help him understand.

6. We need encounters with symbolism. In our busy lives, it is easy to avoid dealing with deep existential questions about life and

death, love and suffering, and so on. The power of symbols is that they capture in an image or object a world of meaning: they open for our imaginations a journey toward an appreciation of the profound mysteries of our lives. The Church is rich in symbolism, from images like the cross or the Alpha-Omega decorations in churches, to the colors of priests' vestments at Mass, to words and phrases in Latin, Greek, and Hebrew like *agnus dei, kyrie eleison,* and *amen.*

Yet symbols both display and obscure; for unless a person knows what a symbol means, it remains lifeless. We need symbols, but first we need catechesis and mystagogy. A vibrant community of faith will be one that knows how to use symbols to bring people out of the ordinary flow of their daily existence, and it will also be a community that knows how to do this in ways that will be evident to newcomers. Primarily, such a community will constantly point to its symbols and use them as ways to instruct. One example that I have encountered was a pastor at a small church in Connecticut who, every Easter, would hand out to all children a small plant. His charge to the children was simple: "this represents new life, just like we are celebrating the new life of Jesus Christ this Easter day. Take care of it as a reminder that we must take care of new life." My preschool-aged daughters were able to understand this symbolism, and it helped them to come to some understanding of what Easter meant.

7. We need to be part of a living tradition. There is something compelling about being part of something larger: a cause, an unfinished story. It motivates athletes who are part of storied teams; it motivates artists who see themselves as inheritors of a legacy; it motivates scholars who believe they are contributing to the improvement of society; it motivates researchers in search of cures. To be part of a living Catholic tradition is to see one's life story as part of the longer story of God's participation in human affairs. In this light, the vagaries of our individual lives are brought into relief: suffering is a real element, but it is not the decisive one.

Participation in the worship of the Church is regular participation in the long story of God's presence to human beings. If one sees life from such a perspective, then the normal frustrations appear to be of less account. An experience of boredom at Mass can be understood as but one movement in a larger story that moves one closer to God, even when we don't realize it.

On a global level, participation in the story of salvation history is cause for hope. The deepest theological truth of Christian faith is that salvation has come to human beings through the death and resurrection of Christ, and that the often tragic vicissitudes of history are but the denouement of a joyful drama. The suffering of the world is real, and we must do everything we can as a people of faith about it; but we know that we are headed for an end in which God will be all in all. We need the constant liturgical reminder of this hope in order not to succumb to the despair that often follows upon the harsh realities of life.

8. The Church needs us. I have focused on developing ideas why cultivating an authentic Catholic spirituality means participation in the public worship of the Church. Here, I take the opposite approach: the authentic life of the Church depends upon cultivating the spiritual lives of its members. Today, the Church needs young people because it is the sacramental presence of Christ in the world, and only the young have the capacity to be Christ's presence among those with whom they live, work, and play. Taking seriously Jesus' promise to be with the Church always (Matt 28:19–20) means recognizing the irreplaceable role of the Christian faithful in the world.

CATHOLIC SPIRITUALITY IS REALISTIC

The objective of the practice of Catholic spirituality is attentiveness to the reality of the world. As I suggested earlier in this chapter, this practice ought to move first in the direction of knowledge of God, and second in knowledge of ourselves. To be more precise, however, it is proper to say that authentic knowledge of God is all-encompassing, for it will enable us to understand ourselves in light of an understanding of the end for which God has created us. The first commandment—to love the Lord with all our heart, all our soul, and all our strength—is a summary of all the commandments. Loving God will necessarily involve loving those around us, with whom God has called us into relationship. And as a result, Catholic realism will entail acute sensitivity to other people around the world, as well as to the world itself that people live in.

It is precisely the realism of Catholic spirituality that gives it a public dimension. Unlike the mystery religions of the Hellenistic world of the first centuries of the common era, Christianity developed as a movement that embraced the world.[146] For while some followers of Jesus advocated a kind of removal from the world, mainstream Christians instead advocated for Christian engagement in the world. Today, this engagement in the world means nothing less than coming to a greater consciousness of suffering than can be found elsewhere. To be a person of prayer ought to enable one to look honestly at the most difficult issues we face in our world today and see them in a broader, richer context. Far from being an attempt to remove oneself from the world, the practice of spirituality ought to help one become more able to enter into a world of suffering and be a sacrament of Christ's healing presence.

For young people today, the realism of Catholic spirituality can be refreshing. When so much of their world is ruled by market forces, characterized by the promotion of false images and the cultivation of false desires, an immersion in the gritty reality of a world of sin and grace can be a welcome oasis. In their song "Iris," the band Goo Goo Dolls wrote insightfully of the difficulty to come to any understanding of what's real today:

> When everything feels like the movies
> Yeah you bleed just to know you're alive.

In a market-driven world, the encounter with suffering represents an opportunity for spiritual growth because at least it is real. Young people live, to a great extent, in an imaginary world, and too frequently it is a traumatic event such as the death of a loved one that causes them to rethink what their lives ought to be about. Invariably I have found among my students that those who take spirituality most seriously can point to some experience of suffering.

VERY TRUE

What is refreshing about Catholic spirituality is the fact that it is not about becoming better, or about developing hidden potential, or about leading a full life—but rather about the paschal mystery. A spirituality that is predicated on the events of Jesus' death and resurrection challenges one to consider suffering and death in a way radically different from what we perceive in daily living. For while so much in U.S. culture seeks to hide these realities from our experience as human beings, drowning them in the endless pursuit of pleasures and various forms of power, the heart of Catholic spirituality is the meditation on the meaning of Christ's life as a foundation for living one's own. Catholic spirituality draws us into consideration of the ways that so much of our energies is devoted to the banal, the meaningless, the fruitless—what the author of Ecclesiastes called "vanity."

It is unsurprising that so many of the early Christians were themselves people on the margins of society, just as it is unsurprising that so many of the most authentic disciples of Jesus today live on the margins. They have no illusions about the world, whereas many of us who live in comparative comfort are likely to be persuaded of the importance of those things that bring us comfort. Catholics of a certain period in U.S. history were on the margins, and saw mainstream (Protestant) Americans as holding the reins of power in the culture. Catholics' yearnings for a better life for themselves and their children made sense under these circumstances; these yearnings could be seen as a movement toward a more just and equitable order. Today, however, when so many Catholic young people already live within the U.S. mainstream, there is great need for a spirituality that challenges them to see themselves and the world in which they live in a much broader context. The realism of Catholic spirituality will encourage them to consider the world from the perspective of the Gospel story.

- Jesus' life was about service to others, not self.
- Jesus was called to suffer and die in testimony to God's love for the world.
- Jesus' promise to the disciples was that the Holy Spirit is always with us, even amid the world's suffering.

168

- Suffering itself does not represent the final reality, but can often be a place of encounter with God's grace.
- To be a person of faith in the God that Jesus proclaimed is to be ready to be an agent of transformation and healing in the world.
- The objective of life is not to win the most toys, but to offer oneself generously in service to others while trusting God's project, the divine order of things.
- We who live in the most prosperous nation on earth have a special responsibility to cultivate structures that recognize the dignity of all human beings: born and unborn, sick and aged, disabled and afflicted, poor and powerless, victimized and disenfranchised.
- Our joy in life will be to discover our talents and discern ways to use them according to God's will.
- We can use our talents within the structures that exist in the contemporary world to work for justice; other times, we can work to change structures that are unjust.
- The Eucharist sustains us in the practice of our faith and helps us to grow in ways we could never have anticipated.
- We learn from those who precede us in faith, and can draw from the Church's living tradition as we consider new challenges.

There is a dual challenge to Catholics who work with and among young people in the twenty-first century. First, while the contours of a Catholic spirituality are in many ways the same today as always, there is nevertheless an imperative to be attentive to the particular culture in which young people live. Second, Catholics must have the courage to shape fresh models of Catholic life that are at once continuous with tradition and responsive to the needs of today—needs that include, for example, greater lay leadership in parishes in light of fewer priests; financial support of Catholic ministries undertaken by lay professionals rather than (often unpaid) religious women and men; emotional support of those who are discerning difficult types of work and ministry that serve the poor and marginalized; and so on. In short, we have the challenge and opportunity to form young people, but we also need to shape a Church that more fully cultivates their spiritual lives.

Chapter Six

Moral Authority: Persuasive Life in the World

Perhaps the greatest impact of the sexual abuse scandal in the U.S. Catholic Church will be its loss of public moral authority among young people.[147] My sense is that many older adults—those who have strong memories of bishops taking thoughtful, public stands on issues such as racism, abortion, economic justice, or peacebuilding[148]—will be able to enter into critical dialogue with the their positions on other issues. Young people, however, who live in a world in which there are many voices claiming authority, will more easily dismiss bishops' statements if they should even encounter them in the first place.

With the breakdown of the Catholic subculture, which fostered a certain reverence for the office of the bishop and his teaching authority, young people will be influenced more and more by the everyday attitudes of the adults in their lives. Because one of the fallouts of the scandal is distrust of bishops, many adults will not easily regard their teaching as authoritative. Yet there remains a significant responsibility for Catholics today to come to a well-formed, nuanced understanding of our tradition and its moral wisdom, in order that we may contribute to intelligent public discourse both in the Church and in the wider society.

It would be a mistake to assert that Catholic moral teaching is coterminous with the teachings of any single bishop: the tradition is significantly more expansive than any single figure can proclaim for simple, practical reasons. The good news, therefore, is that even while many Catholics distrust their bishops, there nevertheless remains a strong tradition of moral reflection that many other Catholics—professors, social workers, priests, religious men and women, doctors, mothers and fathers—are proclaiming. The Church's moral authority will influence many even during this period of the Church's history when trust in bishops is low.

There are two ways in which Catholics can rebuild trust in the moral wisdom of the Church. The first is a rather traditional way: adults can demonstrate through their lives that they are trustworthy to young people, and young people will trust what they say. The second way is more modern and even postmodern, and is predicated in part on the simple fact that many young people are well educated and have developed critical thinking skills. For this group, trust may be a starting point, but will not, in the end, be persuasive enough in the face of strong evidence contrary to the word of a trusted figure. This second way of rebuilding the Church's moral authority, then, will be difficult, for it involves bringing Catholic teaching into dialogue with the challenges in postmodern society, in order that discerning minds will be able to judge the truth of that teaching. This second way is predicated on formation and education of young people, and it is dependent on the dedicated effort of adult Catholics—particularly those in various levels of education.

Handing of the faith to the next generation depends in large part on Catholics' willingness to move beyond the current fractured state of moral discourse within the Church. The shrill tone that exists in debates over many contentious issues speaks very loudly to many on the fringes of the Church: it demonstrates to them that the power struggles within the Church are little different from those in the political arena, suggesting that Catholic faith does little to tame the desire for power. Catholic moral discourse must first be demonstrable. Our Church must show itself capable of being more wise and more loving in the way that it even raises moral questions than one sees in the wider public arena. Catholic laypeople, in particular, must show ourselves able to grapple intelligently with the moral wisdom of the tradition in ways that are neither fideistic nor dismissive. We must be willing to engage the teachings of bishops, even as we attend to the concrete realities of life in the United States and the rest of the world.

The relationships between the official teachers in the Church—the bishops—and laypeople are different from those of the past, and these differences suggest new challenges for discerning and proclaiming moral wisdom. First, then, let us recall the observation in chapter 2 that the dynamic between bishops and a significant number of laypeople in the United States is similar to the dynamic of communication between parents and adolescents. Many laypeople have grown up as a result of both Vatican II and the cultural changes of the late to middle twentieth century. The publication of *Humanae Vitae* (On Human Life, which dealt with artificial birth control) in 1968, in particular, highlighted the onset of this new dynamic. Many in the Church openly dissented from their bishops' teachings on this issue, even while others publicly affirmed the teaching and criticized those who did not. Like adolescents responding to parents, Catholics responded to bishops sometimes with disdain, sometimes with obedience. The emergence of this new dynamic in the Church is predicated in large part on two simple facts: many laypeople are now, in many cases, just as well educated if not better educated than priests and even bishops; and in the rest of their lives they are accustomed to exercising control and authority.

This chapter addresses the situation of those Catholics who have found themselves questioning the authority of the Church in light of cultural changes over the last few decades. It is important for these Catholics to remember, however, that they represent a relatively small yet influential minority in the Catholic Church as a whole. While clear studies on a global scale are not available, it is reasonable to assume that many Catholics in the developing world hold very different views of the Church, views that many U.S. Catholics would consider conservative. Moreover, even in the United States, progressive Catholics arise from a mostly white, middle-class background, and thus do not likely reflect the very significant numbers of first- and second-generation immigrant Catholics. The post–*Humanae Vitae* animus toward the Church is, in some ways, a middle-class phenomenon.

I do not wish to oversimplify the difficult debates that emerged from the publication of *Humanae Vitae*, nor do I wish to suggest that either the dissenters or the (for lack of a better term) assenters are right or wrong.[149] Rather, I wish to focus attention on the fact that many influential Catholics since 1968 have found themselves critiquing the positions of either local bishops or the Vatican. These critiques have crossed ideological boundaries, moreover—both conservatives and liberals have demonstrated strong resistance to certain teachings of the hierarchy. In addition to the teaching on birth control, targets of critique have been female acolytes; homosexuality; translations of liturgical texts; liberation theology; just war; the death penalty; the role of Catholic politicians; and the list goes on. What we have witnessed in the last forty years of U.S. Catholicism is a growing critical consciousness of the moral implications of Catholic faith.

The key point to observe, then, is that neither dissent nor assent in itself represents the flowering of mature faith. If we examine the analogy to adolescence, we can see that teenagers who challenge their parents are negotiating the difficult process of right judgment. Of course their different personalities come into play. Some will naturally agree with their parents on everything out of simple immaturity. Others will do so out of a heightened sense of responsibility for younger siblings. Some will disagree with their parents about everything because of past wrongs, while others will disagree out of insecurity. The adolescent's patterns of communication with parents are complex and multivalent, involving psychology, family dynamics, education, and a host of other factors. What distinguishes the right moral development of the adolescent is not his or her propensity to agree or disagree with parents. It is rather his or her willingness to engage in a constantly self-correcting process of judgment and decision making, rooted in a desire to seek, know, and practice the truth.

I am suggesting that many Catholics in the United States (and elsewhere, of course) are engaged in such a process. There is no recent precedent from which laypeople can draw in the history of the Church; faith formation for laypeople does not share the same long history as monastic or priestly formation. In short, the relationship patterns between bishops and their flocks as a whole share certain similarities with the relationship patterns between parents and adolescents. The primary analog is the negotiation of relationship to the person in authority: for the adolescent, it is the parent; for laypeople, it is the bishop and the hierarchy he represents. The title of the encyclical of Pope John XXIII, *Mater et Magistra* (Mother and Teacher, 1961), is especially apt: it suggests the model of the magisterium that many Catholics today are seeking to challenge.

It would be a serious mistake to judge that all those who challenge the hierarchy do so out of a lack of faith or out of hatred for the Church. Indeed, the opposite may be true: challenging the statements of bishops—even at the level of conciliar or papal teaching—may instead represent the very process by which a community comes to deeper appreciation of the implications of faith. For young people especially, suspicion of the Church's motives is widespread; but the very fact that many continue to question the Church's teachings is hopeful. In my teaching, I have seen students write passionately against certain moral teachings of the Church such as birth control and homosexuality. What is interesting to me, though, is the fact that of all the interlocutors they might choose in their Internet-savvy worlds, they choose the Church. Why? Because they believe that the Church is supposed to teach them how to love, and what the Church teaches they don't understand. The Church's teaching, in short, provokes them to a kind of cognitive disequilibrium.

It is precisely this provocation that can represent the seed of conversion. But we must also recognize that this provocation can also represent the seed of division. Negotiations between parents and adolescents can involve creative tension, but they can also involve rupture. There are responsibilities on the sides of both parents and adolescents, both bishops and laypeople, to promote a healthy relationship. What we are seeing as the primary challenge of the Church in the twenty-first century is the development of both new narratives and new models of relationship between bishops, priests, deacons, religious men and women, and other laypeople—in short, it is a challenge for Catholics to understand their places in this Church. Like adolescents trying to understand their identities and their places in the world, many Catholics are trying to understand what it means to be a person of faith, part of a living tradition that stretches back millennia. What does Christian faith mean for us, as we consider how we use money, sex, and power? What role ought bishops and other religious leaders take in a pluralistic world where many claim religious authority?

Our aim is to explore the dimensions of Catholic moral teaching in the contemporary cultural landscape. We take a look the ways that Catholics come to make moral judgments and the ways that such judgments work in the world we inhabit. Our focus, therefore, is not on the content of moral judgment, but rather the process and effect of such judgment on a world in which Catholics are called to live the gospel. We seek to address how young people perceive the Church's ability to manifest moral truth. I argue that the ways to do this are first to perform the truth and speak from the authority rooted in love; and second to create the conditions that enable the maturing of conscience.

PERFORMATIVE MORAL AUTHORITY

The complexity of the postmodern world in which we live makes moral authority more difficult to manifest than in the past.[150] Although it is easy to romanticize the past, let us observe at least that the Catholic Church has enjoyed the privilege of moral authority unlike any other institution in U.S. society. Catholics themselves in the early to middle twentieth century were a largely loyal flock; and moreover Catholic bishops' influences on political life were formidable. Today, however, the picture is different. The claim to moral authority has been weakened not only by the sex abuse scandal; it has also been affected by many changes in both the Church and U.S. culture. We consider three factors: the influence of the Internet and its impact on the way Catholics view authority; the education of the laity; and the developments in Catholic moral theology.

The Rise of the Internet and Open Source Theology

The paradigmatic example of authority in the modern world— the period in Western history extending from roughly the seventeenth to the early twentieth centuries—was the encyclopedia. The first modern encyclopedia, edited by Denis Diderot in France beginning in 1751, was an attempt to gather all knowledge into a single place. The assumption underlying all encyclopedias has been that it is possible to seek an objective truth in much the same way that scientists gather objective truths about the nature of the universe. The truth is out there, and right observation and thinking will lead rational people to it.

It is worth noting that Diderot himself, and many thinkers of the Enlightenment period that produced this way of thinking about human knowledge, sought to critique the dogmas of the Catholic Church. For them, knowledge was unlike faith. Knowledge could be found through right observation and right thinking, and did not therefore involve the acts of irrational faith that they perceived in Church doctrine. Knowledge, unlike faith, could be proved again and again by any right-thinking person.

In contrast to the encyclopedia, the paradigmatic example of authority in the postmodern world is the Internet. This postmodern world can be seen as a reaction to the modern view of knowledge: it regards knowledge as far more complex than simply being out there and available to any right-thinking person. Unlike the encyclopedia, which is a centralized source for all knowledge, the Internet is a multipolar network of authorities, an *open source* to use the term preferred by many users.[151] There is no single location for knowledge—there are millions. On the Internet, there is an implicit epistemology: knowledge is perspectival, dependent upon the perceiver. For many people (especially young people), news does not come from large media conglomerates; it comes from the individual blogs (Web logs) of writers in various parts of the globe.[152] Authority itself becomes decentralized—one does not go to the encyclopedia, or the government, or the Church for knowledge (let alone wisdom); one goes to a hundred different Web sites for a hundred different perspectives that help to shape one's own unique perspective.[153]

What has emerged in the United States and other economically developed cultures is a kind of open source theological method among young people. What I mean by this is that many young people encounter the gospel from many sources, and have developed a kind of consumer attitude toward matters of faith and morals: I can decide on what's right for me in a manner similar to choosing clothing or food. Conscience, not the magisterium or any source external to oneself, is the primary filter for religious truth. Many call such people "cafeteria Catholics," suggesting that their engagement with the Church is shallow because it is based only on a selfish appropriation of religious truths, rather than a deep-seated conversion to the truth. I am suggesting, however, that we look deeper to the social influences of cafeteria Catholicism.

In the Internet age, any attempt to gather knowledge into one place appears arrogant. For the Internet-savvy consumer, claims to any type of authority—especially religious authority—is like salesmanship, an attempt to entice people to embrace a specific perspective in contrast to any number of others. It is not surprising that many faithful Catholics regard this implicit epistemology with great suspicion. How, they ask, can Christians proclaim the one truth of the gospel if such a proclamation is seen as merely one option among many?

What they forget is that the growth of the Church in its first centuries happened amid a similar epistemological milieu. Christianity did not always enjoy the kind of intellectual hegemony it claimed in medieval Europe; it spread in a pluralistic Middle Eastern world by virtue of the power of its message and (perhaps more) the charisma of its proponents.

The challenge to Catholics in the postmodern world is similar to the challenge of the earliest followers of Christ: to live the gospel in a persuasive manner, illustrating its truth in a performative way. Neither bishops nor theologians can speak their way into authority in the postmodern world, for in this multipolar context the best kind of authority that can emerge from the noise is that which changes lives. What I am speaking of is sainthood: the kind of living that manifests to others one's radical commitment to faith in Christ. The rise of the Internet is a symptom of a changing world, and the change it symbolizes is the move from trust in centralized authority to a kind of critical developmental consciousness—a trust that one's own understanding will develop in right fashion by the corrective developmental process of encountering different worldviews. The critical "consumer" of knowledge will use his or her judgment of other worldviews to develop a unique way of thinking, in a manner

parallel to the way that consumers of products in the grocery store balance objective knowledge of products with the subjective knowledge of personal needs. Sainthood is "persuasive life in the world" because it is the critical decision to subordinate one's subjective judgments to a larger desire to find God's will in all things—in other words, to be a virtuoso at love, which (in the end) is the most persuasive way of living.

Open source theology need not be as much a subject of fear for many older Catholics as might immediately be evident. For while there are rightly strong reservations among those who hold to the traditional model of magisterial authority and apostolic succession—those who do not wish to cede the authority of interpreting revelation to individuals whose religious and intellectual formation may be shoddy—there are nonetheless signs of hope. For what has begun to emerge on a broad scale in the open source age is a certain sophistication in critical consciousness. Consider the example of pyramid schemes as illustrative of this sophistication. The earliest schemes began long before the Internet, as a way of making money with no product to sell.[154] Today, anyone who has become accustomed to using the Internet can spot such schemes immediately. A quick Google search of "pyramid scheme" today yields 4.4 million sites that address this theme—the word about these schemes has gotten around in ways that no single centralized authority could possibly hope to mimic. What happens in the open source age is the rapid clarification and refinement of practical knowledge: people helping people to learn and understand what is necessary, and doing it at the speed of the Internet. Those who have become accustomed to this epistemology are, for the most part, able to develop good judgment about what is good knowledge and what is not.

In the open source age, when people are developing more and more sophisticated approaches to truth-claims, those claims that do not have deep roots in the reality of human experience will be identified and eventually dismissed. Catholic theology, because of its critical realism about the human condition, can emerge in the open source age as refreshingly honest. The sheer number of Catholic Web sites—and, moreover, the quality of these sites, in large part—says volumes about the Church even before a person reads a word.

If what people are seeking in truth-claims is "consumer value," then what many perceive is that the brand "Catholic" is a good product. And very, very often it is produced and marketed by laypeople. Open source theology is emerging as a new kind of evangelization—a way that people can honestly share their own experiences, challenges, hopes, and failings of faith with others. What might be the result if, instead of seeing the bishop as the one whose kerygma brings others to faith (as in the apostolic age), the bishop is seen as the one who orchestrates the millions of kerygmas in ways that produce harmony? What if the principle of subsidiarity[155] were applied to evangelization itself, such that for every person seeking faith there were ways to connect her or him to someone who has lived similar experiences? What if the role of the bishop were seen less as primary moral instructor and more as superintendent or overseer *(episkopos)* over many primary moral instructors?

Let us be clear: there are likely to be some poor teachers, some examples of the blind leading the blind. But in the open source age, there is room for such missteps, because the process of moral growth of the community is self-correcting, particularly in light of the fundamental theological understanding of the presence of the Holy Spirit in the Body of Christ. The sense of the faithful *(sensus fidelium)* will develop even amid some poor teaching. The bishop's performative moral authority will be evident in his willingness to trust the guidance of the Holy Spirit, his willingness to honor the formative experiences of ordinary Catholics, and (finally) his ability to bring these experiences into conversation with the great living tradition of scripture and magisterial teaching. Like a wise teacher, he will allow his students to make mistakes and learn from them, in order that they might grow into maturity. The bishop's charism, then, might be best described as the charism of catholicity: the apostolic mandate to bring the million voices in the diocese into the harmony that befits the Body of Christ around the world.

The Education of the Laity

The days when clerics (and bishops in particular) were the most well educated people in the Church are past. Many gifted laypeople are leaders in government, education, medicine, technology, economics, and a host of other fields, and so when these lay people read episcopal or Vatican statements about moral issues they often do so with a trained, critical eye. Moreover, their prominent roles in the workplace lend them authority in those matters in which they enjoy competence.[156] Because of the increasing complexity and specificity of moral issues that Catholics face today, no one can claim authority in all of them.

The development of moral theology during the Middle Ages into the Reformation period was due in large part to the needs of priests in the confessional. They consulted manuals that ordered the proper penances for many types of sins; these manuals provided a kind of taxonomy of the moral life. Because in many places priests were the only literate members of a community, and because they alone took the time to read and study the manuals, they could rightly claim an authority of judgment about the way the Church deemed the severity of various sins, mortal and venial. Moreover, their experience of being in the confessional—of having privileged access to the testimonies of their faithful over years—added to their authority.

Much has been written, and much more needs to be written, about the slow erosion of the practice of confession. Here it is worth observing, though, that there is a significant loss to the Church because of people's decision not to go to confession more regularly: priests lose the valuable experience of learning their people's struggles against sin. This loss affects that which, I want to suggest, is at the heart of priestly (and therefore of episcopal) authority: sacramental celebration. What gives priests and bishops their special role in the Church is not primarily their learning, but rather the particular relationship they develop with the people of God as pastors. No layperson knows what it is like to act in the sacramental role of the priest absolving another of sin. The cumulative experience of this vocation gives to priests an authority that is unique and irreplaceable.

Yet laypeople have assumed, and will continue to assume, important leadership roles in the Church because many have not only committed themselves to a life of holiness; they have also gained education in matters that gives them competence beyond that of many priests and bishops. Consider the following types of learning that can benefit the Church today:

- Sociologists to study what the pastoral needs of an area are
- Theologians to discern how the traditions of the Church can deepen Catholics' understanding of their faith
- Political scientists to counsel Catholics on how to vote or make laws
- Lawyers to discern the just applications of law both in the Church (canon law) and in society (civil law)
- Doctors to advance our understanding of embryonic growth
- Historians to help us understand the deposit of faith and how it sheds light on contemporary challenges within the Church
- Accountants to manage the considerable funds that pass through parishes and dioceses
- Organizational experts to help address the structures within the Church that allow for the dissemination of information and good working conditions
- Philosophers to diagnose the trends of contemporary thinking that cultivate or harm efforts at evangelization
- Authors to unleash the sacramental imagination of the faithful
- Business leaders who can offer their experience of managing large numbers of people
- Nurses who can minister to the sick of a parish
- Parents who can offer their wisdom on handing on the faith to children
- Teachers who are skilled in cultivating a love for learning
- Computer scientists who can expand the outreach of the Church via the Internet
- Communications specialists who can manage public relations of a parish or diocese via various media
- Artists to give shape and color to the stories from the Bible or Catholic tradition
- Linguists to translate communications from around the globe
- Anthropologists to help Church leaders understand local cultures and the symbols and rituals they produce
- Scholars of religions to help the Church in its relationships with people of other faith traditions

- Diplomats who foster conversations between Church leaders and heads-of-state around issues of global concern, like poverty and education
- Liturgists who produce thoughtful and beautiful ways for Catholics to engage in worship together
- Biblical scholars who illuminate the meanings of texts for the contemporary world
- Physicists who expand our knowledge of the origins of the universe
- Psychologists who help us appreciate the complexity of the human condition
- Economists to provide Catholics with advice on how to use their resources for the common good

The list could go on. The point to underscore, of course, is that no one today can claim competence in more than one or two of these areas. Priests in the United States, for example, usually achieve master's degree–level competence in those areas that touch directly on the practice of the priesthood. Many bishops have doctoral degrees in such areas as ministry, canon law, philosophy, and theology. Yet among those Catholics in the United States who possess the master of divinity degree, or the doctor of philosophy degree in these areas, the clear majority are laypeople.

To be more precise: there are over two hundred Catholic colleges and universities in the United States, at which teach hundreds of lay Catholics who hold doctoral degrees in many fields. Their constant practice of teaching and research suggests that they have greater grasps of their respective fields than do administrators of dioceses and parishes, whose energies are directed toward a host of practical questions. In many areas of Catholic theology, for example, laypeople are the most conversant and influential writers.[157] The many Catholic institutions of higher education are well positioned to be of great service to their local churches if they continue to ask how the talents of their faculty, staff, and administration can be of service.

Of course the key concern among some Catholics is that a loosening of the reins of episcopal authority would usher in a model of Church authority that is antithetical to the apostolic faith entrusted to the disciples. The bishops, as the successors to the apostles, they assert, have the mandate to hand on the faith entrusted to them by Christ. The Church is not a democracy in which different groups vie for authority.

This critique is significant. Those who call for a democratization in the Church, I find, tend to gloss over the very obvious fact that many people in a democracy are not competent to address the very serious issues that affect the world today. Can any of us claim expertise in the panoply of issues that come before the U.S. Congress, let alone the United Nations or the Vatican? Nevertheless, calls for democratization do hit on an important point, which is that educated adults in the United States (and elsewhere) expect to be able to voice their concerns and be heard.

There is a middle path between the traditional model of hierarchical authority and the modern model of democratic authority, and it is this middle path that manifests the performative moral authority that bishops (and even ordinary Catholics) need in the contemporary Church. Performative moral authority is doing the truth: that is, engaging in a process of moral discourse that is itself a manifestation of Catholics' commitment to love of the neighbor. Too often, parties on different sides of moral debate demonize the other and fail to engage in authentic discourse—the kind that reflects a fundamental belief that each human person bears the image of God. This model rests upon a firm belief in the power of the Holy Spirit to guide the Church and its leaders to the truth through the process of prayer and open discussion.

The model is predicated on two observations. First, communities of experts have greater competence in addressing matters within their expertise than bishops. Second, bishops are entrusted with the duty to listen to the voice of the community of experts and to make judgments that are consistent with the tradition of the Church.

The hopeful news is that the U.S. Bishops' Conference and even the Vatican, to some extent,[158] have already adopted this practice. Many of my theological colleagues have served as consultants to bishops on issues ranging from marriage to environmental protection. Frequently, bishops assemble teams of experts to weigh in on controversial issues, giving these teams the freedom to debate among themselves the various merits of different proposals. Bishops stand to gain from greater exposure of the processes that lead to decisions. If they can show that their decisions are informed by the best of current thinking within a field, they leave the burden, in part, on the practitioners within that field. Rather than being accused of arrogant claims to knowledge, they will be seen as administrators informed by the best thinking.

There is, however, a danger, which I suggest is one that bishops—and the Church in the United States in general—can confront and, through this process, grow in holiness. It is this: experts in every field disagree, and their debates can sometimes be fractious. Asking experts to consider how the Church ought to proceed on difficult moral issues, for example, will mean inviting them to question the very foundations of Catholic teaching. Many would see such questioning as a threat to the unity of Catholic tradition.

My argument in response to this danger is that a transparent process of open discussion among Catholics—lay and ordained all bringing their talents and expertise to a difficult moral question—will not only be salutary for the Church; it will provide the opportunity for growth in holiness. First, it will demonstrate to both Catholics and others that the Church is not afraid of tackling difficult questions, guided by the Holy Spirit and the law of charity. Intra-ecclesial debates can manifest greater humanity, greater desire for beauty, truth, and goodness than we see, for example, in so much of the contemporary political landscape. Catholic moral dialogue can perform the truth that is love even before issuing a final judgment on a topic.

Second, such debates will recognize what is already a reality in the Church: disputes between liberals and conservatives that take place often without either side really talking to the other. The various publications and Web sites that different Catholics consult do not offer opportunities for Catholics to actually meet face to face; and as a result, many Catholics have never had the opportunity to have personal encounter with someone who thinks very differently. Even different parishes today break down along liberal or conservative lines, such that members of one parish may be suspicious of the members of another parish. Such balkanization is antithetical to authentic catholicity, and so it is important that we start finding ways to bridge these divides. The polarizations that exist between conservatives and liberals in the Church are the fruits of postmodern culture and its open source epistemology. When traditional structures of authority break down, what emerges is a kind of epistemological musical chairs: each person must find the community with which he or she identifies, and that community therefore will have a formative influence on the person's thinking. In the postmodern milieu, then, the Church must assume the task of reconciliation, drawing attention to the Church's fundamental kerygma in order to nurture a communion within which Catholics can discern the fruits of faithful living.

Let us manifest our faith that all people bear the image of God, and seek to understand those who think differently by engaging them in serious conversation about moral teachings, under the auspices of the Church itself. It would be a great service to adult Catholics today if good ecclesial discussion could be modeled in parishes and dioceses, in order that many might have opportunities to learn more than what they encounter in liturgy. Adults in the United States think democratically, meaning that many consider it a duty to become informed on issues in order to vote on them. Could we not take this desire to become informed and invite adults into conversation that benefits the Church community? Practically, couldn't parishes sponsor town-hall meetings as ways of giving voice to the adults in their communities, which would then help inform the pastoral imperatives of the Church as a whole? This kind of healthy moral discourse within the Church need not compromise the apostolic mandate of the episcopal office; there would be no referenda on crucial teachings. The very practice of this discourse, however, would assist the bishop because it would enable him to understand more fully what the people of his diocese are really thinking.

The proposal that discourse in the Church involve not only the bishops, but also laypeople who sincerely practice their faith is not new. In a well-publicized debate in 1859, the prominent English theologian John Henry Newman argued against Monsignor George Talbot that the faithful ought to be consulted on matters of Catholic doctrine.[159] His specific observation involved the way Catholics believed in the Immaculate Conception of Jesus' mother Mary, but it was based on his earlier studies of the Arians of the fourth century. Ordinary Catholics of that early period, he argued, held fast to the Nicene Creed even in the absence of good leadership, suggesting that their habits of devotion carried a certain kind of authority distinct from the teachings of the bishops. The "shared feeling of the faithful" (*consensus fidelium* or, in its shortened form, *sensus fidelium*)—the common proclamation of faith of bishops, priests, and laypeople together—was a sign of authentic Christian teaching.[160]

Newman's theology was an important precursor to Vatican II and its two constitutions on the Church (*Lumen Gentium* and *Gaudium et Spes*). His optimism about the cooperation of the clergy and laity provided a backdrop for more specific developments in moral theology—in particular, the strong emphasis on the properly formed conscience of the person of faith, and his or her role in proclaiming faith through action. In addition, his writings on the development of doctrine in the Church have influenced contemporary thinking about the very process of moral thinking within Catholic tradition. As we shall see, this contemporary thinking on moral theology has also affected the ways that Catholics think about moral issues, and must therefore influence the ways that we consider how to bring the Catholic moral tradition into conversation with contemporary questions.

The Developments in Moral Theology

We see in the neuralgic debates over moral issues how Catholics have different views on the process of moral decision making. There are fundamentally two distinct narratives at work.

The first narrative is what I describe as "revelatory." In the revelatory narrative, there is strong emphasis on moral wisdom being revealed by God in the scriptural traditions—the Ten Commandments, the Mosaic Law, and the teachings of Jesus. The revelatory narrative begins with scripture, emphasizes the role of the magisterium in authentically interpreting scripture, and points to key scriptural and magisterial texts. For example, the revelatory narrative treats homosexuality by appealing to biblical texts that show it as a moral evil.[161] Because of its divine origin, the teaching that derives from these texts is perceived as unchangeable; hence the duty of the true pastors of the faithful is to stand strong against those social currents that are seen to undermine belief in the divine truth. Contemporary U.S. attitudes toward homosexuality, by contrast, are the relatively recent byproduct of the sexual revolution. According to this view, the Church must transcend the vicissitudes of history and culture in order to proclaim the unchangeable truth that we know only through divine revelation.

The second narrative rests upon a process of discernment. In the discernment narrative, moral wisdom is seen as the culmination of the long process of thinking across generations. Scriptural texts are weighed against the *sensus fidelium* across the ages, which in turn is weighed against magisterial teachings. Two examples are the issues of slavery and capital punishment, both of which are condoned in the scriptures and in older magisterial teachings, but which more recently have come to be proscribed because of the strong evidence of the *sensus fidelium* and more recent magisterial teachings. According to the discernment narrative, the moral teachings of the Bible and the magisterium reflect the thinking of the time, and must be balanced by the accumulated wisdom of Christians over the ages as they wrestle with the evidence presented in their lives. The lived experiences of Catholics wrestling with difficult moral questions carry a certain authority, because they are manifestations of the Holy Spirit breathing life into the faith community struggling to live according to the demands of truth and love.

Underneath the current debates about serious moral questions in the Church are disputes about which of these two narratives provides the right template. Also at issue is a fundamental question about the balance of individual conscience and religious obedience. Ought the teachings of bishops override individual conscience, or do Catholics have a duty to obey the dictates of conscience even when it contradicts current Church teaching?

We must remember that in light of the ways that Americans think, and in light of the kind of culture that exists in the United States today, it is important to be realistic about how to address questions of moral authority. Catholics have a duty to obey the dictates of conscience,[162] but they also have a duty to form conscience rightly according to the scriptures and the teachings of the Church.

We are to regard the Church's teaching with religious assent,[163] but we also have the ability to help the Church develop its understanding of issues about which there is a lack of moral clarity.

The two narratives of moral decision making must be seen as complementary in the life of the Church today; both must inform the consciences of Catholics seeking to exercise faithful judgment. In short, neither narrative provides a one-size-fits-all template for moral reasoning. Indeed, what distinguishes Catholic moral thinking today is its dialectical nature: it involves not only the subjective dimension of conscience development, but also the more objective dimension characterized by attention to a history, a scripture, a tradition of moral teaching.

There are dangers in either one of these narratives becoming exclusive in Catholic reasoning about moral norms. On the surface, the revelatory narrative seems more authentically Catholic to many, who argue that it militates against the secularist, liberal tendencies to treat moral reasoning as a sophisticated kind of individualism or relativism. Holding fast to scripture and magisterial teaching, they assert, gives greater credence to the objective nature of divine revelation— the words that God has spoken to us about how to grow in love in holiness according to the laws that God himself has set in place. The revelatory narrative brings us out of our selfish tendencies, our predilection for seeing the world through the lenses of our own limited self-interests, by attending rather to the deep question of how God has created order out of chaos. Moreover, this revelatory narrative reminds us that our views tend to be overly conditioned by historical and cultural myopia; God's truth transcends the fads of our often-flighty American cultural mores. Whereas contemporary pop culture extols false values of money, sex, and power, the revelatory narrative opens us up to consider the theological values of poverty, chastity, and obedience.

Yet the revelatory narrative can descend into a kind of biblicism or even a kind of ecclesiasticism. What distinguishes the trajectory of Catholic moral theology over the centuries is its willingness to be self-corrective, recognizing that indeed the moral prescriptions of the Bible need to be seen against a larger commitment to moral reasoning,[164] and further that the Church's own proclamations of moral truth develop over time. Abortion, just war, usury, capital punishment, religious freedom, and relations with non-Catholics are just some of the issues about which the Church has developed its understanding over the years; and it is to be expected that over time it will continue to refine its thinking on other issues as well. Without the complementary discernment narrative, the reliance on the revelatory narrative risks making revelation itself appear irrelevant or even flatly wrong. God's will is greater than our ability to articulate it or practice it.

On the other hand, many today see the discernment narrative as more amenable to the sophisticated epistemologies of the modern and postmodern worlds. For those attracted to this narrative, the natural law tradition represents a model: with Aquinas, they believe that human beings have the capacity to discern God's order in creation and need not rely solely on revelation for an understanding of moral truth. The discernment narrative places the onus on the perceiving, thinking person in community—much like the epistemology of those empirical philosophers who so strongly influenced the rise of modern science. To achieve truth, one must pay attention to the world, ask all the relevant questions, then make sound judgments. Knowledge develops and grows with accumulated experiences that bring forth new evidence, enabling the human community to discern more fully the structures of reality. Scripture and the Church's tradition are resources that can be drawn into the larger conversation about what God demands of us today.

Yet the discernment model can descend into cultural relativism that lacks an adequate view of history. Whereas the revelatory model emphasizes the authority of the Bible and the magisterium, the discernment model emphasizes the authority of the conscience, whether alone or in community. And the danger for anyone seeking to interpret data is to overemphasize the local, the immediate, the contemporary over the universal, the traditional, the ancient. The discernment model involves someone or some people doing the discernment, and there will always be the danger of bias. Moreover, discernment itself is the process of sorting the relevant from the irrelevant, and thus the further danger is evident when, for example, people perceive that too much attention is paid to the data within culture and not enough attention is paid to the data of scripture and magisterial teaching.

We return to the issue of birth control, which was a catalyst for the widespread emergence of these differing models of moral reasoning. According to the revelatory model, which Pope Paul VI espoused in *Humanae Vitae*, the way to approach the issue is to learn from scripture and tradition what the Church has understood about human sexuality in the context of married life. The emphasis is on the reading of key scriptural texts and their interpretation by key figures like Augustine, Aquinas, and earlier popes. On the other hand, the commission that Paul VI appointed to study the topic of birth control espoused more of the discernment model of reasoning, drawing into their study the testimonies of married couples.[165] Their recommendations emphasized the pastoral implications of the teaching, suggesting that married couples ought to decide for themselves how to engage in sexual practices in the context of their married lives.

The example of the debate that emerged from *Humanae Vitae* illustrates the kind of challenge that exists today in reconciling—or better, bringing into authentic dialogue—the two narratives of moral reasoning. To oversimplify, let us observe that the revelatory narrative says "trust the magisterium," whereas the discernment narrative says "trust the community of believers." The Catholic Church is, of course, both of these groups, and so the more adequate counsel would be to "trust the Church," with all the nuances that the term implies. To trust the Church is to trust, ultimately, in the presence of the Holy Spirit. It is to regard with great care the many writings of the Church's ordinary magisterium, but it is also to regard with great care the many testimonies of people who lead prayerful lives. The fact that there is sometimes divergence within the Body of Christ need not necessarily be seen as a source of scandal, but rather as ordinary human limitation—as those who study the Church's history have seen time and again. The Church lives not only in the moment, but also in the trajectory of history that leads to the eschaton. Divergence is a sign of the need for deep dialogue predicated on a spirituality of communion, analogous to a marriage. The experience of divergence itself can become a *kairos*, a graced moment of reconciliation, so that it not descend into schism. As couples who have been married wisely for a long time understand, *kairos* moments, when approached in a spirit of communion, are opportunities for growth. The Church can approach its experiences of divergence similarly as opportunities for growth.

CRITICAL MORAL JUDGMENT

U.S. Catholics are, as other Americans, likely to believe that they have a responsibility to form their consciences in ways that enable good judgment. It would be a great service if parishes had the habit of fostering discussions around papal encyclicals, bishops' pastoral letters, and so on. It would benefit liberal-leaning Catholics by inviting them to more seriously consider the original sources; and it would benefit conservative-leaning Catholics by exposing them to objections firsthand. Many U.S. Catholics, whether we like it or not, will make up their own minds about moral issues. It cannot be the Church's goal to force people to behave morally; rather, it is the goal of all Catholics to live and proclaim their faith and thereby to perform the truth of the gospel.[166] What made the birth control question particularly contentious was the fact that many of those who proclaimed the moral norm were not called to the vocation of married life to live through its implications. Today, with forty years of hindsight, it is possible to revisit the question in light of the experiences of married couples who have sought to adhere to the guidelines in *Humanae Vitae*. Their experiences in marriage can help inform younger couples who grapple with the same basic questions today. Do the marriages of those who eschew artificial birth control manifest the truth of the gospel and enable them to lead holier lives? Do those who use artificial birth control show themselves to be more committed to the gospel and capable of more perfectly living out God's will? Who, in the end, performs the moral truth?

We began this chapter by observing that the dynamic that exists in the Church in the United States today is much like the relationship between parents and adolescents. Here, we take that observation one step further, to suggest that the family model can offer us a way forward in thinking about the roles and relationships in the Church.

People who are responsible for raising children, I believe, have an advantage in understanding the persuasiveness and limits of moral authority. Good parents—those whose love for their children is constantly evident to the children, such that they feel safe as they grow—will of course pass on values to their children. Young children naturally agree with their parents on just about everything; their naiveté is based on loving trust of the parents. As they grow older, though, children begin to develop a critical consciousness; they realize that sometimes their parents make mistakes or misunderstand situations, and need correction. As noted earlier, moments of disagreement can often be privileged moments of growth—a parent who loves a child will accept critique and appreciate the child's growing sense of self. Ideally, a good parent-child relationship will allow the parent to communicate his or her beliefs to the child, manifesting in action and word the lived value of the parent's faith. Yet every parent knows that it is simply impossible to make the child see the world in the same way as the parent does. I cannot make my child believe anything: the best I can do is live what I believe, share it with my child the best I can, and hope that my life and my words are persuasive enough to guide the child's judgments. My duty as a parent—indeed, my vocation as a parent—is to be a witness *(martyrion)* to God's truth in my life and in what I teach. I simply do not have the power to influence a child's judgment any further. I must anticipate, in fact, that there will be times when my child's judgments conflict with my own, and be ready to respond in a manner consistent with my faith.

At a certain stage, finally, my child will have the maturity to reach moral judgments independent from any coaching on my part. My hope as a parent is that my life and words will have had a positive impact on my child's life, and that her judgments lead her to freedom. Perhaps my good parenting will even enable her to show me the deficiencies and biases in my own judgments.

Leaders in the Church today—not only bishops and priests, but also catechists, educators, lay ministers, deacons, religious men and women, journalists, writers, and so on—can learn from the parenting model. In the previous section, I sought to suggest that a key challenge for the Church today is to perform its moral authority. Catholics must manifest in their actions and words that a commitment to the gospel of Jesus Christ, and an obligation to live that faith in the community that professes faith in the one, holy, catholic and apostolic Church, enables them to be better human beings than if they had not made such choices. Neither participation in the sacramental life of the Church, nor close listening to what the Church teaches, can make people holy. The Church cannot make people believe in God; it cannot make people believe that contraception, or abortion, or homosexual activity is wrong. What it can do—through the individual commitments of ordinary Catholics and through the teachings of the magisterium—is proclaim faith in Christ, worship the triune God, disseminate the gospel, and perform the corporal and spiritual works of mercy. If it does these things well, then the critical moral judgments of those whose lives proclaim God's truth will become morally persuasive. Right living must precede right moral judgment. In short, if the moral witness of the Church—all Catholics—is like the moral witness of a parent, then the best it can do is to promote critical moral judgment.

Practically, this commitment to fostering critical moral judgment means that the Church can manifest what it means to love: celebrating the sacrament of communion; feeding the hungry; honoring and nurturing the sacrament of marriage; curing the sick; seeking reconciliation in the wake of sin; visiting prisoners; and so on. It can teach what it already performs, as a way to reinforce in words what is already present in deeds. It can bring the gospel to the many people around the globe, both in loving service and in welcoming invitation to liturgy. It can bring to the public square the fruits of its reflections on social issues, but it cannot expect that lawmakers will be able to appropriate these reflections and translate them into laws without difficulty.

The Synoptic Gospels describe a Jesus who came not for those who already have committed themselves to right relationship with God, but rather for sinners. This refreshingly honest description of the mission of Jesus offers us an important consideration of how the Church today will regain its moral authority. In a soundbyte culture, condemnations are easily perceived as being central to the raison d'etre of the Church, and nothing could be further from the truth. The Church's moral authority derives precisely from the fact that *it cares about human beings unlike any other institution.* The clear message—in the pulpit, in the news media, in the interactions of faithful Catholics with one another and with others—must be that Catholic faith in the risen Christ leads us to draw sinners close to the heart of the Church. Catholics must demonstrate that their being immersed in the ecumenical "school of humanity"[167] gives them the ability to translate the experience of their lives into practical wisdom for the wider society.

A CONSISTENT MORAL VISION

Catholics (including their leaders) will carry persuasive moral authority when their public lives—and by extension, their public image—manifest a consistent moral vision based in the gospel demand to love. This authority must encompass those moral issues that garner the attention of those who live in the communications age: war and peace, migration, hunger and poverty, slavery and trafficking, terrorism, inter-religious strife, economic justice, fair labor policy, access to health care and education, sexuality and marriage, vocation and spirituality. Young people can sniff out hypocrisy with great ease, and so in all the ways Catholics manifest their commitment to the gospel, there must be a common thread.

At root, that thread is the gospel itself; and thus the Church's original mission to spread the gospel amounts to a mission to draw people into discerning the will of God in all moral questions. One contemporary flowering of the tradition of Catholic moral theology is Catholic Social Teaching, which may be described as the public implications of the personal turn away from sin to embrace the will of God. What, the Church asks, are the ways that God calls us into right relationship with both God and one another? What are our responsibilities to other human beings today, and what are the forces that strangle people's abilities to live according to the right order that God intends?

The first message that young people need to hear from Catholics is that there is an integrity in the Church's moral vision that enables it to address all issues, from the global to the personal, and that people are willing to take the risk to live out that vision.

Unlike nation-states that act out of limited self-interest, or corporations driven by a need for self-sustainability, the Church's concern is right relationship with God. Its focus, therefore, is on the distinctly human. In his 2006 encyclical *Deus Caritas Est,* Pope Benedict XVI highlighted this concern:

> In today's complex situation, not least because of the growth of a globalized economy, the Church's social doctrine has become a set of fundamental guidelines offering approaches that are valid even beyond the confines of the Church: in the face of ongoing development these guidelines need to be addressed in the context of dialogue with all those seriously concerned for humanity and for the world in which we live.[168]

The Catholic moral vision is distinctly human: it is neither nationalistic nor profit-driven. Moreover, as the pope avers, it is in dialogue with all who seek the fundamental human good. Unlike so many organizations that seek finite ends, the communion of Catholic organizations is based in a moral vision that seeks an integrated, unified approach to human flourishing. It is remarkable—and indeed, hopeful—that these Catholic organizations freely pool resources in the common desire to help the people of the world. They do so without much central oversight; they are unlike various nation-led efforts or United Nations–led efforts in that their funding most often comes from private sources. While there are some organizations like Catholic Relief Services or the Catholic Campaign for Human Development that benefit from relationships with the United States Conference of Catholic Bishops (and parallel organizations with ties to the bishops' conferences in other countries), many more are driven by Catholic Social Teaching and work independently from the bishops. The very existence of these myriad organizations[169] testifies to the efficacy of the principle of subsidiarity. For just as these local organizations are apt to address the local needs of a population, so too are they more apt to promote the public face of the Church in the societies in which they live.

In the open source age, Catholic organizations can lead in ways that Catholic bishops and priests cannot, in large part due simply to the numbers of people involved. The public face of the Church will be enhanced if Catholics themselves, and the wider public, perceive the Church as the "on the ground" groups of people seeking to bring healing and care to all of God's children. When complex moral issues arise in the public square, it ought to be those people on the ground who address them. Catholics who work in adoption ministries and post-abortion counseling can address public policy around abortion. Catholics who work in migration and refugee services can address policies toward immigration. Catholics who are psychologists, theologians, or college campus ministers can address issues of sexuality. Catholic doctors, biologists, and other researchers can address bioethical issues. In general, the authority of the Church will depend less on the specific person of the local bishop and more on his ability to bring faithful members of his community to public discourse around the issues in which they have expertise.

Of course, even the most eloquent Catholic voices in the public square must wrestle with the simple fact that the Catholic moral vision is different from what many Americans believe. There is no whitewashing the fact that the Church's teaching on issues like homosexuality, the death penalty, birth control, the priesthood, and a number of other contentious issues is perceived by many as wrong. In light of such differences, Catholics must wrestle with serious questions. Does disagreement with Church teaching constitute a barrier to divine grace? Does the Church's firm stand on such issues imply a need to take a stand against the culture, to fortify itself (as it were) against the encroachments of the sinful world? How do such teachings affect the Church's missionary and evangelical activity? How ought the Church respond to the many within the Church who disagree with these teachings? Are there criteria by which to judge which Catholics are authentically Catholic, and which are really just kidding themselves? How, in the end, is Christ summoning people to himself by the actions of the Holy Spirit—and are we getting in the way?

Differences of opinion are to be expected within a pluralistic society. The attitudes that many people of faith bring to public debates around moral issues have now come to seem like a remnant of an earlier era in which Christianity (more specifically, its Protestant iterations) amounted to a kind of civil religion in the United States. Morality was understood as more or less coterminous with the demands of the Bible, and hence variations from the accepted moral norms often elicited from people of faith a kind of righteous indignation. Now that the age of Christian moral hegemony in U.S. public life is largely behind us, such indignation can come across as arrogant, even when promulgated by such late-comers as the children of Catholic immigrants. The duty of people of faith is not to ensure the retaining of power, but rather to witness humbly to the gospel in a persuasive way. More precisely, our duty is first to live "the basics"—to be people committed to justice and works of mercy. Our contributions to public life must demonstrate that we are capable of living the moral truth even as we engage with those who understand it differently. Can our commitment to the gospel be obvious even to those with whom we disagree?

There is one final point that must be addressed. It is this: the Catholic moral tradition has never sought to articulate a vision of the moral good that is beholden to a narrow time frame, even if that time frame spans centuries. It is properly described as "teleological" in the language of Aristotle—that is, it seeks to articulate the good that points to our ultimate happiness. Developments in moral teachings—such as those around slavery, for example—have taken centuries precisely because only through the accumulated wisdom of many different cultures can we distill what is temporary from what is lasting. In the United States, our reflection on the fruits of the sexual revolution, for example, is a paltry few decades old, and so our contributions to the world's understanding of sexuality is still limited. What this means for the Church is mixed. On the one hand, it suggests that a certain humility is in order for those who would urge significant change in the Church's understanding of such a complex moral issue. On the other hand, it suggests that the role that such progressives play within the Church is vital, even if their urgings go unheeded in the short term. For we must remember that among those progressive thinkers in the Church were (at one time) people like Saint Thomas Aquinas, Saint Catherine of Siena, Saint Francis of Assisi, and Saint Teresa of

Avila. What Newman called the *consensus fidelium* is very different from "the will of the people" as it is often understood in democratic societies. Majorities can be wrong—we need look no further than the examples of our own history to recognize that majorities can justify evils such as racial discrimination. That the Church takes positions that seem contrary even to a majority in a given era is not a sign that the teaching is wrong. It may be prophetic.

The bottom line is this: we live in an age when many claim moral authority; and in the midst of such moral fog, young people are often not equipped to easily discern what constitutes an authentic claim. The Church must lead not only by word, but by example, and its message must be clear: we love human beings the way that God did, to the extent that he sent his Son to die for them. Catholics must be the ones that give up wealthy jobs to be teachers and let their lives manifest the meaning of faith. Catholics must adopt children and show young women that there are real, powerful, life-giving alternatives to abortion.[170] Catholics must show in their marriages and family lives that fidelity to the teachings of the Church enables growth in holiness. Catholics must show that their commitments to working with the poor, immigrants, people with AIDS, the elderly, drug abusers, and others on the margins of society are rooted in the bedrock of the gospel, and that this bedrock sustains them in their ministries. Catholics in public life must be willing to make explicit the ways that their commitments to balanced budgets, social programs, foreign aid, security, and all other tools of statecraft are rooted in an integral reading of Catholic tradition of political thought.

The net effect of such witness in our society ought to be kerygmatic, very much as in the apostolic age: it ought to lead many to ask what motivates us. If our answer is clear—"my faith"—people will want to know more. There is no more hopeful sign of God's presence in the world than people who are committed to manifesting it. In this age when membership in the Church must be an intentional choice, rather than an obligation arising from family heritage or historical precedent, those who choose to live their faith become sacraments for the world. It is not a surprise that in this age, a seam between the modern and postmodern worlds, there are significant changes in the membership in the Church, especially in a country like the United States. What is a surprise to many—and will continue to surprise, for that is the way that God works—is that many young people are choosing the Church even in spite of its problems. Their faith must be nourished by the witness of mature Catholics, both in their works of love and in their critical thinking that engages and even challenges the current thinking in the Church. It is precisely the seeds of this nascent faith that are the seeds of hope for U.S. Catholicism.

Appendix

Some Suggestions for Building a Twenty-First-Century Parish Community

1. Build a parish e-mail list. Learn who prefers e-mail to postal service mail and send all parish correspondence electronically to these people. It will save money and time, and create a parish network that will grow.

2. Extend the invitation to younger members of the community to be the parish Web master or leader of the e-mail list. This is a valuable new ministry that many young people are capable of doing even in high school.

3. Send the digital version of the bulletin to the e-mail list. Include links to good Catholic Web sites—the local diocesan office, Catholic Charities and Catholic Relief Services, the Vatican, various prayer sites like Sacred Space (www.sacredspace.ie), age-specific sites like Busted Halo (for young adults: www.bustedhalo.com). Like printed bulletins, it can include local sponsors.

4. Encourage parishioners to consider regular donations using their bank's Web bill pay service. Many now use these services to pay regular bills, and it allows them to consider the way their church donations relate to the rest of the items in their monthly or yearly budget.

5. Forge relationships with other parishes in the region, and pool resources. Now that many parishes are without resident priests, it will be important for parishes to recognize the talented people who are catechists, financial advisors, contractors, plumbers, and so on. Develop a consulting service of talent within the region that any parish can use. Consider working with other parishes to finance a resident theologian, or counselor, or nurse.

6. Provide thorough guides to the Mass, the artwork, the language, the traditions of the Church at the front door. Display them prominently so first-time visitors or returnees after many years will not feel lost.

7. Use the parish Web site to link people to good information about all things relating to the Church: the origins of prayers, the history of vestments, saints, Eucharistic theology, and so on. Imagine what it would be like to enter a Catholic Church for the first time and ask: what does such a person need to know?

8. Develop small prayer groups among parishioners in order to encourage the practice of spirituality outside of the Mass.

9. Talk with others after Mass about the readings. Find ways to encourage "water-cooler" discussion about the sacred text: What does it mean today? How do different people understand it?

10. Model respectful conversation in the parish by inviting people with different views on an issue (e.g., voting in the next election) to express how their faith informs their judgment.

11. Consider tithing as a parish, donating a portion of all collections to a poorer parish elsewhere. There are a number of tithing parishes today. Such a practice can help foster a sense of catholicity and responsibility for our brothers and sisters in different parts of the Church.

Notes

1. Raymond Flynn related this quotation in an interview on NBC's *Meet the Press* on April 3, 2005, shortly after the pope's death. The transcript for this broadcast was retrieved on April 20, 2005, at the MSNBC Web site: http://www.msnbc.msn.com/id/7361533/.

2. In view of the fact that there is no other adequate adjective to describe only the residents of the United States, I use the term *American* frequently throughout the text. In a later section, I address the objection that the term *American* can also refer to other people in North, Central, and South America. The terms *U.S. Catholic* and *American Catholic* are not meant to have any technical sense, but rather describe those Catholics who live in the United States or (more broadly) in the Americas.

3. Terence Tilley has critiqued the view of Catholic tradition that suggests that it is fundamentally about a body of teaching, a view that is suggested even in some teachings from the Vatican itself. He suggests instead that an authentic understanding of tradition must stress the creative process of integrating the insights of the past into a dynamic approach to present issues. See his *Inventing Catholic Tradition* (Maryknoll, NY: Orbis Books, 2000).

4. Cornel West, "The Moral Obligations of Living in a Democratic Society," in *The Good Citizen*, ed. David Batstone and Eduardo Mendieta (New York and London: Routledge, 1999).

5. See Dean R. Hoge et al., *Young Adult Catholics: Religion in the Culture of Choice* (Notre Dame, IN: University of Notre Dame Press, 2001); Patrick H. McNamara, *Conscience First: Tradition Second* (Albany: State University of New York Press, 1992).

6. Tom Levinson, *All That's Holy* (San Francisco: Jossey-Bass, 2003), pp. 19–24.

7. I do not know of such an organization; he may have meant the Jesuit Volunteer Corps or the Mercy Volunteer Corps, or a related organization.

8. Cf. John R. Quinn, "The Internet and the Church of the Future," *The Way* 42/4 (October 2003), pp. 21–31.

9. See Michael L. Budde's analysis of the forces of consumerism and Catholicism, which is provocative over a decade later. See his book *The Two Churches: Catholicism & Capitalism in the World-System* (Durham and London: Duke University Press, 1992).

10. On the way that children have become the fastest-growing market in the United States, and how advertising seeks to tap this market, see James U. McNeal, *The Kids Market, Myths and Realities* (Ithaca, NY: Paramount Market Publishing, 1999). For a critique of the extent to which children have become entangled in consumerism, see Juliet Schor, *Born to Buy: Marketing and the Transformation of Childhood and Culture* (New York: Scribner, 2004).

11. Wade Clark Roof's analyses of the baby boom generation's approaches to religion are helpful. See especially his book *Spiritual Marketplace: Baby Boomers and the Remaking of American Religion* (Princeton: Princeton University Press, 1999).

12. Dan Brown, *The DaVinci Code* (New York: Doubleday, 2003).

13. Cf. Philip Jenkins, *The Next Christendom: The Coming of Global Christianity* (Oxford and New York: Oxford University Press, 2002).

14. The development of the Catholic Church in Asia reflects and draws on the development of the Church in Central and South America. See Tom Fox, *Pentecost in Asia: A New Way of Being Church* (Maryknoll, NY: Orbis Books, 2002). On the Church in Africa, where Catholicism is growing the fastest, see Maura Browne, *The African Synod: Documents, Reflections, Perspectives* (Maryknoll, NY: Orbis Books, 1996).

15. Cited in Daniel C. Maguire, *Sacred Energies: When the World's Religions Sit Down to Talk about the Future of Human Life and the Plight of This Planet* (Minneapolis: Fortress Press, 2000), p. 34.

16. The Center for Applied Research in the Apostolate (CARA) suggests that the Catholic Church in the United States is "one of the only religious bodies that can truly be considered national in scope" (Bryan T. Froehle and Mary L. Gautier, eds., *Catholicism USA: A Portrait of the Catholic Church in the United States* [Maryknoll, NY: Orbis Books, 2000], p. 19).

17. See Hoge et al., *Young Adult Catholics*, p. 61, which shows results of their poll of young Catholics. When asked to respond to the statement "All the major world religions are equally good ways of helping a person find ultimate truth," 70 percent of the respondents answered in the affirmative.

18. See the statement from the gathering of world religious leaders that took place in Moscow in summer 2006 for an example of the ongoing attempts to bind different religious communities in a community dedicated to advancing the flourishing of the human community: http://www.cwnews.com/news/viewstory.cfm?recnum=45156 (Catholic News Service).

19. This and the following excerpts are from Gao Xingjian, *Soul Mountain*, trans. Mabel Lee (New York: HarperCollins, 2000), pp. 237–40.

20. According to CARA at Georgetown University, the Catholic population in the United States has grown steadily since 1965, from 45.6 million (24 percent of the population) to the 2002 figure of 62.2 million (22 percent of the population). See their Web site at http://www.georgetown.edu/research/cara/bulletin/index.htm.

21. Of the largest group of Catholic immigrants, those clustered under the term *Hispanic*, Arturo Valenzuela writes, "The conventional wisdom, for example, is that Hispanic immigrants will bolster the sagging fortunes of the Roman Catholic Church. And yet, many of the immigrants are evangelical protestants or convert to Protestantism in coming into the United States, replicating patterns that are also occurring in the sending countries" (in Nueva Mayoría.com: www.nuevamayoriacom/english/analysis/valenzuela/ivalenzuela230301.htm). Also, Gaston Espinosa, Virgilio Elizondo, and Jesse Miranda head a three-year study funded by the Pew Charitable Trusts entitled "Hispanic Churches in American Public Life" (www.hcapl.org/HCAPL_Summary_of_Findings_English.pdf), in which they write that 70 percent of Latinos in the United States are Catholic. This percentage has remained constant for at least fifteen years. But 18 percent of first-generation Latinos are Protestant, compared with 33 percent of the third generation, meaning that many children of immigrants are leaving the Catholic Church. As many as 600,000 Catholics are leaving the Church every year. Perhaps the greatest challenge for Church leaders in the coming years is to minister to the youngest group of Catholics in the United States (less than ten years old), of which fully 50 percent are Hispanic today (see the statistics compiled by the Instituto Fe Y Vida at http://www.feyvida.org/research/fastfacts.html).

22. See Froehle and Gautier, *Catholicism USA*, p. 23. Cf. William D'Antonio et al., *American Catholics: Gender, Generation, and Commitment* (Walnut Creek, CA: AltaMira Press, 2001); James D. Davidson et al., *The Search for Common Ground: What Unites and Divides Catholic Americans* (Huntington, IN: Our Sunday Visitor Publishing, 1997).

23. According to the CARA study, only 21 percent of young adults (ages eighteen to thirty-five) go to Mass weekly, and half go to Mass a few times a year or less (Froehle and Gautier, *Catholicism USA*, p. 23).

24. The CARA study states that in 1960, there were five hundred parishes without a resident pastor. In 2000, about 13 percent, or 2,500, of the parishes in the United States had no resident pastor (Froehle and Gautier, *Catholicism USA*, p. 121).

25. Karl Rahner, "Toward a Fundamental Theological Interpretation of Vatican II," *Theological Studies* 40/4 (December, 1979), pp. 716–27.

26. Samuel P. Huntington, *Democratization in the Late Twentieth Century* (Norman: University of Oklahoma Press, 1991).

27. Are We On Track To End Hunger? Hunger Report 2004, Bread for the World Institute, http://www.bread.org/institute/hunger_report/index.html.

28. United Nations Food and Agriculture Organization, *Mobilizing the Political Will*, no. 3.3 (2002), online at http://www.fao.org/DOCREP/004/Y1780e/Y1780e00.HTM.

29. The number of people living on these amounts of money have steadily decreased since the 1980s, according to a study done by Shaohua Chen and Martin Ravallion of the World Bank research group: "How have the world's poorest fared since the early 1980s," online at http://www.worldbank.org/research/povmonitor/MartinPapers/How_have_the_poorest_fared_since_the_early_1980s.pdf.

30. "Household Food Security in the United States, 2002," ERS Research Briefs, http://www.ers.usda.gov/publications/fanrr35/fanrr35.pdf.

31. Examples are the following: Mark Massa, *Catholics in American Culture: Fulton Sheen, Dorothy Day, and the Notre Dame Football Team* (New York: Herder and Herder, 2001); David J. O'Brien, *Public Catholicism* (Maryknoll, NY: Orbis Books, 1996); Jay Dolan, *In Search of an American Catholicism: A History of Religion and Culture in Tension* (Oxford and New York: Oxford University Press, 2002); John Tracy Ellis, *American Catholicism* (Chicago: University of Chicago Press, 1969).

32. Budde, *The Two Churches*, p. 96.

33. Hwee Hwee Tan, *Foreign Bodies* (New York: Persea Books, 1999), p. 39.

34. The studies of Hoge and Davidson noted in the Introduction indicate that young adults, even though they may not be practicing (regular churchgoing) Catholics, nevertheless retain a sensibility of being Catholic, and could not envision being anything other than Catholic.

35. Andrew Greeley has written of the "Catholic imagination," which is also an accurate description. I use the rich theological term *sacramental* because it is the lens through which Catholics, as well as other Christians (and, arguably, many non-Christians), view the world. See Greeley's *The Catholic Imagination* (Berkeley: University of California Press, 2000).

36. Julian of Norwich, *Showings* [short text], trans. Edmund Colledge, OSA, and James Walsh, SJ (New York: Paulist Press, 1978), p. 130.

37. Consider, for example, Leonard Swidler's proposal in his book *Toward a Catholic Constitution* (New York: Herder and Herder, 1996), which argues that the Church must incorporate lessons from American democracy.

38. Cf. James O'Toole's essay, "The Six Ages of Catholicism in America," in *Church Ethics and Its Organizational Context*, ed. Jean Bartunek, Mary Ann Hinsdale, and James F. Keenan (Lanham, MD: Rowman and Littlefield, 2005), which describes the challenges faced by early U.S. Catholics before the establishment of an organized hierarchy and presbyterate.

39. Cf. the July 12, 2003 *Washington Post* editorial by Henry G. Brinton, a Presbyterian pastor, on how democracy within church bodies is not always a good thing. In anticipation of the first Voice of the Faithful conference, he writes, "While having a voice and a vote certainly gives people more opportunities for institutional involvement and may even inspire greater commitment to the church's benevolent works, the process of democratization dilutes the purity of the church's moral message, and can undermine its influence in larger political and social spheres."

40. *The Theological Dictionary of the New Testament*, ed. Gerhard Kittel, trans. Geoffrey W. Bromiley (Grand Rapids, MI: Eerdmans, 1981) suggests the following about the term *latreia:* "The service which Christians are to offer conists in the fashioning of their inner lives and their outward physical conduct in a way which plainly distinguishes them from the world and which corresponds to the will of God…Paul describes this sacrifice as a *logike latreia*, a service of God which corresponds to human reason, in which, however, divine reason is also at work" (vol. 4, p. 65).

41. For more on *latreia* and the church's liturgy, see chapter 4.

42. Paul Lakeland, *The Liberation of the Laity: In Search of an Accountable Church* (New York and London: Continuum, 2003), p. 245.

43. This is an excerpt from a sermon that the archbishop gave on January 22, 1978.

44. Czeslaw Milosz, "A Theological Treatise," *Spiritus: A Journal of Christian Spirituality* 2/2 (2002), pp. 193–204.

45. David Nantais, "'Whatever!' Is Not Ignatian Indifference: Jesuits and the Ministry to Young Adults," *Studies In the Spirituality of Jesuits* 36/3 (Fall 2004), pp. 1–38; Andrew Greeley, "Like a Catholic: Madonna's Challenge to Her Church," *America* 160/18 (May 13, 1989), pp. 447–50.

46. Vincent Miller, *Consuming Religion: Religious Belief and Practice in a Consumer Culture* (New York: Continuum, 2003).

47. See the article by John Cavadini, "Ignorant Catholics: The Alarming Void in Religious Education," *Commonweal*, April 9, 2004, which argues a similar point.

48. The story was reported by the Catholic News Service in 2004: http://www.iobserve.org/wn0713b.html.

49. Ada Maria Isasi-Diaz, *En La Lucha/In the Struggle: Elaborating a Mujerista Theology* (Philadelphia: Fortress Press, 1993, 10th anniversary edition, 2003).

50. The term comes from an interview with Sheila Larson, whose articulation of personal spirituality the authors take as representative of the individualism that has come to pervade American religious life. See Robert Bellah et al., *Habits of the Heart: Individualism and Commitment in American Life* (New York: Harper and Row, 1986), p. 221.

51. Cf. one of the late writings of the great twentieth-century Catholic theologian, Karl Rahner: "attachment to the Church must be a part of the spirituality of the future. Otherwise it is elitist arrogance and a form of unbelief, failing to grasp the fact that the holy Word of God has come into the flesh of the world and sanctifies this world by taking on himself the sin of the world and also of the Church. The ecclesial aspect of the spirituality of the future will be less triumphalist than formerly. But attachment to the Church will also in the future be an absolutely necessary criterion for genuine spirituality: patience with the Church's form of a servant in the future also is an indispensable way into God's freedom, since by not following this way, we shall eventually get no further than our own arbitrary opinions and the uncertainties of our own life selfishly caught up in itself." *The Practice of the Faith: A Handbook of Contemporary Spirituality* (New York: Crossroad, 1992), p. 26.

52. James Davidson et al. document certain measures of religious literacy among the pre–Vatican II, Vatican II, and post–Vatican II generations of the church, concluding that the last of these have the lowest measure. See James D. Davidson et al., *The Search for Common Ground: What Unites and Divides Catholic Americans* (Huntington, IN: Our Sunday Visitor Books, 1997).

53. Salient examples include the following: Robert Schreiter, *The New Catholicity: Theology Between the Global and the Local* (Maryknoll, NY: Orbis Books, 1997); Stephan B. Bevans, *Models of Contextual Theology* (Maryknoll, NY: Orbis Books, 1992; revised ed., 2002); Richard G. Cote, *Re-Visioning Mission: The Catholic Church and Culture in Postmodern America* (Mahwah, NJ: Paulist Press, 1996).

54. The term is traced to the theology of Saint Augustine, who wrote that the person who undergoes conversion in Christ joins his or her free will

to the grace of God in order to bring forth good works (*On Grace and Free Will*, chapter 27, sec. 33).

55. The audio archive of Gifford's story can be found on the NPR Web site at http://www.npr.org/programs/morning/features/2002/aug/chineselives/#dongmei.

56. See, for example, the Travel China Guide Web site at http://www.travelchinaguide.com/cityguides/guangdong/shenzhen/. This site is hosted by a tour company located within China, and shows highlights of those places deemed most attractive to foreign visitors.

57. See, for example, Barbara Ehrenreich's book *Nickel and Dimed: On (Not) Getting By in America* (New York: Metropolitan Books, 2001) for her experiences trying to make a living under blue-collar working conditions in various parts of the United States.

58. The example of the Church's condemnation of slavery is illustrative of the Church's previous engagement with a social issue, an engagement with an ambiguous history. Diana Hayes ("Reflections on Slavery," in *Rome Has Spoken*, ed. Maureen Fiedler and Linda Rabben [New York: Crossroad, 1998]) has chronicled documents from the Church's magisterium from the fourth century to Vatican II, demonstrating that at times the Church has clearly supported slavery while at other times it has condemned it. In 1537, for example, Pope Paul III condemned the practice of slavery of the natives of the newly discovered Americas in *Sublimus Dei* (On the Enslavement and Evangelization of Indians). Pope Gregory XVI reiterated this condemnation in *In Supremo Apostolatus* (Condemning the Slave Trade) in 1839, and Pope Leo XIII himself issued an encyclical against slavery in 1890, *Catholicae Ecclesiae* (On Slavery in the Missions). Yet as late as 1866 the Holy Office supported the institution of slavery, and so Leo's encyclicals sought to define a final condemnation of the practice.

59. Pope Pius XI, *Quadragesimo Anno*, paragraphs 2–3. Available online at http://www.papalencyclicals.net/Pius11/P11QUADR.HTM.

60. Pope Pius IX, "The Syllabus of Errors," online at http://www.papalencyclicals.net/Pius09/p9syll.htm.

61. Pope Leo XIII, *Rerum Novarum* (On Capital and Labor), paragraph 1, online at http://www.vatican.va/holy_father/leo_xiii/encyclicals/documents/hf_l-xiii_enc_15051891_rerum-novarum_en.html. See also Donal Dorr, *Option for the Poor: A Hundred Years of Vatican Social Teaching* (Maryknoll, NY: Orbis Books, 1992) and David J. O'Brien and Thomas A. Shannon, eds., *Catholic Social Teaching: The Documentary Heritage* (Maryknoll, NY: Orbis Books, 1992) for treatments of the context and substance of *Rerum Novarum* and the later social encyclicals.

62. The National Labor Committee reported in 2004 that many bobblehead dolls were produced in the He Yi Electronics and Plastics Products Factory in Dongguan (China) for Major League Baseball, the National Football League, the National Basketball Association, the National Collegiate Athletic Association, the Collegiate Licensing Association, NASCAR, Disney, and Wal-Mart. In their report, they document abusive conditions among workers, including an hourly wage of 16.5 cents per hour. See the report at http://www.nlcnet.org/campaigns/he-yi/he-yi.opt2.pdf.

63. Friedrich Nietzsche, *The Will to Power: A New Translation* by Walter Kaufmann and R. J. Hollingdale; ed. Walter Kaufmann (New York: Vintage Books, 1967).

64. For a positive appraisal of the influence of American economic power on world culture, see Philippe Legrain, "Cultural Globalization Is Not Americanization," *The Chronicle of Higher Education* 49/35 (May 9, 2003), p. B7.

65. The wealthier countries are able to determine the agendas of these organizations, due to their greater representation among their leaderships. Many poorer countries, those suffering from the greatest debt, do not have direct representation. For an overview of the Bretton Woods initiatives, see the following: The Center of Concern's Rethinking Bretton Woods Initiative (www.coc.org/focus/?ID=902) and the British Bretton Woods Project (www.brettonwoodsproject.org/). In addition, the International Monetary Fund site (www.imf.org) and the World Bank site (www.worldbank.org) gives overviews of the leadership structures and agendas for these organizations. In both cases, the United States has the greatest influence, followed by the other industrialized countries.

66. Pax Christi USA, in particular, sponsored the "God is not a Republican...or a Democrat" campaign, which involved advertisements in U.S. newspapers. The ads rejected the notion that single issues could define a party as consistent with the Catholic Church's concern for the entirety of human experience. See the campaign at http://www.paxchristiusa.org/news_events_more.asp?id=934.

67. The Common Ground initiative founded by Cardinal Joseph Bernardin is an example of the kind of irenic emphasis that I am advocating. Controversial when it was announced, due to the perception that it would lead to a compromise of ecclesiastical authority and orthodox teaching, its leaders have consistently maintained that "common ground" is a metaphor for a method of approaching tough issues, rather than a compromise of doctrinal positions. See its Web site at www.nplc.org/commonground.htm.

68. Cf. the book of the same title: Robert C. Fuller, *Spiritual But Not Religious: Understanding Unchurched America* (New York and Oxford: Oxford University Press, 2001).

69. For an exploration of the significance of this text for contemporary spirituality, see my book *The Ignatian Workout: Daily Spiritual Exercises for a Healthy Faith* (Chicago: Loyola Press, 2004) and my essay "Postmodern Spirituality and the Ignatian *Fundamentum*," *The Way*, January 2005.

70. See Michael Amaladoss, SJ, "Mission in Asia: A Reflection on *Ecclesia in Asia*," in *The Asian Synod*, ed. Peter Phan (Maryknoll, NY: Orbis Books, 2002), pp. 222–35.

71. Cf. *Unitatis Redintegratio* 3: "the separated Churches and Communities as such, though we believe them to be deficient in some respects, have been by no means deprived of significance and importance in the mystery of salvation. For the Spirit of Christ has not refrained from using them as means of salvation which derive their efficacy from the very fullness of grace and truth entrusted to the Church."

72. Thomas Ryan, CSP, "The Ecumenical Landscape," *America* (June 19–26, 2006).

73. The initiatives of Pope John Paul II to reach out to other churches and religious groups are well documented. In his message for the 2002 World Day of Peace, for example, he wrote, "The various Christian confessions as well as the world's great religions need to work together to eliminate the social and cultural causes of terrorism. They can do this by teaching the greatness and dignity of the human person and by spreading a clearer sense of the oneness of the human family. This is a specific area of ecumenical and interreligious dialogue and cooperation, a pressing service which religion can offer to world peace." Cf. his 1995 encyclical *Ut Unum Sint* (5): "Together with all Christ's disciples, the Catholic Church bases upon God's plan her ecumenical commitment to gather all Christians into unity. Indeed, 'the Church is not a reality closed in on herself. Rather, she is permanently open to missionary and ecumenical endeavour, for she is sent to the world to announce and witness, to make present and spread the mystery of communion which is essential to her, and to gather all people and all things into Christ, so as to be for all an 'inseparable sacrament of unity.' " Yet the pope's commitment to ecumenism has not been without controversy, especially in light of the 2000 document from the Congregation of the Doctrine of the Faith (under then-Cardinal Joseph Ratzinger, the future Benedict XVI) *Dominus Iesus*. In response to the writings of various thinkers on the theology of religions and the ecumenical question, the document pointed out what were perceived as errors against the tradition of the

Church. Response to the documents has been varied, some accusing it of setting back ecumenical and inter-religious discourse, while others indicate that there was nothing in the document that cannot be found in other Vatican documents.

74. On the importance of these figures for Catholic identity in the United States, see Mark Massa, *Catholics and American Culture: Fulton Sheen, Dorothy Day, and the Notre Dame Football Team* (New York: Herder and Herder, 2001).

75. I am sympathetic to the call for a "moratorium on Church renewal" by Tom Fox, former editor and publisher of the *National Catholic Reporter*. His point is that the promotion of Catholic Social Teaching depends upon a unified voice from the Catholic community. See his article "The Moment, the Message, the Messenger," *America* (April 24–May 1, 2006).

76. In his column "All Things Catholic" of July 14, 2006, John Allen Jr. put it very well. Speaking of a conference in July 2006 in Padua that gathered theological ethicists from around the world, he wrote, "Since two-thirds of the 1.1 billion Roman Catholics in the world today live in the global south, the gathering in Padua may provide an intriguing hint about what the coming 'southern moment' in Catholicism will look like—more focused on changing the world, and correspondingly less on changing the church" (online at http://www.nationalcatholicreporter.org/word/word071406.htm).

77. Cf. Pope John Paul II in the encyclical *Sollicitudo Rei Socialis* (On Social Concern, 1987): "The teaching and spreading of her social doctrine are part of the church's evangelizing mission" (41). This sentiment is echoed in his encyclical *Centesimus Annus* (The Hundredth Year of *Rerum Novarum*, 1991): social doctrine is "an instrument of evangelization."

78. Jesus does preach the more difficult theme of hell and condemnation. The tree that does not bear fruit is thrown into the fire (Matt 7:19); the sheep are separated from the goats and the sinners from the righteous (Matt 25:31–46).

79. The term *metanoia* is found in the New Testament twenty-two times. It is usually translated as "repentance," as in the description that Peter gives to his fellow Jews about God's offer to the Gentiles in Acts 11:17–18: "'If then God gave them the same gift he gave to us when we came to believe in the Lord Jesus Christ, who was I to be able to hinder God?' When they heard this, they stopped objecting and glorified God, saying, 'God has then granted life-giving repentance *[metanoian]* to the Gentiles too.'" The term signifies the change that a person undergoes when responding to God's gift of grace.

80. It is notable that at the 2004 conference of the Catholic bishops, the U.S. prelates voted for membership in an ecumenical group, Christian Churches Together in the U.S.A, for the first time.

81. Allen, the Rome correspondent for the *National Catholic Reporter*, polled Catholic observers from several countries. Their agreement that there has developed a polarization in the contemporary Church led him to develop a spirituality of dialogue, in which the first suggestion is epistemological humility.

82. The full text is online at http://www.ncronline.org/mainpage/specialdocuments/allen_common.htm.

83. On the history of practices of dialogue within the Church, see Bradford E. Hinze, *Practices of Dialogue in the Roman Catholic Church: Aims and Obstacles, Lessons and Laments* (New York: Continuum, 2006).

84. The story of Jesus dialoguing with the Canaanite woman (a pagan) in Matthew 15:22–28 is illustrative. Jesus' own position is changed during the dialogue; he indirectly calls the woman a dog, but her tenacity persuades him that he was wrong about the nature of her faith.

85. This was the substance of the reaction against Cardinal Joseph Bernardin's establishment of the Catholic Common Ground Project, which promoted dialogue among conservatives and liberals within the Catholic Church. The reaction was put forth by other American cardinals, including John O'Connor and Bernard Law. For an overview of both sides of the issue, see Peter Steinfels, *A People Adrift: The Crisis of the Roman Catholic Church in America* (New York: Simon and Schuster, 2003), pp. 22–29.

86. These were the closing words of Glendon's response to John L. Allen Jr.'s Catholic Common Ground Initiative speech of 2004 (see note 73).

87. Pope John Paul II, encyclical *Redemptoris Mater* (1987) (34), online at http://www.vatican.va/holy_father/john_paul_ii/encyclicals/documents/hf_jp-ii_enc_25031987_redemptoris-mater_en.html#-2E.

88. The summer 2006 meeting in Moscow included a large Vatican delegation as well as leaders from other Christian, Muslim, Jewish, Buddhist, Hindu, and Shinto religious communities from forty-nine countries. In particular, their focus on the human good paid attention to the question of economics: "Human life is also interrelated with economy. International economic order, as all other spheres of global architecture, should be based on justice. All economic and business activities should be socially responsible and carried out using the ethical standards. It is this that makes the economy really efficient, that is, beneficial to the people. A life lived only for financial profit and facilitating production progress becomes barren and meager. Being aware of this, we call on the business community to be open and responsible towards the civil society, including religious

communities, at the national and global levels." The full joint statement is online at http://www.cwnews.com/news/viewstory.cfm?recnum=45156.

89. United Catholic News Service, reprinted on the Australian Mission and Justice site, December 37, 2004: http://www.missionand justice.org/modules.php?name=News&file=article&sid=877.

90. As reported on the Union for Reform Judaism Web site, http://urj.org/csa/.

91. From the Ecclesia (UK) Web site, May 11, 2004: http://www.ekklesia.co.uk/content/news_syndication/article_04115oco.shtml.

92. See Jean-Francois Lyotard, *Postmodern Fables*, trans. Georges Van Den Abbeele (Minneapolis: University of Minnesota Press, 1999) and *The Postmodern Condition: A Report on Knowledge*, trans. Brian Massumi (Minneapolis: University of Minnesota Press, 1985).

93. For example, Karl Marx and the communist movement accused religion of being a cultural force that kept peasants in their place; Sigmund Freud posited religion as a phenomenon that grew out of the human psyche reaching toward a father figure; Friedrich Nietzsche critiqued Christian morality as a set of rules to keep people from realizing their freedom.

94. The following is a representative sample of texts over the past two decades: R. Scott Appleby, *The Ambivalence of the Sacred* (Lanham, MD: Rowman and Littlefield, 1999); Gil Baile, *Violence Unveiled: Humanity at the Crossroad* (New York: Crossroad, 1997); Christopher Catherwood, *Why The Nations Rage: Killing in the Name of God* (revised and updated edition, Lanham, MD: Rowman and Littlefield, 2002); H. A. Drake, *Constantine and the Bishops: The Politics of Intolerance* (Baltimore: Johns Hopkins University Press, 2002); J. Harold Ellens, *The Destructive Power of Religion* (4 vols., Westport, CT: Praeger, 2003); Marc Ellis, *Unholy Alliance: Religion and Atrocity in Our Time* (Minneapolis, MN: Augsburg, 1997); Mark Jurgensmeyer, *Terror in the Mind of God* (Berkeley: University of California Press, revised 2003); Charles Kimball, *When Religion Becomes Evil: Five Warning Signs* (San Francisco: HarperSanFrancisco, 2003); Oliver McTernan, *Violence in God's Name: Religion in an Age of Conflict* (Maryknoll, NY: Orbis Books, 2003); John F. Murphy Jr., *The Sword of Islam: Muslim Extremism from the Arab Conquests to the Attack on America* (New York: Prometheus Books, 2002); Jack Nelson-Pallmeyer, *Is Religion Killing Us? Violence in the Bible and the Quran* (Harrisburg, PA: Trinity, 2003); David Nirenberg, *Communities of Violence* (Princeton: Princeton University Press, reprint 1998); Christoph Reuter, *My Life Is a Weapon: A Modern History of Suicide Bombing* (Princeton: Princeton University Press, 2004); Regina Schwartz, *The Curse of Cain: The Violent Legacy of Monotheism* (Chicago: University of Chicago Press, 1998); Charles Selengut, *Sacred Fury:*

Understanding Religious Violence (Lanham, MD: AltaMira Press, 2004); Jessica Stern, *Terror in the Name of God: Why Religious Militants Kill* (New York: Ecco, 2003); Andrew Wheatcroft, *Infidels: A History of the Conflict Between Christendom and Islam* (New York: Random House, 2004); Hent de Vries, *Religion and Violence: Philosophical Perspectives From Kant to Derrida* (Baltimore: Johns Hopkins University Press, 2002).

95. He wrote in *The Gulag Archipelago* (1973), "Gradually it was disclosed to me that the line separating good and evil passes not through states, nor between classes, nor between political parties either, but right through every human heart, and through all human hearts. This line shifts. Inside us, it oscillates with the years. Even within hearts overwhelmed by evil, one small bridgehead of good is retained; and even in the best of all hearts, there remains a small corner of evil." Translated by T. P. Whitney, vol. 3–4 (New York: Harper and Row, 1974–78), pp. 615–16.

96. Perhaps the best example in the contemporary world is China, which has seen the most concerted effort to eliminate religion from popular practice over its recent history. Yet some project that within a relatively short time China may be the largest Christian nation in the world, even as a significant proportion of those who practice Christian faith do so illegally—that is, outside the boundaries of the government-recognized Three Self Patriotic Movement (Protestant) and Catholic Patriotic Association churches.

97. See, for example, G. Marsden, *Fundamentalism and American Culture* (New York: Oxford University Press, 1980); M. E. Marty and R. S. Appleby, eds., *The Fundamentalism Project* (Chicago: University of Chicago Press, 1991–95).

98. Cited in Mary Ann Glendon, "Catholicism and Human Rights," Marianist Award Lecture, 2001 (University of Dayton, 2001), p. 8.

99. See the International Theological Commission's document "Memory and Reconciliation: The Church and the Faults of the Past." They write about the pope's public act of repentance: "The Church is invited to 'become more fully conscious of the sinfulness of her children.' She 'acknowledges as her own her sinful sons and daughters' and encourages them 'to purify themselves, through repentance, of past errors and instances of infidelity, inconsistency and slowness to act.' The responsibility of Christians for the evils of our time is likewise noted, although the accent falls particularly on the solidarity of the Church of today with past faults. Some of these are explicitly mentioned, like the separation of Christians, or the 'methods of violence and intolerance' used in the past to evangelize" (sec. 1.3). The document is online at http://www.vatican.va/roman_curia/congregations/cfaith/cti_documents/rc_con_cfaith_doc_20000307_memory-reconc-itc_en.html.

100. Luke Timothy Johnson has made a similar observation of contemporary spirituality in his article "A New Gnosticism," *Commonweal* 131 (November 5, 2004), pp. 28–31.

101. For a helpful overview of the state of the Asian churches from an institutional perspective, see Peter Phan, ed., *The Asian Synod: Texts and Commentaries* (Maryknoll, NY: Orbis Books, 2002). This collection of texts related to the 1999 synod, as well as theological reflections on the synod, gives the Western reader a sense of the challenges facing the churches of Asia in the new millennium. See also Thomas C. Fox, *Pentecost in Asia: A New Way of Being Church* (Maryknoll, NY: Orbis Books, 2002); Gaudencio B. Rosales, DD, and C. G. Arevalo, SJ, eds., *For All the Peoples of Asia: Federation of Asian Bishops' Conferences Documents from 1970 to 1991*, vol. 1 (Maryknoll, NY: Orbis Books; Quezon City, Philippines: Claretian Publications, 1997); Franz-Josef Eilers, ed., *For All the Peoples of Asia, FABC Documents from 1992–1996*, vol. 2 (Manila: Claretian Publications, 1997); Franz-Josef Eilers, ed., *For All the Peoples of Asia, FABC Documents from 1997 to 2001*, vol. 3 (Manila: Claretian Publications, 2002).

102. Thomas Fox *(Pentecost in Asia)* reports that a good example is South Korean Cardinal Stephen Kim Sou-Hwan, who was named "Man of the Year" by one of South Korea's largest newspapers, *Dong-a Ilbo:* "His vision of democracy—his vision that people be respected, his going out to seek the marginalized and the oppressed, to be with them, to comfort and pray with them—is the reason we have chosen Kim Sou-Hwan man of the year." Today Korea is experiencing the highest rate of adult baptism in the world.

103. For a critique of Natural Law theory in postmodernity, see my essay "Postmodern Moral Theology and Holiness: A Critique of Natural Law," in *Moral Theology: Fundamental Issues and New Directions*, ed. James Keating (Mahwah, NJ: Paulist Press, 2004).

104. On anti-Catholicism in the United States, see Philip Jenkins, *The New Anti-Catholicism: The Last Acceptable Prejudice* (New York: Oxford University Press, 2003); and Mark Massa, *Anti-Catholicism in America: The Last Acceptable Prejudice* (New York: Crossroad, 2003).

105. Mother Teresa of Calcutta wrote and spoke frequently of her work with people across religious boundaries, indicating that it was possible to respect their religion even while being committed to one's own. "I've always said we should help a Hindu become a better Hindu, a Muslim become a better Muslim, a Catholic become a better Catholic." *Meditations from a Simple Path* (New York: Ballantine, 1996), p. 40.

106. For the Vatican response to Dupuis, see "Commentary on the Notification of the Congregation for the Doctrine of the Faith regarding the book *Toward a Christian Theology of Religious Pluralism* by Father Jacques

Dupuis, S.J.," Congregation for the Doctrine of the Faith, March 20, 2001, online at http://www.vatican.va/roman_curia/congregations.cfaith/documents/rc_con_cfaith_doc_20010312_dupuis-2en.html. The 2001 account of the Vatican inquiry into Haight's book *Jesus Symbol of God* (Maryknoll, NY: Orbis Books, 1999) can be found on the *Los Angeles Times* Web site, http://www.hvk.org/articles/0401/117.html. In February 2005, Haight was forbidden by the Vatican to teach as a Catholic theologian. See the response of the Catholic Theological Society of America (CTSA), which argued that the Vatican's action was not justified: online at the CTSA's Web site, http://www.jcu.edu/ctsa/haight.html.

107. For a treatment of both of these figures, see Ronald Modras, *Ignatian Humanism: A Dynamic Spirituality for the 21st Century* (Chicago: Loyola Press, 2004), pp. 85–130.

108. On Bretton Woods, see note 65.

109. The charter of the International Military Tribunal (which can be found online at the Avalon Project of Yale Law School, http://www.yale.edu/lawweb/avalon/imt/proc/imtconst.htm) describes crimes against international law over which the new tribunal would exercise jurisdiction.

110. Mary Ann Glendon, "Catholicism and Human Rights," Marianist Award Lecture (University of Dayton, 2001). The text is reproduced in James L. Heft, *Believing Scholars: Ten Catholic Intellectuals* (New York: Fordham University Press, 2005).

111. Pope Benedict XVI, *Deus Caritas Est* (31).

112. See Robert Royal, *Catholic Martyrs of the Twentieth Century: A Comprehensive World History* (New York: Crossroad, 2000).

113. Cf. the *Catechism of the Catholic Church*, 1397: "The Eucharist commits us to the poor. To receive in truth the Body and Blood of Christ given up for us, we must recognize Christ in the poorest, his brethren."

114. See note 34.

115. Kristeen Bruun, "Hospitality at Church," *America* 191/7 (September 20, 2004).

116. These quotations are from anonymous young adult Catholics, interviewed for John C. Cusick and Katherine F. DeVries' book *The Basic Guide to Young Adult Ministry* (Maryknoll, NY: Orbis Books, 2001), pp. 13–15.

117. The perceptive reader will recognize a possible source of conflict in this observation, for we have seen examples of how the imperative to be welcoming can sometimes be perceived as a violation of Church positions on controversial issues. Two examples from the recent history of the Church in the United States will illustrate this point. The first is the pastoral care to homosexuals, which in the cases of Sr. Jeanne Gramick and Fr. Robert Nugent led to disciplining (see the commentary by Richard Gaillardetz,

"The Ordinary Universal Magisterium," *Theological Studies* 63 [2002], pp. 447–71, esp. 454–55). The second is the question of communion for politicians who take public positions counter to official Church teaching; this issue came to a head during the presidential campaign of John Kerry. In both examples, the local practice of faith and pastoral care was seen as antithetical to magisterial teaching. The neuralgic issue is ecclesiological: can the Church welcome those who are regarded as practicing or teaching that which is seen as contrary to Church teaching?

118. Cf. the Vatican II document *Sacrosanctum Concilium* (8): "In the earthly liturgy we take part in a foretaste of that heavenly liturgy which is celebrated in the holy city of Jerusalem toward which we journey as pilgrims, where Christ is sitting at the right hand of God, a minister of the holies and of the true tabernacle."

119. This topic is too extensive to treat here. There are certain liturgical formulas that would be nearly impossible to render inclusive in a responsible way: the Sign of the Cross; the Glory prayer; the baptismal formula. However, a great deal of liturgical language can and should be rendered more inclusive, sometimes because the inclusive language better renders gender-neutral terms from Hebrew or Greek (e.g., Jesus Christ "became *human*" in the Nicene Creed) and sometimes because the gender-specific terminology is dated (e.g., Paul's *adelphoi* in several letters).

120. An anonymous young adult Catholic, cited in Cusick and DeVries, *The Basic Guide to Young Adult Ministry*, p. 15.

121. See their Web site at http://www.usccb.org/laity/ygadult/index2.htm.

122. The term *kairos* is one of the New Testament Greek words for "time," but the connotation is different from *chronos* or "clock time." It suggests opportunity, event—in this case, the opportunity for God to speak to a person by means of another's compassion.

123. One example of a parish that has taken seriously the task of welcoming is described in the British Catholic journal, *The Tablet*. In short: parishioners at Holy Ghost Parish in Balham, south London, were enlisted to help spread the word about the parish through posting flyers in their windows and talking to their family, friends, and neighbors (James Roberts, "Confidence is Key," *The Tablet*, May 6, 2006, p. 17).

124. Cf. Pope John Paul II, "Apostolic Letter on the 40th Anniversary of the Constitution on the Sacred Liturgy *Sacrosanctum Concilium*," *Spiritus et Sponsa* (13): "One aspect that we must foster in our communities with greater commitment is *the experience of silence*. We need silence 'if we are to accept in our hearts the full resonance of the voice of the Holy Spirit and to unite our personal prayer more closely to the Word

of God and the public voice of the Church.' In a society that lives at an increasingly frenetic pace, often deafened by noise and confused by the ephemeral, it is vital to rediscover the value of silence." Online at http://www.vatican.va/holy_father/john_paul_ii/apost_letters/documents/hf_jp-ii_apl_20031204_sacra-liturgia_en.html.

125. John Henry Newman, *An Essay on the Development of Christian Doctrine* (Notre Dame, IN: University of Notre Dame Press, reissued 1989).

126. The difficult observation is that many marriages among Catholics in the United States effectively end in divorce, regardless of declarations of nullity, thereby raising the question whether we still celebrate the indissolubility of marriage in reality and not just as a juridical category. Furthermore, since many Catholics enter marriage already sexually active, there are difficult theological and canonical questions that the Church has not adequately addressed.

127. There are a number of examples that support this claim. One is the multilingual site hosted by the Irish Jesuits, Sacred Space (www.sacredspace.ie), which offers people Ignatian-based daily prayer using the readings from the liturgical year. Another is the U.S. bishops' site, which allows people to access the daily readings for several months at a time (http://www.usccb.org/nab/index.htm).

128. Even the Liturgy of the Hours, for example, which many vowed religious pray privately, is in essence a communal prayer. I would argue that all private prayer must be predicated on a public prayer of the Church as a whole, because of the Church's identity as the Body of Christ. Each instance of private prayer is a participation in the whole prayer of the Body.

129. Julian of Norwich, *Showings* [long text], trans. Edmund Colledge, OSA, and James Walsh, SJ (New York: Paulist Press, 1978), p. 315.

130. See, for example, Wade Clark Roof, *Spiritual Marketplace: Baby Boomers and the Remaking of American Religion* (Princeton: Princeton University Press, 1999).

131. Cf. Reid Locklin, *Spiritual but Not Religious?: An Oar Stroke Closer to the Farther Shore* (Collegeville, MN: Liturgical Press, 2005). The author's own story of conversion provides the backdrop for his meditation on what he calls a "spirituality of institutional commitment."

132. An important recent contribution to reflection on the state of lay ministry today is the U.S. bishops' document "Co-Workers in the Vineyard of the Lord," approved in November 2005: http://www.usccb.org/laity/laymin/co-workers.pdf.

133. I do not mean to suggest that only Christians working together can provide a counterpoint to prevailing economic norms. Indeed, work toward justice is one of the most promising areas of inter-religious dialogue.

134. Luke Timothy Johnson illustrates the necessity of the early Christian faith community in addressing the question of who Jesus was and what his mission was about. According to Johnson, there is no way to access the real Jesus apart from those stories that early Christians told about him. The quest for the historical Jesus that gained momentum in the late nineteenth and early twentieth centuries was limited in that it sought to isolate Jesus the person from Jesus the proclaimed Messiah—a move that, Johnson argues, is not sufficiently attentive to the extant sources about Jesus' life and work. See his *The Real Jesus: The Misguided Quest for the Historical Jesus and the Truth of the Traditional Gospels* (San Francisco: HarperSanFrancisco, 1997).

135. Saint Ignatius of Loyola suggested in his *Spiritual Exercises*, for example, that the aim of spiritual growth is ridding oneself of what he called "disordered affections," in order to grow in understanding of the purpose for which God created one.

136. The cardinal's position was described in the archdiocesan newspaper, *The Tidings*, on February 17, 2006 (online at http://www.the-tidings.com/2006/0217/cardinal.htm).

137. The Spanish term roughly translates as "United Staters"—an adjective proper to those Americans who live in the United States.

138. Cf. Tom Beaudoin, *Consuming Faith: Integrating Who We Are with What We Buy* (Lanham, MD: Sheed and Ward, 2004).

139. Cf. William Portier, "Here Come the Evangelical Catholics," *Communio* 31 (Spring 2004), pp. 35–66.

140. In a study of seniors at Boston College, for example, a significant predictor of those who describe themselves as both "spiritual" and "religious" is participation in the university's International Studies Program.

141. I borrow the term *downward mobility* from Dean Brackley, SJ. See his book *The Call to Discernment in Troubled Times: New Perspectives on the Transformative Wisdom of Ignatius* (New York: Crossroad, 2004).

142. A search of the Vatican Web site's archive of his writings reveals over 1,500 hits for the word search "solidarity." The term represents a central theme in several of his writings. Further, in the *Catechism of the Catholic Church*, the production of which he oversaw, there are nineteen subcategories under the category "solidarity."

143. The full contours of this theological trajectory cannot be explored here. The *Catechism of the Catholic Church* articulates the basic point, namely, that all people are invited by God to salvation: "It is from God's love for all men that the Church in every age receives both the obligation and the vigor of her missionary dynamism, 'for the love of Christ urges us on.' Indeed, God 'desires all men to be saved and to come to the

knowledge of the truth'; that is, God wills the salvation of everyone through the knowledge of the truth. Salvation is found in the truth. Those who obey the prompting of the Spirit of truth are already on the way of salvation. But the Church, to whom this truth has been entrusted, must go out to meet their desire, so as to bring them the truth. Because she believes in God's universal plan of salvation, the Church must be missionary" (par. 851).

144. In paragraph 1397 of the *Catechism*, the explicit connection between the Eucharist and commitment to the poor cites a homily of Saint John Chrysostom on 1 Corinthians: "You have tasted the Blood of the Lord, yet you do not recognize your brother…You dishonor this table when you do not judge worthy of sharing your food someone judged worthy to take part in this meal…God freed you from all your sins and invited you here, but you have not become more merciful."

145. I wonder whether it is precisely the otherness of older Church rituals that attracts younger Catholics today. Now that post–Vatican II rituals and music are a few decades old, they appear to many young Catholics as outdated and incapable of bearing the weight of divine mystery.

146. I oversimplify here for the sake of clarity. To be certain, *Christianity* is an ambiguous term when used of the churches of the first through third centuries; not until the time of Constantine was there a more univocal sense of the term. Moreover, the ways that early followers of Jesus looked at the world were complex: some moving more in the direction of rejecting the sinful world in Gnostic fashion; others embracing the world because of a belief that ultimately it was of little significance. What I underline in this claim is that the trajectory of Christian belief and practice went the way of rejecting these extremes, ultimately finding a certain balance between acceptance of the world ("living in the world but not of the world") and rejection of the sinfulness that tarnished our experience of it. The crystallization of this belief took form in the Chalcedonian doctrine of Jesus' full humanity and full divinity, which amounted to an embrace of both the reality of God and the reality of the world.

147. I do not address here the very serious question of reparation in the wake of the crisis: what ought Church leaders do in order to repair the broken relationships with survivors of abuse, and with other Catholics whose trust has been breached due to poor judgment on the part of leaders? I refer readers to other treatments of this issue: for example, Jean Bartunek, Mary Ann Hinsdale, and James F. Keenan, *Church Ethics and Its Organizational Context* (Lanham, MD: Rowman and Littlefield, 2005); and Francis Oakley and Bruce Russett, *Governance, Accountability, and the Future of the Catholic Church* (New York: Continuum, 2004).

148. Two examples are the pastoral letters written by the U.S. Bishops in the 1980s, *The Challenge of Peace* (1983) and *Economic Justice for All* (1986).

149. For a synthetic approach to the debates that emerged in the wake of *Humanae Vitae*, see Julie Hanlon Rubio, "Beyond the Liberal/Conservative Divide on Contraception," *Horizons* 32/2 (Fall 2005), pp. 270–94.

150. Some of this material I have explored in greater length in an essay entitled "Postmodern Moral Theology and Holiness," in *Moral Theology: Fundamental Issues and New Directions*, ed. James Keating (New York: Paulist Press, 2004).

151. The term originally applied to computer programming, but has come to represent a kind of unique epistemology. The definition of "open source" proposed by the Open Source Initiative is as follows: "When programmers can read, redistribute, and modify the source code for a piece of software, the software evolves. People improve it, people adapt it, people fix bugs. And this can happen at a speed that, if one is used to the slow pace of conventional software development, seems astonishing" (at www.opensource.org).

152. This phenomenon of accessing news from sources different from traditional media conglomerates has practical ramifications, as there have recently been layoffs of reporters at many large newspapers such as the *Philadelphia Inquirer* and the *New York Times*.

153. Cf. the site www.opensourcetheology.net for an Evangelical example of this kind of emerging method of discerning religious truth.

154. The earliest known pyramid scheme was orchestrated by Charles Ponzi in 1920. At one point, he took in over a million dollars in one three-hour period, because he promised returns on investment that were far greater than those promised by banks. Debra A. Valentine gave a talk to the International Monetary Fund in 1998 describing the potential harm of these schemes today, at the Federal Trade Commission Web site: http://www.ftc.gov/speeches/other/dvimf16.htm. It is interesting to note that pyramid or Ponzi schemes still happen today even at high levels, such as the one reported by the *Boston Globe* on June 7, 2006 (online at http://www.boston.com/business/globe/articles/2006/06/07/sec_says_adviser_ran_ponzi_scheme/). Such "heresies" will never be extinct, but the point is that in a sophisticated, information-driven society, they are not likely to take hold as influential movements.

155. This principle has been articulated in a number of Catholic social documents, according to which "a community of a higher order should not interfere in the internal life of a community of a lower order,

depriving the latter of its functions, but rather should support it in case of need and help to coordinate its activity with the activities of the rest of society, always with a view to the common good" (Pope Pius XI, *Quadragesimo Anno* I, 184–86; also cited in Pope John Paul II, *Centesimus Annus* 48 #4).

156. Cf. Vatican II, *Gaudium et Spes* (62): "In order that they may fulfill their function, let it be recognized that all the faithful, whether clerics or laity, possess a lawful freedom of inquiry, freedom of thought and of expressing their mind with humility and fortitude in those matters on which they enjoy competence."

157. Membership in the Catholic Theological Society of America is a symptom of a change in the field. At its founding over fifty years ago, the membership was overwhelmingly clerical. Today, the majority of the Society is lay.

158. I am thinking here of the Pontifical Academies, which act in advisory ways to the Holy See. One example, the Pontifical Academy of Social Sciences, is headed by an American laywoman, Mary Ann Glendon (online at http://www.vatican.va/roman_curia/pontifical_academies/acdscien/index_social_en.htm).

159. John Henry Newman, "On Considering the Faithful in Matters of Doctrine," originally published in *The Rambler*, July 1859, online at http://www.newmanreader.org/works/rambler/consulting.html.

160. Michael Sharkey explores the impact of Newman's doctrine of the *sensus fidelium* in his essay "Newman on the Laity," *Gregorianum* 68, 1/2 (1987), pp. 339–46. He underscores Newman's use of the term *consult*—as when one consults a barometer to understand the weather, but also when a bishop consults parents in order to learn about the state of schools.

161. The texts cited in the 1975 document of the Congregation for the Doctrine of the Faith *Persona Humana* are Romans 1:24–27; 1 Corinthians 6:10; 1 Timothy 1:10. There are several other relevant documents of the Congregation, including *Homosexualitatis Problema* (1986); "Some Considerations Concerning the Response to Legislative Proposals on Non-discrimination of Homosexual Persons" (1992); and "Considerations Regarding Proposals to Give Legal Recognition to Unions Between Homosexual Persons" (2003).

162. Cf. *Gaudium et Spes* (16): "In the depths of his conscience, man detects a law which he does not impose upon himself, but which holds him to obedience. Always summoning him to love good and avoid evil, the voice of conscience when necessary speaks to his heart: do this, shun that. For man has in his heart a law written by God; to obey it is the very dignity of man; according to it he will be judged."

163. Cf. *Lumen Gentium* (25): "In matters of faith and morals, the bishops speak in the name of Christ and the faithful are to accept their teaching and adhere to it with a religious assent."

164. Catholic theology has never embraced a full literalism as one finds, for example, in some forms of contemporary Evangelical strains of Christianity. To cite one example, Saint Augustine—who himself leaned in his later writings toward a more literal interpretation of scripture in *The Literal Meaning of Genesis*—nevertheless articulated the rudimentary contours of just war theory, which rests upon a rather sophisticated balancing of scripture and reason.

165. See Robert McClory, *Turning Point: The Inside Story of the Papal Birth Control Commission* (New York: Crossroad, 1997).

166. In his address for the World Day of Peace in 2006, Pope Benedict XVI repeated a theme of John Paul II about the Church's nonviolent witness: "To try to impose on others by violent means what we consider to be the truth is an offence against the dignity of the human being, and ultimately an offence against God in whose image he is made" (online at http://www.vatican.va/holy_father/benedict_xvi/messages/peace/documents/hf_ben-xvi_mes_20051213_xxxix-world-day-peace_en.html).

167. The Vatican II document *Gaudium et Spes* (52) describes the family as a "school of deeper humanity." It goes on to suggest that "if it is to achieve the full flowering of its life and mission, it needs the kindly communion of minds and the joint deliberation of spouses, as well as the painstaking cooperation of parents in the education of their children." I am suggesting that if the domestic church becomes the model for our deliberations about moral authority in the Catholic Church today, such counsel is provocative. The fathers and mothers in the Church today must seek such communion of minds if they are to model faith for the youngest members of the Body of Christ.

168. Encyclical *Deus Caritas Est* (27), online at http://www.vatican.va/holy_father/benedict_xvi/encyclicals/documents/hf_ben-xvi_enc_20051225_deus-caritas-est_en.html.

169. Some examples include Jesuit Refugee Service, The Catholic Worker, and many of the over two hundred agencies affiliated with Caritas International (www.caritas.org). In this last group are many organizations that are approved by national episcopal conferences, but there are also a number of independent Catholic organizations. A full list of the member organizations is available at http://www.caritas.org/Upload/d/directorylist9_05.pdf.

170. I offer my own essay, "A Life-Giving Choice," *America* (November 29, 2004) as an example.

Index